Sandplay Therapy in Vulnerable Communities

Sandplay Therapy in Vulnerable Communities offers a new method of therapeutic care for people in acute crisis situations such as natural disasters and war, as well as the long-term care of children and adults in areas of social adversity including slums, refugee camps and high-density urban areas.

This book provides detailed case studies of work carried out in South Africa, China and Colombia and combines practical discussions of expressive sandwork projects with brief overviews of their sociohistoric background. Further topics covered include:

- the social aspect of psychoanalysis
- the importance of play
- pictographic writing and the psyche.

Providing the reader with clear, practical instructions for carrying out their own sandwork project, this book will be essential reading not only for psychotherapists involved with sandplay therapy but also for those with an interest in cross-cultural psychotherapy, as well as all professionals working with those in situations of social adversity.

Eva Pattis Zoja is a clinical psychologist, Jungian analyst and sandplay therapist based in Italy. She is currently working in South Africa, China, Colombia and Argentina for the International Association of Expressive Sandwork.

Sandplay Therapy in Vulnerable Communities

A Jungian approach

Eva Pattis Zoja
Translated by Benjamin Seaman

Routledge
Taylor & Francis Group

LONDON AND NEW YORK

First published in the UK in 2011
by Routledge
27 Church Road, Hove, East Sussex BN3 2FA

Simultaneously published in the USA and Canada
by Routledge
711 Third Avenue, New York, NY 10017

Routledge is an imprint of the Taylor & Francis Group, an informa business

© 2011 Eva Pattis Zoja
English Translation © 2011 Benjamin Seaman

The right of Eva Pattis Zoja to be identified as author of this work has
been asserted by her in accordance with sections 77 and 78 of the
Copyright, Designs and Patents Act 1988.

Typeset in Times by
RefineCatch Limited, Bungay, Suffolk

Paperback cover design by David Mumelter

British Library Cataloguing in Publication Data
A catalogue record for this book is available from the British Library

Library of Congress Cataloging in Publication Data
Pattis Zoja, Eva, 1952–, author.
  Sandplay Therapy in Vulnerable Communities: A Jungian Approach/
Eva Pattis Zoja.
    p.; cm.
  ISBN 978–0–415–59271–0 (hbk) — ISBN 978–0–415–59272–7 (pbk)
  1. Sandplay—Therapeutic use. 2. Jungian psychology. I. Title.
  [DNLM: 1. Play Therapy—methods. 2. Jungian Theory. 3. Stress
  Disorders, Traumatic—therapy. WM 450.5.P7]
  RC489.S25P38 2011
  616.89′1653—dc22

                                        2010043730

ISBN: 978–0–415–59271–0 (hbk)
ISBN: 978–0–415–59272–7 (pbk)
ISBN: 978–0–203–81795–7 (ebk)

To Luigi

Contents

Acknowledgements

Warmest thanks go to my Jungian colleagues Heyong Shen and Gao Lan and to my friend Irmgard Thom: without them, the method of Expressive Sandwork would not exist today, nor would this book have been written at all.

I am profoundly grateful to the tireless and talented volunteers Ali Mabitsela in South Africa, Siyuan Chen and Liang YingYe in China, and the colleagues in the Jungian Association ADEPAC in Colombia: Juan Carlos Alonso, Ines della Ossa Izquierdo, Maria Camila Mora, Monica Pinilla Pineda, Claudia Munevar, Maria Patricia Quijano and Liliana Alvarez.

I am grateful to Kate Hawes for her support, and to Sarah Gibson and Christine Firth for their careful reading and patient editing.

I thank Andrew Samuels, who many years ago gave me the idea to write about Freud's free clinics.

My deep gratitude goes to Ruth Ammann, with whom I had the opportunity to discuss many theoretical and practical questions, especially regarding the distinction between Expressive Sandwork and Sand Play Therapy.

Special thanks go to Benjamin Seaman, who has not only provided an excellent translation, but also raised important questions during the writing process, and to David Mumelter, who has captured the spirit of an African shanty town in his cover design. The support of Henry and Glenyce Seaman and of Martin Mumelter has been important to me over many years.

Words are not enough to describe the support of my husband Luigi Zoja and children Stefano, Sara and Elisabeth, who have collaborated – each with his or her own skills – in all of the projects described in this book.

Eva Pattis Zoja

Introduction

This book arose out of practical work, and was written with practical work in mind. However, in the course of the experience, a rich theoretical backbone also emerged: for the sake of clarity it has been put at the beginning of the book. The text is intended as a resource for anyone who would like to care for other people psychologically, even in precarious situations.

The method of Expressive Sandwork evolved out of psychoanalytic work that is based on a Jungian approach, and it has proven successful in Chinese kindergartens and orphanages as well as in South African slums since the 1990s. In 2008, Expressive Sandwork was successfully applied on a broad basis for the first time, as a therapy for posttraumatic stress disorder in the earthquake area of Sichuan.

The method, which relies primarily on non-verbal image processes, is suited for acute crisis situations such as natural catastrophes or wars, where there is a huge need for psychological assistance and a chronic lack of trained psychotherapists to meet it. Today we are able to observe physiological cerebral processes that are caused by posttraumatic stress disorder, and we know how important it is to treat affected people as soon as possible. Every week that passes decreases the patient's chance of being treated successfully, and increases the severity and length of ensuing depressions. Expressive Sandwork has also proven helpful in the long-term care of children and adults in areas of social adversity, such as slums and refugee camps, as well as in project-based assignments in high-density urban areas and in the countryside.

The position that Expressive Sandwork holds in psychotherapy could be compared to that of the 'Arte Povera' movement in the Italian world of art in the 1960s and 1970s. As the art critics of the time emphasized, what may look 'poor' and 'simple' is by no means just that. On the contrary: after long experience and refinement everything superfluous has been removed, revealing a crystallized essence. This is the art of 'leaving out'. One might ask the same question regarding a psychological method: 'What can be left out?' This leads inevitably to a whole row of theoretical considerations and especially to the next questions: 'What indeed is essential in a psychotherapeutic technique? What theoretical instruments do we have for telling ballast from essence in new situations?'

Since every future builds on the past, a glance at history is called for. The beginnings of psychotherapy were characterized by a great social vision, an almost forgotten enthusiasm and idealism of its founders.

Chapter 1 in this book deals with this history, and describes the social roots of psychotherapy. The psychoanalytical institutions that Freud founded in the 1920s, where patients were treated for free, paved the way for the spread of psychoanalysis. The countless patients receiving psychological help were not just members of the higher social classes but came to a great extent from socially disadvantaged classes. This chapter tries to provide a short overview of the assumptions on which they were based and of how these clinics worked.

Chapter 2 explores a further theoretical aspect of psychotherapeutic work which is just as important. How can a concept of psychotherapeutic intervention that was developed in Europe be applicable in different populations, linguistic systems and cultures of the world? With the help of C.G. Jung's childhood memories, one of the central basic assumptions of his theory can be illustrated: the collective unconscious and the function of the psyche's ability to create images independently from the culture and stimulation of its surroundings. This chapter also deals with the psychological meaning of children's play.

Chapter 3 deals specifically with the search for the essence of child psychotherapy. Two historical developments in psychotherapy will be examined more closely: Margaret Lowenfeld's *World Technique* and Dora Kalff's *Sandplay*.

The book's actual subject begins in Chapter 4 – 'Psychotherapy in precarious situations' – which focuses on two questions: 'To what extent does psychotherapy even make sense in situations of social adversity?' And: 'Is a minimalist, cross-cultural form of psychotherapy that can achieve a maximum of psychological help with just a minimum of training even conceivable?' Theoretical aspects and practical experience complement one another to answer these questions.

To complete the psychoanalytic understanding of precarious situations, Chapter 5 offers some reflections on psychological trauma.

Chapter 6 describes the method of Expressive Sandwork systematically and with the help of many examples. Both the practical and the psychological requirements are considered: sandtray, sand and miniatures, as well as the attitude of the therapists and their assistants. The term 'assistants' in this case pertains to all people who are not specifically trained psychologists themselves but who apply Expressive Sandwork under the direction of a licensed psychotherapist. These can be volunteer helpers, social workers, teachers, educators and students. This chapter also describes some examples of symbolic play processes from private practices in order to further illustrate the method.

The following three large chapters on South Africa, China and Colombia feature individual sandwork projects, as well as brief overviews of the relevant sociohistoric aspects of their backgrounds. Series of sand images by individual children demonstrate clearly how psychological dynamics can change over the course of many sessions.

At the end of the book in Chapter 10, the reader will find clear, practical instructions for a complete project of Expressive Sandwork, consisting of four group sessions.

These projects would never have been possible without the untiring, dedicated and enthusiastic work of countless students and volunteer helpers. At this point I would like to thank all of them, because they could not all be named individually in the following text.

Chapter 1

The social aspect of psychoanalysis
Freud's polyclinic

> . . . to mix some alloy with the pure gold of analysis. . .[1]

Although the First World War had not yet come to an end, the city of Vienna had largely already lost its sheen of a cultural and political metropolis. The Viennese saw themselves facing a future of historical insignificance. Esteemed psychiatrist Sándor Ferenczi's suggestion to hold the Fifth International Congress on Psychoanalysis in Budapest met with agreement because life was thought to be safer there than in Vienna. Ferenczi, the son of a radical journalist and publisher, belonged to a circle of progressive Hungarian intellectuals and artists including György Lukács and Béla Bartók.

The psychoanalysts whom Freud had once assembled around himself in Vienna had been dispersed across Europe since the beginning of the war, because many of them had had to do military service for their own countries. Each of them knew that he might one day have to face friends and colleagues in the enemy's lines. Many of them experienced the war's psychological consequences, in the form of posttraumatic stress disorder (as we call it today), at close range. The main purpose of the conference was to discuss the psychological costs of war and to try to find methods of treating war neuroses. Official representatives of the Central Powers were attending the congress, and were interested in establishing psychiatric wards according to new criteria. They had high expectations of psychoanalysis: the psychological damage that this war had caused was to be repaired.[2]

It is surely thanks to psychoanalysis that this psychological damage received a general description for the first time in the history of war. According to the German army's official medical report,[3] between 1914 and 1918, a total of 613,047 soldiers had been treated in military hospitals for 'nervous afflictions'. This equalled almost 10 per cent of an estimated 6.5 million soldiers. The official term of the time was 'war hysteria',[4] and electric shocks were the usual form of treatment in military hospitals. There was obviously a big challenge awaiting psychiatry and especially psychoanalysis, which had already proven that it was able to leave its consultation rooms and make its knowledge available to the general public. It was time 'to make the psychoanalytic healing method available to wider parts of the population'.[5]

The time was right for Sigmund Freud's and Sándor Ferenczi's idea of universal access to psychotherapy, which was voiced for the first time at this congress, to meet with strong approval.[6] In his talk, Freud said: 'The poor man should have just as much right to assistance for his mind as he now has to the life-saving help offered by surgery'.

One circumstance in particular, which also had to do with the political events of the time, paved the way for this suggestion's acceptance. The years of war had led to a shortage of patients in Vienna. Freud's entire fortune had fallen victim to inflation. His separation from Swiss psychiatrist C.G. Jung had happened four years ago. He could now devote all of his attention to developing psychoanalysis according to his own ideas. These included the founding of training institutes. Over the past years, several questions had started arising in psychoanalyst circles: 'How does one become a psychoanalyst? Where should training institutes be founded? How should supervision be governed? Could lay analysts (psychoanalysts without a degree in medicine) be trained?' In any case, future trainees would certainly require a large number of patients. Given the entire population's current precarious psychological state, patients would no longer come only from Europe's highest social classes. Therefore, the idea of a clinic in which patients could be treated without charge seemed attractive from this point of view as well.

But Freud's proposal was also an expression of a special historical moment of socio-political reformation in which liberal and social ideas were poised to overcome conservative, monarchist and clerical attitudes.

> Then institutions and out-patient clinics will be started, women who have nearly succumbed under the burden of their privations, children for whom there is no choice but running wild or neurosis, may be made capable, by analysis, of resistance and efficient work. Such treatments will be free.[7]

Freud's idea met with great approval. It took root in the psychoanalysts' minds and was soon to become reality.

In February 1920, Ernst Simmel and Max Eitingon opened the first polyclinic for psychoanalysis at Schloss Tegel sanatorium in Berlin. The cultural programme for the opening ceremony reflected the spirit of the time: Karl Abraham gave the opening speech, Ernst Simmel read from Rainer Maria Rilke's *Book of Hours*, and there was music by Chopin, Schubert and Schönberg. Everyone was filled by a spirit of optimism. The list of psychoanalysts who agreed to devote a fifth of their working time to the free clinic reads like an index of pioneers in this field: Karl Abraham, Paul Federn, Therese Benedek, Otto Fenichel, Edith Jacobson, Karen Horney, Erich Fromm, Helene Deutsch, Hanns Sachs, Sándor Radó, Wilhelm Reich, Annie Reich and Melanie Klein. From the start, the clinic was so popular that its founders decided against further promotion and advertising.

In the first two and a half years alone, 700 patients had sought admittance: 'from the 6-year-old child to the 67-year-old man, from workers and maids to generals' daughters'.[8] Psychoanalytical treatment was indicated for about half of the patients. Analysis was free of charge if patients declared that they could not pay for the treatment. Otherwise they were to pay 'as much or as little as they can or think they can'.[9] Proper financial support for the clinic was found eventually. Ernst Simmel wrote to the relevant ministry at the time that the very group of patients who needed treatment most were usually also the ones without resources, precisely because of their psychoneurosis.

Regarding a clinic in Vienna, Freud was sceptical at first: he had not considered Vienna to be a suitable city for a clinic in which people in need could be treated free of charge. He would have preferred Budapest. Indeed, the initiative had met with resistance for the longest time. The medical association expressed their concern that such a clinic could damage the status and image of doctors. But the atmosphere in Vienna under the influence of the social-democrats was favourable. In 1922, Eduard Hitschmann, Helene Deutsch and Paul Federn founded the Vienna Ambulatorium, which was integrated into the university clinic at Pelikangasse 18. Just as had been the case in Berlin, there was no form of funding at first. The patients were treated in the rooms of the cardiology ward, which were empty during the afternoons. The *couch* was a narrow, unpadded treatment table for heart patients, which was so high that the patients had to reach it with the help of a stool. Nevertheless, from the start it was barely possible to deal with the rush of patients. Craftsmen, civil servants, nuns, factory workers, housemaids, lawyers and students all came to the ambulatorium. Between 1920 and 1931, hundreds of patients of all ages, many of them welfare cases, were treated for psychosomatic illnesses, depression and phobia.[10] The most common diagnosis was hysteria; the second most common was neurotic compulsion. Anna Freud, Wilhelm Reich, Siegfried Bernfeld, August Aichhorn, Willi Hofer and Grete Bibring were among the psychoanalysts who were active there. They saw the ambulatorium itself as an instrument for social reform. The psychoanalysts were convinced that they would be able to bring about a change in society towards greater social justice. Free services were extended to the analysts as well. Specifically, Pappenheim recalled that 'every training analyst in Vienna was obligated to train two students for free'.[11]

Treatment of children and adolescents was one of the ambulatorium's priorities.

> Vienna's focus on children's needs and rights increased in parallel with the emergence of new scientific studies of child development and treatment techniques, and a developing interest in early education. Child analysis itself emerged from the social context of radicalism and service.[12]

Anna Freud held a series of seminars on the relation between psychoanalysis and upbringing. August Aichhorn, a former teacher and director of a municipal kindergarten, developed a psychoanalytical model of social help for disturbed or delinquent adolescents.[13]

At the Berlin Polyclinic, up to 10 per cent of patients treated every year were children of school age. They first underwent a general medical and neurological examination and were then entrusted to a psychoanalyst. Sessions took place three times a week, as they did for adults.

An outpatient file from 1921 titled 'Case History and Diagnosis' bears a comment by Max Eitingon:

> Brought from the youth office in Wilmersdorf. Petty thieving (broke into a school cupboards led by [?] another boy) and sexual aggression towards little girls. Very difficult environment; appears to have been encouraged to steal from a very early age by a sister. Cries when asked if he knows he has done something that is not allowed. Speaks very little the first time, is visibly intimidated, despite otherwise having many characteristics of the uninhibited suburban child. Has difficulty learning, but gives no impression of being intellectually backward.[14]

Suggested therapy for the boy was: Attempted analysis: Frau Klein.[15] The young patient was asked to lie down on the couch and to associate freely – both requests apparently always met with his resistance.[16] Though more sessions had been intended (three sessions weekly), only fourteen of them took place (from April 1921 until the last session on 9 June), because – as Melanie Klein says – 'his foster mother did all she could to keep him away from me'.[17] The analyst's resentment is hard to miss in this statement.[18] This was one of Melanie Klein's first child analyses, and she began by interpreting the boy's associations according to Freud's Oedipus complex. She tried to understand the boy with the help of S. Freud's essay 'Verbrecher aus Schuldbewusstsein' (1916).[19] But she also made a note of everything that did not necessarily fit this concept. In the seven pages of session notes there are two mentions of the boy's 'fantasies of the electric'. The 'electric' (the tram) would derail on the way home from his therapy session, and the conductor would not give the passengers tickets to board another tram.

The boy's fear of derailing (in German this word is also used for immoral behaviour in particular) and the impossibility of making reparations for lack of a positive fatherly authority (the conductor), are obvious to us today. The second time that Melanie Klein remarks on this fantasy, she adds that the boy is also 'preoccupied with elevators whose ropes could tear'.

Later, the analyst remarks on 'the boy's completely new interest in metalwork and the exact construction of elevators.' It is easy to imagine that the boy had begun to draw hope at this point, and that new, inner-psychological dynamics were becoming activated inside him.

The boy's pictographic associations on the couch could have taken a similar form if he had been sitting at a table with paper and colour pencils – or at a sandtray with toys: he could have, for example, let a miniature train derail. Perhaps he might have shown less initial resistance to the sessions if this had been the case. It might have made the situation a little easier for both parties. (Later in life, Melanie Klein developed a form of treatment for children with miniature toys.) But there is an important difference between the two approaches, which influences their

respective ways of expressing unconscious content. In his freely associated fantasies on the couch, the boy himself is sitting in the tram when it derails. If, however,
he is playing with a miniature train and makes it derail, he keeps the event at a
certain distance. Naturally, this has advantages and disadvantages for the therapy's
progress.

The psychoanalysis of this boy from Berlin's suburbs could not be successfully
completed. Melanie Klein reported that 'the boy didn't commit a single offence
during his highly sporadic analysis', but that he 'became delinquent once more
during the interruption and was immediately admitted to a reformatory.'[20] This
interruption lasted a few months and was due to the analyst's 'absence from
Berlin for personal reasons', as she put it. Later, she lamented: 'All of my attempts
at bringing him back to analysis, after my return, were in vain. In view of all
circumstances, I do not doubt in the least that he pursued a career in crime.' There
is no way that we can know if Melanie Klein's view was too pessimistic. However,
if we consider what reformatories for youths were still like in Germany of the
1920s, we probably must share her fears.

After more than a hundred years of psychoanalysis, there is no lack today – and
maybe also back then – of analytical understanding, empathy or techniques of
treatment. What was known as 'free association' then is essentially still the core of
depth-psychological treatment today, even if we have developed a whole spectrum
of different methods for evoking unconscious content in the mean time, as well as
diverse theoretical systems for understanding the same. Far more, our therapeutic
approach today – and in 1920 – seems to suffer from the fact that the transforming
and healing effect of the therapeutic *relationship* is underestimated, especially by
therapists themselves. The therapist's simple presence, as a person with his or her
own thoughts and feelings about the child, is experienced by the child as being
symbolic for the child's own complete and fundamental acceptance or rejection in
the world. The therapist, who is reliably present during every session, becomes a
surface for projection: he or she is made to represent outwardly the parental roles
that are laid out in the child's psyche. Whether the child will be able to compensate
for the shortcomings in the environment depends on the therapist's ability to let
him or herself be used as such a 'primary object' within the therapeutic relationship. Too long an interruption – as was for example the case in Melanie Klein's
analysis – and the glimmer of hope, which was awakened in the child, will go out.

By no means does it merely depend on the therapists and their training if children find their way to therapy in the first place, and whether these therapies are
interrupted too easily or not. The cultural and societal connections go further and
lie deeper. In the end it depends on the adults' abilities to perceive consciously the
vulnerability in children's lives *and* to relate to the feeling emotionally.

Many new processes along these lines were set in motion on a collective level
in the time between the two wars. An example is the development of pedagogic
ideas such as the Montessori schools. Different forces were working in the exact
opposite direction at the same time and ended up determining the course of events
in Europe and the world.

For more than ten years, the psychoanalysts worked at their dream of being able to influence society as a whole. They were able to train many young psychoanalysts, because the clinics provided enough 'patient material'. Most of the trainees also received free analyses themselves. Psychological thoughts enriched art, literature and film, and in the minds of many people it seemed that a great movement towards social and humanitarian values was imminent. But things were to come differently.

In 1933, everything that Berlin's polyclinic for psychoanalysis had achieved disappeared into one of the darkest abysses in history. Freud's works were burnt; the aryanization of Germany had begun. Max Eitingon no longer wanted to set foot in the polyclinic, for fear of 'being arrested in those rooms'. He emigrated to Palestine. Ernst Simmel was arrested. The archives were largely destroyed so as not to compromise any of the patients. In 1936, those in power tried to convert the clinic into an instrument of national socialism.[21] Matthias Göring (a cousin of Hermann Göring's) was made the new director of the 'German institute for psychological research and psychotherapy'. In a telegram to the Reich's head doctors and to the interior ministry, Göring and Böhm assured their complete support of the national socialist cause.[22] C.G. Jung was offered a position at the institute, but he declined and remained in Switzerland. Most of the Jewish psychoanalysts emigrated to the USA. There, psychoanalysis was developed further, and eventually returned to Europe after the war.

The Vienna ambulatorium had already closed in 1931 due to a lack of funding. It took until 1999 for it to reopen as the Ambulatorium for Psychoanalysis in Vienna.[23]

Chapter 2

The cross-cultural aspect of analytical psychology

Carl Gustav Jung

> Sometimes the hands reveal a secret around which the intellect struggles in vain.[1]

The 10-year-old Carl had a small yellow pencil case that contained not only his pen and pencils but also a wooden ruler. This was in 1885, a time when children were used to crafting and inventing their own toys. Therefore it was not unusual that Carl began carving away at his ruler one day, without having anything partic- ular in mind. Without sparing a thought to the fact that this would render his ruler completely unusable, he carved a little man about six centimetres tall 'with frock coat, top hat, and shiny black boots'.[2] He coloured the little figure with black ink, sawed it off his ruler and laid it in his pencil case,

> where I made him a little bed. I even made a coat for him out of a bit of wool. In the case I also placed a smooth, oblong blackish stone from the Rhine, which I painted with water colours to look as though it were divided into an upper and lower half [. . .] This was *his* stone.[3]

Carl took the case containing his little man upstairs to the attic of his parents' house, where children were not allowed, and hid it behind one of the roof beams. Decades later, he remembered that day:

> No one could discover my secret and destroy it. I felt safe, and the tormenting sense of being at odds with myself was gone. In all difficult situations, when- ever I had done something wrong or my feelings had been hurt, [. . .] I thought of my carefully bedded-down and wrapped-up manikin and his smooth, pret- tily coloured stone.[4]

The episode with the carved manikin lasted about a year of the boy's life:

> From time to time – often at intervals of weeks – I secretly stole up to the attic when I could be certain that no one would see me. Then I clambered up on

the beam, opened the case, and looked at my manikin and his stone. Each time I did this I placed in the case a little scroll of paper on which I had previously written something. [. . .] The addition of a new scroll always had the character of a solemn ceremonial act. [. . .] The meaning of these actions, or how I might explain them, never worried me. I contented myself with the feeling of newly-won security, and was satisfied to possess something that no one knew and no one could get at.[5]

Thinking of the little man was always particularly helpful when Carl's self-esteem started to dwindle. This was, for example, the case when he had been invited to visit important people. Despite preparing for the event for a long time, and despite very thorough personal hygiene, which was repeatedly interrupted by his mother's admonitions to 'wipe your nose – do you have a handkerchief? Have you washed your hands?',[6] his identity would begin to get weaker and weaker the closer he came to the house he had been invited to. When he finally rang these more or less important people's doorbell, he felt as 'as timid and craven as a stray dog. [. . .] My shoes are filthy, and so are my hands; I have no handkerchief and my neck is black with dirt',[7] he could hear it ringing in his ears.

   What is more, Carl then disregarded his mother's admonitions and recommendations out of defiance, and 'would act with unnecessary shyness and stubbornness'.[8] But inside he felt something different as well:

   If things became too bad I would think of my secret treasure in the attic, and that helped me regain my poise. For in my forlorn state I remembered that I was also the 'Other', the person who possessed that inviolable secret, the black stone and the little man in frock coat and top hat.[9]

After 25 years of having 'completely forgotten the whole affair, [. . .] this fragment of memory rose up again from the mists of childhood with pristine clarity',[10] to the psychiatrist Carl Gustav Jung. This occurred when he was reading about the soul stones of Arlesheim and the 'churingas' of the Australian Aboriginals, while doing research for an anthropological study. These stones were not just painted in the same way as his own; the soul stones even seemed to have a similar function for these people as they had had for him as a child.

   'Along with this recollection there came to me, for the first time, the conviction that there are archaic psychic components which have entered the individual psyche without any direct line of tradition.'[11] The basis for the notion of a 'collective unconscious' had been created.

   Jung later succeeded in fitting his childhood play into a greater cultural context:

   Ultimately, the manikin was a *kabir*, wrapped in his little cloak, hidden in the *kista*, and provided with a supply of life-force, the oblong black stone. But these are connections which became clear to me only much later in life. When

I was a child I performed the ritual just as I have seen it done by the natives of Africa; they act first and do not know what they are doing. Only afterwards do they reflect on what they have done.[12]

What Jung describes here can be seen as an example for the self-regulation of the psyche through childhood play. Thinking of his little man – whom he himself had created but who can nevertheless also be found elsewhere in human history – enabled him to overcome his inner feeling of disunion with himself at least to a certain extent. This autonomous mechanism for the psyche to bridge an inner conflict naturally must not be overrated. Jung certainly had a difficult childhood, which left its traces and influenced his personal relationships up until late in his life.[13]

The mysterious manikin, who was hidden away in the attic of his parents' house, could be seen as a precursor, as the ancestor, of all sandplay miniatures that were yet to come. Everything that would later be written about the effect of sandplay was already anticipated by this episode of Jung's childhood. Jung's narration offers an impression of how his theories developed more or less out of the 'objective' observation of his own subjective inner life.

The concept of a psychological matrix that is common to all humans, from which similar figures – the archetypes – appear under different geographic and historic circumstances, is known to most psychologists, anthropologists and philosophers today as the *collective unconscious*.

So what was the importance of Jung's views, especially for developmental psychology? Contrary to the common opinion that Jung was hardly interested in child psychotherapy, his thoughts on the relationship between parents and children actually seem like pioneering work today. In 1924, in the foreword to Frances G. Wickes' book *The Inner World of Childhood*,[14] Jung writes: 'Parents should always be conscious of the fact that they themselves are the principal cause of neurosis in their children.'[15] This may strike us as self-evident today, but that was by no means the case in the 1920s. Jung continues:

> For all Lovers of theory, the essential fact behind all this [he is referring to the fact that children are influenced by their environments] is that the things which have the most powerful effect upon children do not come from the conscious state of the parents but from their unconscious background.[16]

The consequences of such a view are considerable, even on a social level. He continues:

> For the ethically minded person who may be a father or mother this presents an almost frightening problem, because the things we can manipulate more or less, namely consciousness and its contents, are seen to be ineffectual in comparison with these uncontrollable effects in the background, no matter how hard we may try.[17]

The aforementioned episode with Jung's mother illustrates this: she intended well in doing all she could to allow her son to be able to stand his ground, clean and shining, even in front of especially important people. But this *conscious* intent of hers – *unconsciously* she probably suffered herself under the pressure of higher social classes – provoked the exact opposite in her child: her well-meaning, somewhat obsessively repeated admonitions didn't make her son stronger, they made him weaker! They permeated his inner life deeply but were transformed there as if under a demonic influence. In the end it was the *unconscious* message that echoed loudly in the child's head. It might have told him something like this: 'We are worthless, but we have to conceal this fact behind our good appearances. In actual fact, we are pathetic.' The child could not help but follow the *unconscious* message, and therefore did not take notice of his mother's well-meant recommendations, which originated from just a thin layer of consciousness in her personality. He behaved shyly and stubbornly, and worst of all, he suffered under the contradictory world of the adults.

In Jung's descriptions of his few therapies with children, his main focus lies on the feeling of trust that can be established between the child and the therapist. This has nothing to do with psychoanalytical techniques; it depends not only on the therapist's personality, but also on whether the therapist is able to communicate with the child in the child's own language, and this, in turn, is naturally not limited to the verbal level. Jung himself had had intimate experience with the effect of non-verbal forms of expression, not only as a child, but also as an adult. At a time of great crisis, he reverted to play:

> After the parting of the ways with Freud, a period of inner uncertainty began for me. It would be no exaggeration to call it a state of disorientation. [. . .] This moment was a turning point in my fate, but I gave in only after endless resistances and with a sense of recognition. For it was a painfully humiliating experience to realise that there was nothing to be done except play childish games. [. . .] Nevertheless, I began accumulating suitable stones, gathering them partly from the lake shore and partly from the water. And I started building: [. . .] I went on with my building game after the noon meal every day, whenever the weather permitted. As soon as I was through eating, I began playing, and continue to do so until the patients arrived; and if I was finished with my work early enough in the evening, I went back to building. In the course of this activity my thoughts clarified, and I was able to grasp the fantasies whose presence in myself I dimly felt.[18]

Jung describes something here that might be similar to what a child experiences during free play and also during play therapy.[19] When Dora Kalff came in contact with Margaret Lowenfeld's *World Technique*, Jung, who had already heard a lecture about it in France in 1937, supported her greatly in developing this technique into a child psychotherapy.

Jung's focus on the importance of images instead of concepts led to the development of diverse imaginative methods in the second half of the twentieth century.[20] Everything that is nowadays summed up under the term 'expressive therapies' can be taken as an example: 'At the beginning of the 20th century C.G. Jung anticipated everything we do today in the expressive therapies.'[21]

Expressive therapies are very widespread in the USA and are exceptionally broadly defined; first in the type of expression,[22] and second in respect to their theoretical basic principles: 'Expressive Therapy draws from psychoanalytic theory, ego psychology, object relations theory and brain research.'[23]

The supporters of expressive therapies sometimes point out that the latter theory has many similarities to Jung's method of 'Active Imagination'.[24] It is important to clear up this misunderstanding because Expressive Sandwork can also be counted among the expressive therapies. While the conditions for active imagination might have a certain formal similarity to many an expressive therapy's approach, the heart of the method – conscious confrontation of unconscious content – is the exact opposite of a spontaneous expressive process.

Therefore active imagination is suited neither for children nor for groups. Far more, it is a possibility for people with enough personal strength and perseverance to attempt an actual analysis of themselves.

Other terms that were coined by Jung in the 1920s have also become commonplace. The concepts that have even entered our colloquial language have, however, also suffered a reduction in their meaning. The terms 'introversion' and 'extroversion' are apt examples. In his typology, Jung describes four types of psychological function, which can each be expressed either in an introverted or an extroverted way, equalling eight psychological types. But today, only the crude distinction of two types is commonly known; the typology as a whole is reserved for specialists. The ongoing discussion of whether introversion should be counted as a pathological disorder in DSM-V (the forthcoming fifth edition of the *Diagnostic and Statistical Manual of Mental Disorders*)[25] shows how far the current usage of the term has drifted from Jung's original meaning.

Sometimes concepts of analytical psychology are also mingled with anthropological or theological terms, resulting in a confusing lack of distinction between such words as 'archetype', 'individuation', 'initiation' and 'ritual'.

It was very important to Jung to use the language of objective science. His definitions and distinctions between terms like symbol and sign, interpretation and amplification, and finality and causality, are unmistakeably clear. C.G. Jung's importance today does not lie only in his emphasis on imaginative processes as opposed to conceptual forms of thought. Other aspects of his person appear to be gaining continuous importance for psychology in the twenty-first century. Those aspects came to light in 1906 and 1907, when the brave, young psychiatrist in a clinic in Burghölzli first confronted the general view of his colleagues. Jung was the first to suspect a meaning behind the 'meaningless' fantasies of his schizophrenic patients, and also to argue against the pathologization of psychological phenomena.

Today, one need only consider the fervid discussion over the diagnosis of 'posttraumatic stress disorder' and its controversial treatment, or think of the exponential increase in diagnoses of manic-depressive disorder in US American children and how frivolously attention deficit disorders are diagnosed and treated with medication, in order to see that Jung's approach of searching for the unconscious purpose behind a psychological disorder is as modern as ever.

The work of Jungian analyst and psychiatrist Renos Papadopoulos with refugees – which might seem simplified only at first – is a good current example of a broad and social application of Jungian theory. He writes: 'the healing of these painful experiences due to atrocities may not lie in devising sophisticated therapeutic techniques but in returning to more "traditional" forms of healing based on assisting people to develop appropriate narratives.'[26]

Although most of the Bosnian refugees with whom Papadopoulos worked fulfilled the diagnostic criteria for posttraumatic stress disorder, he did not initially reveal himself to them as a therapist who was seeking to relieve them of their trauma.

> I did not impose any therapeutic schema, such as debriefing, abreaction, catharsis, re-living previous trauma, developing coping skills. Respecting that they where 'in charge', I did not direct their conversations in any way but allowed them to talk to me about anything they wanted following their own pace.[27]

Above all, he tried to avoid pathologization as much as possible. For example, terms such as 'dissociation' or 'regression' were replaced with 'petrification'. Papadopoulos decided to try to find an 'unclassic' therapeutic setting that was, however, suitable in this specific situation of his work with refugees. The fact that the psychiatrist was not to be found in a consulting room treating patients – at least not initially – did not mean that he had merely intended to assume a compassionate role in the group. At first he spent unstructured time with the severely traumatized people and tried to assist 'with anything I was capable of doing (from making cups of tea to cleaning, from translating between Serbo-Croatian and English to liaising between them and various authorities)'.[28]

But at the same time he made sure of adopting a therapeutic attitude in his daily conversations,

> for example to remind them of their painful losses and their disorientation as we would talk about everyday issues. Moreover I would appreciate their reserved stance as appropriate and not treat it as resistance. [. . .] In a respectful and discreet way, my 'interpretations' would aim to normalize their experiences (that is as 'normal reactions to abnormal circumstances') within a framework which emphasized the tragic but not pathological dimensions. [. . .] The attention here was on empowering them to develop their own new narratives within which their experiences would acquire different meaning.[29]

On the one hand Jung's therapeutic approach found a very subtle form of expression here, and on the other hand it was consistently practised. Pathologization is also avoided by the fact that no actual 'treatment' is intended. One relies on past experience that the psyche can unfold its self-regulatory powers, provided that the minimum preconditions – a protected framework and a therapeutic presence – are given. The focus lies on a prospective view: could it be that even the most terrible events produce something valuable in life, something that was not there before? This view towards a possible meaning behind a disorder, a symptom or a crisis, be it individually or collectively, is one of C.G. Jung's great achievements. It goes without saying that such a concept is nothing new. It has always been deeply rooted in the world's great cultures, and it has manifested itself in the most diverse forms. One of these forms is the Chinese character for the word 'crisis', which contains the character for the word 'creativity'. Creativity, so to say, is the other, as yet concealed and potentially yet to be developed side of every crisis. Some of Jung's terms will be introduced in the following chapters, but they will occur only implicitly in the text.

According to Jung, the term S*elf*, and the *transcendent function* that is connected with it, signify an instance which is superordinate to the ego and which directs psychological processes. Jung speaks of a religious human instinct. By that he means that humans are interested since childhood in questions that go beyond our material world. Our mental equilibrium even depends on whether we can find satisfactory answers to these questions during the course of our lives. These answers are never final. The questions must be asked again after every dramatic experience and in every stage of life. In Jung's view, the psyche creates images or figures spontaneously. They result in a context of meaning when enriched by a greater, cross-cultural setting. Their character can be symbolic, which means that they have an excess of meaning that can be perceived holistically. Through their energetic load, *symbols* are able to transcend mental opposites, contradictions and blockages; they are able to take them to another level.

Expressive Sandwork, as it is described in the following, is not a specific and independent method. It understands itself as a practical application of Jungian theory.

Chapter 3

Margaret Lowenfeld's *World Technique* and Dora Kalff's *Sandplay*

All children are difficult sometimes, but some children are difficult all the time. Some children seem always to be catching something and never to be quite well. Some children are nervous and find life and school difficult for them. Some children have distressing habits.

This clinic, which is in charge of a physician, exists to help mothers in these kinds of trouble with their children, and also to help the children themselves.[1]

This statement was in the brochure announcing the opening of the 'Children's Clinic for the Treatment and Study of Nervous and Difficult Children', which Margaret Lowenfeld founded in 1928 in a working-class area of London. Lowenfeld, an English paediatrician who applied sandplay as a therapeutic medium for the first time, was born in London in 1890 into a wealthy Jewish family. Her father had lost his entire estate in the Polish struggle for freedom, and came to London penniless, where he succeeded in rebuilding his fortune and gaining a high social reputation. He was an art collector and was friends with musicians, actors and writers. The family spent a few months of every year in Poland, where he had bought back his entire former estate. Mrs Lowenfeld, a captain's daughter, was always the perfect hostess. Her active social life did not seem to be affected by the birth of their two daughters, Helena and Margaret. The girls were looked after by nurses, and spent a lot of time on their own. Margaret was sickly and reclusive, and seemed to have trouble learning. Helena was more outgoing, very popular, and her achievements at school were excellent. Margaret's parents were divorced when she was 13 years old. The daughters lived with their mother, who started to suffer from various illnesses. Margaret's health deteriorated as well. While the father, who continued to provide generous financial support, had good marriages in mind for his daughters, the mother attached great importance to the girls' education. They both studied medicine. After completing her studies, Helena began a brilliant career in the field of gynaecology.[2] Margaret took a little longer than her older sister to complete her studies. She finished in the last year of the First World War, and started work as an assistant doctor at the

Women's Hospital. This was in 1919, when Poland was at war with Russia. Army doctors were desperately needed, and England and the USA supported Poland in this respect against the communist enemy. Margaret decided to return to the country where she had spent so much of her childhood, and worked for the British typhoid unit and the American Young Men's Christian Association (YMCA). She was mainly responsible for prisoners of war, but also worked as a secretary for the Polish student aid. The years of war left their mark on Lowenfeld, as they did on so many other psychoanalysts of the time.

> The living of several distinct mutually incompatible lives did for me what the preliminary analysis does for the therapists-to-be, that is, it opened doors on to an interior world I would not otherwise have reached. Later when reflecting upon this experience, I realised that the living of roles totally different from and even hostile to each other, in a constant atmosphere of fear, and with a lack of any overall direction is of the essence of the experience of unhappy children and the black misery of prisoners of war is very like the depression of infancy.[3]

This account is already suggestive of the differences of opinion that she would have with established psychoanalytical concepts in the following years.

When the young doctor returned to London after four years, there was no work to be had at the hospitals, because all the positions were being given to male physicians returning from war. Margaret Lowenfeld opened a private paediatric practice and started studying developmental psychology on the side. Her main interest lay in helping socially disadvantaged children. In 1923 she was awarded a research scholarship by the Royal Hospital for Sick Children in Glasgow, to study the relationship between rheumatic afflictions in children and their family milieu. She also conducted a study about breast feeding of infants, and published its results in 1928. That same year, she finally achieved a goal towards which she had been working persistently for a long time: her children's psychological clinic. Children between the ages of 12 months and 18 years were treated with a new method, which Lowenfeld called the *World Technique*. In just a few years this clinic became a centre of research in the field of child psychotherapy – the Institute of Child Psychology – and a centre of attraction for psychotherapists from around the world. The field of research was ground-breaking for its time: children's experiences, which could not be expressed verbally, were being studied.[4]

Lowenfeld recalls:

> My own approach to the use of a toy apparatus with children derives from a memory of H.G. Wells' *Floor Games*,[5] the first edition of which had made a deep impression upon my youth.When, therefore, in 1925, I came from orthodox paediatrics to the associated study of emotional conditions in childhood, I began to put this memory to use. I collected first a miscellaneous mass of material, coloured sticks and shapes, beads, small toys of all sorts, paper

shapes and match boxes, and kept them in what came to be known by my children as the 'Wonder Box'; with this I began to experiment with my children patients.[6]

After just two years the clinic had to move into a larger building. Lowenfeld had two sandtrays made out of zinc, one for dry and one for wet sand. During their sessions, the children could now work with the sand as well as place the objects from the wonder box in the trays.

> Less than three months after a metal tray with mouldable sand placed on a table and a cabinet containing small miniature objects were included in the playroom equipment, a spontaneous new technique had developed, *created by the children themselves*.[7]

At the same time Melanie Klein had also begun using small toys in her treatment sessions. However, the theoretical approach of the two therapists, the ways in which they assessed the observed play and the therapeutic procedures themselves, could not have been more different. Melanie Klein was of the following opinion: 'Because the therapist imparts to the child his interpretations of the child's play, drawings and behaviour, he slowly loosens suppressed fantasies, which lie behind the child's play, and frees them.'[8]

Margaret Lowenfeld, on the other hand, said about her work:

> My own endeavour in my work with children is to devise an instrument with which a child can demonstrate his own emotional and mental state without the necessary intervention of an adult either by transference or interpretation, and which will allow a record being made of such a demonstration. My objective is to help children to produce something which will stand by itself and be independent of any theory as to its nature.[9]

It is not surprising that such a statement met with resistance from all the psychoanalysts of the age. But it was not Margaret Lowenfeld's intent to oppose psychoanalysis as a whole. She was merely opposed to the tendency to view children's non-verbal forms of expression only through the eyes of a theory – whichever theory that may be. She was convinced that play had an important psychological function *in itself* – a completely new concept, which was not even shared by Donald Winnicott at the time. Children's desire to play during psychoanalytical treatment was seen by Freud's students not only as trivial and secondary, but even as an expression of resistance against the treatment itself.

When Margaret Lowenfeld began to present her work at international conferences, she met with harsh criticism. Melanie Klein thought that Lowenfeld was 'sacrificing the valuable possibilities that lay in transference'.[10] Winnicott wrote to Lowenfeld that he did not understand the aim of her work, and that the abundance of play material used in the World Technique would surely only confuse children; drawings would allow for a much more individual form of expression.[11] (Winnicott later developed the squiggle game as an instrument of communication between the therapist and the child patient.)[12]

Margaret Lowenfeld's counter-argument – that the miniature toys were sorted in drawers and would therefore not create confusion – showed not only her determination on the one hand, but also a certain helplessness on the other hand. The mainstream psychoanalytical opinion that the effect of therapy lay *only* in transference and counter-transference must have loomed before her like a brick wall.

Lowenfeld could not agree with Melanie Klein's view that 'the aim of the psychoanalytical play technique with children is to explore the child's feelings, desires, fantasies and thoughts'.[13] She did not see play as a means of reaching a diagnosis, but believed that it was in itself a chance for healing. She countered Klein with the argument that transference in her method did not go from the child to the therapist, but from the child to the sandtray. She says the following very clearly, thereby expressing the core of her pioneering work:

> In psychoanalysis, the therapist confronts the child with the 'meaning' of his play by interpreting it. In the 'World Technique', the child is confronted with parts of his own emotional world, thoughts and memories, by the fact that the child himself has laid them out for his own inspection.[14]

This formulation, 'laying out life for one's own inspection',[15] puts Lowenfeld's vanguard concept in a nutshell. As we saw in Chapter 2, the same view was proposed by C.G. Jung. It received further confirmation from infant research by authors like Daniel Stern in the 1990s.[16] Nowadays – almost a hundred years later – it is in the course of asserting itself in child psychotherapy. Seen from an anthropological point of view, the work of Arno Stern,[17] who spent decades studying and comparing thousands of children's drawings in many different ethnic groups, leads to the same conclusion: *children themselves can be accorded competency for their own mental processes.* Not one of the psychoanalysts of the time shared this view. Lowenfeld was alone in her conviction.

Margaret Lowenfeld's book *Play in Childhood* was published in London in 1935, but was not published in New York until 1976,[18] when it appeared with a foreword by Margaret Mead, an anthropologist and friend of Lowenfeld's:

> Margaret Lowenfeld was one of the great pioneers in the discovery of childhood – the discovery was itself an outstanding human and scientific event of the 20th century – and part of the whole intellectual adventure of seeking ways to explore children's thinking and feeling.[19]

Lowenfeld had decided not to have the book published in the USA, because she thought that American therapists were not concerned with play but with other aspects of childhood. She had not reckoned with the fact that this would be the same in Europe.

In the book's summary, Lowenfeld expresses clearly and concisely what significance a child's play has in her eyes, namely that normal emotional development is not possible without adequate and sufficient room for play. 'Play has been regarded in this book not as an accident, but as an essential function in childhood'.[20]

It almost seems like a stroke of Lowenfeld's personal fate that she continued to find herself in the shadow of other great personalities throughout her life. As a child she had always lagged behind her capable and extroverted sister (later Helena Wright). Today, Winnicott's *Playing and Reality* is regarded as an absolute classic,[21] while Lowenfeld is not even cited. The idea of working with miniature toys in child therapy is generally accredited to Melanie Klein. Even the World Technique itself, which Lowenfeld had worked out down to the very last detail,[22] is outshone today by Dora Kalff's internationally well-known Sandplay Therapy. The World Technique was not only incorporated into today's Sandplay Therapy, but also transformed by Charlotte Bühler into a diagnostic test procedure – something which Margaret Lowenfeld opposed.[23] Two other test procedures which Lowenfeld *did* invent and elaborate were integrated into the widely known 'Sceno Test' without her name even receiving a mention. Margaret Lowenfeld's book *The World Technique* appeared in 1979 – six years after her death.[24]

Dora Kalff met Margaret Lowenfeld in 1956 in Zurich, where Lowenfeld was giving a lecture on the World Technique.

Dora Kalff was studying at the Jung Institute at the time, and was impressed by the method.[25] She decided to develop it into a Jungian method of child therapy, and C.G. Jung himself encouraged her to do so. She went to London for a year to learn from Margaret Lowenfeld, Michael Fordham and Donald Winnicott.

She adapted the World Technique without making any significant changes to its practical procedures. But she described the processes that are to be observed in the sand in the terms of analytical psychology and of the developmental stages of human consciousness, which were put forward by Erich Neumann. Dora Kalff named this new form of therapy 'Sandplay'. She published her first article on Sandplay Therapy in 1966, 'The archetype as a healing factor'.[26] Her emphasis lay on the 'Self', which Jung had defined as the totality of the unconscious and the conscious, and which stands in tension with the 'ego'. She saw it as a sign of mental health when an axis forms between the Self and the ego, with the ego allowing the Self to take the upper hand.

Dora Kalff's interest in eastern philosophy, especially Tibetan Buddhism and Japanese Shintoism, is expressed in all of her works. One of her great merits is that she succeeded in integrating a spiritual dimension into a psychotherapeutic method, as if it were a matter of course. Sandplay's prominence grew rapidly through Dora Kalff's lecture tours to the USA and Japan, and not least through her charismatic personality. From the 1970s until 1990 – shortly before her death – therapists came from all over the world to Zollikon to study with Dora Kalff. In 1985 she founded the International Society for Sandplay Therapy (ISST), which offers a standardized training programme and has individual national subgroups throughout the world.

Although Dora Kalff had cautioned against using sandplay therapy in the case of severe psychiatric disorders, today it has also become an inherent part of psychiatric clinics and achieves good results in treating psychoses, psychosomatic illness and personality disorders – provided it is part of an overall plan of therapy.

Not only have the symbolic levels of expression in sandplay been researched and described in the past years, but also pre-symbolic processes from earliest childhood,[27] including such complicated transference processes as, for example, projective identification, have been studied. This is especially the case when only the sand is used, and hardly any miniatures. Psychodynamic processes, which take place in the 'mental field' between the therapist and the patient, can potentially be grounded in the third, neutral medium of the sandtray, by taking on a concrete form there.[28] When this happens, the patient, whose hands have just aimlessly and as if in a trance formed something in the sand, is confronted with his own mental state as if it were something that had come at him from outside himself, from the sandtray.

I did a number of sandplay sessions with Dora Kalff in 1988. She insisted that the sessions not take place on consecutive days, and not more often than once or twice a week. She asked questions and was generally very vivacious and talkative, while her eyes paid close but almost unnoticeable attention to my hands. It is not easy to describe the feeling of freedom that overcame one upon entering that room full of miniatures in her presence. It had not simply to do with a lack of judgement or control: it was, far more, as if everything that one thought or did was precisely what she seemed to expect. Everything humanly conceivable, no matter how absurd the action might be, would have provoked only a curious and accomplice-like smile in her face, accompanied by the singsong of her Swiss German: 'Ah, so that's how it is!' It always seemed to be she who was learning from what one did.

What Heinz Kohut meant by the gleam in the mother's eye or reverie was a characteristic that Dora Kalff had mastered perfectly in her therapy.[29] Her person conveyed a sense of respect for the patient's psyche, while a certain homespun manner about her promoted the necessary degree of relaxation at the same time. This manner was surely also the reason that her intellectual capabilities were sometimes underestimated. Dora Kalff's medium-like skills could have become a great danger for trainees. Luckily, sandplay has so far been spared this. It has neither degenerated to a mystical-magical message of salvation, nor been reduced to a scientific diagnostic testing method. It maintains a balance between clinical method and cultural, anthropological approach, between psychoanalytical theory and empirical experience, between science and wisdom, and between influences from the West and from the East. So far it has also maintained quite an openness to innovation, be it in regard to the patient groups, or to variations in its application. There is hardly another psychotherapeutic technique that offers such a broad range of application.

One could describe the path which unconscious content takes during psychotherapy in this way: based on a general physical sensation, the next step is to become aware of a specific emotion. In sandplay, for example, this emotion is transformed into a shape or an image, which is created in the sand. This grows to a series of images that can be arranged to form a narrative, and which can eventually also be expressed in words. This line, which we can schematically describe between body, emotion, image and word, is travelled in both directions in sandplay therapies. A process can begin at any position along this line. A single one of these steps from one mental level of expression to another is mostly drawn out over numerous sessions. Successfully reaching a new level is always connected with a feeling of great relief, and it makes no difference if this is a 'higher' or more 'primitive' level along the line of development. The simple fact that a level of expression could be switched already has a vitalizing effect, and mostly the vegetative nervous system is the first to react to this. Children who lose their stutters or their nervous tics, or ask for the toilet after just half a session of working intensely in the sand, are very simple examples. Another typical aspect of sandplay, compared to other psychoanalytical procedures, is that mechanisms of resistance are manifested less in the relationship between patient and therapist (for instance when the patient arrives late, or talks about irrelevant things), but become immediately visible in the sand itself. They manifest themselves not only as walls or fortresses, for example, but also as particularly symmetrical, empty or crowded images. This has numerous advantages. The therapist is not directly affected and can therefore recognize resistance more easily. But above all – and this is surely the most important point – the mechanisms of resistance show in an intuitive way that their function is *not* limited to mere resistance, but that they also have a constructive side to them. One can tell at a glance that a wall in the sand not only divides and excludes, but also protects and includes. An empty sand image conveys not only a sense of deficiency, but *also* a feeling of freedom and space. An obsessively orderly structure arouses not only a feeling of constriction, but *also* a sense of security. These opposites, which underlie all mental dynamics and must be recognized by the therapist, are relatively easy to see in sandplay.

Another point, which has in fact already been mentioned, is the presence of the neutral 'third party'. Traumatic experiences that cannot be conveyed verbally find a way of being expressed through the sandtray. This may sound abstract, so I would like to illustrate it by using the example of the Grimms' fairy tale 'The Goose Girl'. It is commonly known that fairy tales can be seen as descriptions of inner-psychological processes. When interpreted accordingly, they can prove helpful in understanding many psychological dynamics.

The fairy tale begins with a scene of farewell between a queen and her daughter, who is to travel to a faraway land to meet her betrothed bridegroom. During the journey, the princess is overpowered by her maid, and is made to exchange clothes, horses and roles. When they reach their destination, the prince – like so many princes in fairy tales – does not notice the charade and marries the impostor. The real princess is made to work at court as a goose girl. After a few days, the prince's father – whose powers of perception appear to be a little keener than his son's – becomes suspicious, and asks the goose girl to tell him about her life. Since she refuses, having been forced into an oath of secrecy, the king makes a suggestion: if she wanted to, she could confide all her troubles to the iron stove. When she does this, the king eavesdrops at the stove pipe – taking a circuitous route similar to one that a psychotherapist would adopt today.

The sandplay situation is like the iron stove in this case. One feels safe by its side, and can express unhappiness without fear of disturbing anyone, and without fear of being punished, misunderstood or laughed at. Traumatic, inhuman experiences, which cannot be shared because they are too much for anyone to bear, are thereby made human again little by little.

Chapter 4

Psychotherapy in precarious situations

One question pervades this book's pages like an irritated nerve: can psychotherapy be of use in situations of social destitution? Should not a safe home, food and education be assured first, before any attempt at psychological intervention is made? How should an undernourished child profit from psychological therapy? Concerns like these influenced the planning of all the projects described in this book. During the preparatory phases, young therapists and volunteers who had never before worked in situations of social destitution felt doubtful and anxious. Often a simple briefing on the little biographic data available for the children was enough to trigger feelings of helplessness, anger and despair in the adults. Even before any practical work had begun the facilitators had already identified with the children's emotional situations. 'What if we can't take it?'

The moment in which the children entered the sandwork room for the first time was always awaited with great anticipation by inexperienced and experienced therapists alike. But once children and adults had each taken a seat at one of the sandtrays, and once the creation of miniature worlds had begun, a new and unexpected atmosphere filled the room. The children worked with such seriousness and purpose that the resulting silence felt like a frame, holding everything together. Even those notoriously known as troublemakers worked away quietly, having seemingly forgotten their provocative behaviour. During play one could already perceive the children's expressions and body language changing. Worry lines disappeared from foreheads and breathing became slower and more relaxed. During sandwork processes, 'unspeakable' psychological injuries children may have sustained begin to take shape. First steps of progress were already plain to see in the sandwork images. After a few weeks, changes of behaviour followed. As most of the children came from extremely chaotic family situations or had no family at all, feedback was hardly to be expected from that direction. The teachers at school, however, quickly noticed changes in social behaviour and study motivation. These changes occurred, although the children's family and social surroundings had remained the same.

Obviously, successful psychological therapy will never be able to able to replace social, financial or political intervention. But effective psychological therapy can help an individual gain access to personal resources, either lost or not yet developed. The ideal would be a combination of psychological and financial intervention.

George, a youth from one of the shanty towns near Johannesburg, sowed fields and made vegetable patches during the course of his sandwork sessions. In the miniature world of his sandtray he was able to realize precisely what he had so far been denied in the outside world: a chance to let something grow and thrive (see plate section: p. 1, Plate 1).

In his picture one sees people working in the fields and one man sitting slightly above the others, overseeing everything. The glass pearls in the centre represent water for irrigation. The image's structuredness and order are all the more striking when one has seen in what chaotic and destructive surroundings the boy lives. George said that his picture contained a wish: he would like to grow a garden and sell the harvested vegetables.

Let us assume that George were granted a small loan and given the opportunity to realize his wish. In this case inner and outer reality would have worked together constructively. A depressive youth without psychological intervention might spend the same small loan on drink within a week. *Before* the sessions, not even George had known that he had this wish to create a garden. He had given up on wishes. Within the free and protected space of sandwork, he was able to create something that would further him in his development. Above all, he had experienced that *things are possible*. Strength of mind and endurance arise along with this sense of *being possible*.[1] Not only had George envisioned his wish as if it were a daydream, but also through the help of sandplay he had already made it reality in a miniature world or, as it were, on a symbolic level. He had actually used his very own hands to work in a field, to arrange and shape it. This has a psychological effect.

But what would happen if George were not granted a small loan? Would he be able to beg for vegetable seeds and have the strength of mind to carry water to his patch of earth day after day, enduring the mockery of the other children? All that is certain is that he was able to experience inwardly what it is like to let plants grow and thrive and that, by creating this inner order and beauty, he was temporarily relieved of his depressive mood.

Let us consider things a little further. In many situations, mere financial aid is not simply inadequate, it can actually aggravate existing pathological behaviour.

Daniel, a 6-year-old boy, was living with his grandmother and older brother in a poor part of Bogotá. He did not speak with anybody and trusted only his brother, who had been diagnosed with a severe form of cancer. Daniel had both physical and psychological developmental deficits. During the course of his therapy with Expressive Sandwork, his family situation became even worse. His father had committed murder and was sentenced to

16 years in prison. His grandmother was taken ill and could no longer look after him. He now lived with his alcoholic mother, who took all the food and money she received through charity to her husband in prison. This husband, who had never looked after her, nor their children, now held a special position in her fantasy. In her idealized vision of the future, he would come back after 16 years and all would be well. She did not realize that *in the present* her children were lacking the very basics they needed to survive. She did not notice that Daniel was undernourished and almost autistically withdrawn. She refused to come to a counselling interview, but did not object if the boy took part in the sandwork project, as long as nothing was demanded of her. After six months of sandwork, taking place every two weeks in a group, the boy had gained weight and was talking and socializing without problems.

In the case of families that are both impoverished *and* pathological, psychological intervention is essential. No matter how generous financial aid might be, if it only ends up in the hands of abusive parents it will not help the children at all: they will continue to be treated like objects. But if, through therapy, children can experience that they possess an inner world that is theirs alone, a place in which they can decide and act independently, then there is a chance that their potential for healthy development will prevail over their destructive environment. In these cases, all other measures designed at structuring social life are only made effective through psychotherapy.

For the time being we have answered the question posed at the start of the chapter. This, however, does not mean that it will not pose itself again in a new form.

Psychotherapy tends to be least accessible to the very children who would require it most. Studying psychotherapy takes a long time and there is a lack of qualified professionals. At the same time, in situations of social destitution there are often volunteers who are prepared to offer their time and energy, but who do not have psychotherapeutic training. Time and again I have met young psychologists, fresh from university, working in public or state-run institutions in South America, who are completely overburdened. As they do not have proper psychotherapeutic training, they do not know how to cope with the masses of people asking for help in their clinics every day. When they suffer burn-out syndrome, it is not because of the amount of work or even the severity of problems, but because they feel inadequate. They know they have less to offer than, for instance, a doctor, who can at least prescribe pain-killers. They were never given the necessary tools to help, and are often assigned by the governments merely in order to show the public that things are being done. They know that the adults and children who come to them, usually after waiting some months for an appointment, will most likely go back home empty handed. Rotation in these positions is very fast. Given the opportunity, most of these young psychologists change their profession after a few months or, at most, a few years.

This is where our question fits in, which, in the light of these facts, may seem as unlikely as it is urgent: *is there a method of treating psychological problems that is both simple in practice, and cross-cultural in its nature? Might it even be possible to train lay therapists?*

Let us widen our horizons even more and begin by considering what experience has taught us in disaster areas. Be it after an earthquake, a flood, or in a refugee camp, there is always a degree of uncertainty as to how best to put unskilled volunteers to use. A helper's good will alone is not sufficient. Traumatized people are numbed and unapproachable. If one makes the mistake of issuing volunteers with questionnaires with which to interview survivors, it will only lead to the latter's withdrawal from any further attempt at reaching them. What might have been meant as a simple statistical appraisal of the situation can already have caused serious side-effects. Responding to the question, how many family members a person has lost, is not even possible without deep emotional involvement. Insufficiently trained helpers underestimate this, and further traumatization is often the consequence. Psychological methods, even ones as seemingly harmless as ten questions on a piece of paper, are never neutral. Relief work in the earthquake province of Sichuan in August 2008 demonstrated this time and again. Chapter 8 on China describes how easily accidental re-traumatization can occur through inadequate intervention.

People understandably want to help – but how? This problem is further intensified in situations of chronic social destitution. Should one try to encourage people to talk? Those in need of help could be illiterate and unaccustomed to using words the way educated volunteers from outside might take for granted. Even asking a question in the first place might be taken very differently in some cultures than in a volunteer's country of origin. Talking about one's feelings, especially to strangers, is simply not usual in many parts of the world. If a helper has nothing useful to offer, he will soon feel rejected by the seeming 'passivity' and 'lack of motivation' in those requiring help.

People frequently dare enter this no man's land with individual projects. These are often artists, who simply offer to teach a skill: music, dance, drama, painting or sport. Such projects can boast of extremely high therapeutic effect and efficiency. A striking example is offered by the music education project of the Berlin Philharmonic Orchestra under Sir Simon Rattle, in which 250 underprivileged youths from Berlin staged a performance of Stravinsky's 'Le Sacre du printemps'.[2]

Another well-known example is the network of music centres established in Venezuela by José Antonio Abreu since the late 1970s. Today, *El Sistema* gives over 300,000 underprivileged children the chance to learn a musical instrument.[3]

Slightly less spectacular, though no less successful, are projects in Africa like AIDS prevention by means of theatre,[4] or football grounds built by the Philipp Lahm foundation. During a project of the Italian Cultural Institute after 11 September, New York school children were given the task of designing the 'new twin towers'. The drawings show clearly how the 6 to 18 year olds were coming to terms with their fears, concerns and hopes (Pictures 2.1, 2.2, 2.3 and 2.4).

A further noteworthy example is a model for lay helpers, developed by the Indian psychiatrist Dr Gauthamada after the 2004 Indian Ocean tsunami. The aim

TUESDAY, OCTOBER 9, 2001 – 6:00 P.M.

Picture 2.1

Picture 2.2

TUESDAY, OCTOBER 9, 2001 – 6:00 P.M.

Picture 2.3

TUESDAY, OCTOBER 9, 2001 – 6:00 P.M.

Picture 2.4

was to care for the population of 51 remote villages in the Cuddalore district in Tamil Nadu,[5] some of which had rarely come into contact with civilization to that point. Free creative expression has in itself proven to be helpful in many situations: 'Give any group of 6 year-old children a set of coloured pens and a few sheets of paper and watch their eagerness to use them', Haroon Ahmed, a psychiatrist in Karachi, writes about his work with children in remote areas of Kashmir.[6] In another case, a social worker from a project with street children in the Philippines deplores the fact that the children seem to lack 'creativity'. She finds they do not know what they should draw and simply end up copying each other. This case underlines that it is most important *how* a creative method is implemented, and that results cannot be expected without at least a minimum of therapeutic understanding.

In view of such initiatives' success and necessity, one wonders why no cross-cultural concept of psychological intervention has yet been developed for unschooled helpers. However, one can understand resistance towards developing such a method coming from psychotherapists themselves. How should a volunteer helper cope without the necessary psychological skills one learns in years of study? Where to draw the line between psychological assistance and psychotherapy? Is it right to assume that, in emergency situations, limited help is better than none at all?

Various trains of thought begin at this point, depending on the nature of the crisis and the implemented psychological methods.

First, one must differentiate between poverty, the consequences of wars or natural catastrophes, and chronic social destitution. Poverty alone does not necessarily lead to emotional problems. On the contrary, knowing one's chances of survival are better together can also bond a community. Becoming homeless due to an earthquake or a war is not one and the same thing. The latter is accompanied by unspeakable human violence and, at the same time, would seem within our power to avoid. Natural catastrophes, on the other hand, are often followed by an irrational search for explanations, usually revolving around guilt and punishment. After the tsunami in 2004, in which the majority of victims were Muslim, the Buddhist communities surmised that the tsunami had been divine punishment. In reality, Muslims – not being vegetarian – often work in fisheries, and were either at sea or near the coast when the deadly waves struck.

When children lose both parents through natural catastrophes, this in itself does not necessarily lead to psychological problems. Up until the tragic event, these would usually have been healthy children of equally healthy parents. Even though their parents are now dead, the children still carry a potential of constructive behavioural patterns within them, ingrained in their personalities. Due to the suddenness of their loss, and extended adverse situations thereafter, children can lose touch with this treasure within. It can, however, readily be reactivated through simple yet precise psychological intervention.

The Qiang, a mountain people in the province of Sichuan, offer a fitting example. The Qiang are an ethnic minority with their own language and a culture going back 2000 years. This people's family life and social cohesion were intact until the day in May 2008 when every wall in the high valleys of Beichuan collapsed.

Given the opportunity to observe Qiang youths and children processing the loss of their family members in sandplay, one is astounded at their inner strength. They show deep pain, but not necessarily despair. There is something else, however, which these young people find very hard to cope with. In order to be guaranteed an education, all children between the age of 6 and 18 had to leave their native villages in the Beichuan area; not just temporarily, but permanently, because new settlements are being built down in the lowlands. Only in some scattered villages that are especially hard to reach did some Qiang remain and are trying to rebuild their lives. In distant Mianyang the children have had to adapt to unfamiliar food, customs, language and landscapes. For many of them, the memory of the earth opening up to devour their parents and grandparents is still perilously present. Their fear is quite understandable from the point of view of cultural psychology as well. With the disappearance of almost an entire generation of people, these young people are likely to see their own future identity in danger as well. Strengthening their identity and allowing it to re-emerge is the key to successful therapeutic intervention. We will see how, in due course.

The situation is very different in populations whose social cohesion suffers from chronic self-destruction, and often has done so for generations. One of the delayed consequences of devastating external interference – such as colonization was in so many parts of the world – is always a creeping erosion of traditional ways of life. One finds countless examples of such situations, ranging from South America over Africa to Asia, from Greenland to Madagascar. Decades of war or systematic destruction of economic and natural resources through overexploitation can be the reasons. Traditional trades that had been passed down over generations are lost, along with their associated knowledge, rituals, and ways of life. At the same time a very specific form of everyday 'connectedness with the world' on the inside and outside disappears. Once a people have lost their cultural and spiritual roots, they are emotionally broken. They die, as it were, a psychosomatic death through addictive behaviour, violence, perversion or apathy.

In South Africa, where immigration from the North has never ceased since the end of apartheid, and people from different origins live penned up in abject poverty, the psychological consequences are devastating. Small children normally enjoy special protection in any society, but in this misery they are considered fair game by 'others'. They are persecuted, abused and often killed. In healthy societies, other adults can assume the role of parents for children who no longer have their own. But these children not only lack parents, but also have lost trust in other people in general. Self-destructive behaviour is a logical consequence – the only way out of an impossibility of existence.

Things are no different in South America. A social worker from Buenos Aires described to me how her working conditions have deteriorated between 2000 and 2010. These ten years represent Argentina's economic collapse and, as one of the consequences, the first emergence of organized crime in this hitherto wealthy and culturally diverse country. Today, the scale of crime is enormous and still incomprehensible for most of the city's inhabitants. Never had people needed to scavenge through rubbish for food in Argentina. Nowadays, every tourist returning from Buenos Aires will recount such a scene. Most tourists should also have noticed how discreetly the poor beg for alms and how respectfully the wealthier Argentinians treat them. As they have just so recently become poor, they still 'belong'; they have not yet become 'others'. Just a few years ago, when social workers came to work in the infamous 'barrio 24', children would come running happily to greet them. They had been awaiting the helpers' arrival and knew that they would be given something to eat, would receive books and clothes, or that a theatre project would take place. Nowadays, not a single child comes to welcome the social workers any more. They have to go looking for them. Even 7 year olds are to be found staggering around somewhere between the shacks, intoxicated by a highly poisonous mix of drugs called Paco. They do not know who or where they are, and they have long since forgotten that they need help.

Our question takes on a sense of desperation: is psychological intervention even conceivable in such situations? To avoid despairing, let us try to hold fast to the theoretical framework of analytic psychology and bring to mind the following: despite the downfall of a society as a whole, a potential of cultural identity still persists in each individual, and expresses itself continuously in fantasies, dreams, or symptoms. If we want to believe C.G. Jung, we can assume that we each inherit such a potential, from which psychological life is formed again and again. 'Soul is image'.[7] The soul is where images are created. This idea has been a part of various cultures' mythical narrations throughout the history of humankind. They describe destruction and recreation in countless variants as a never-ending, self-repetitive cycle. Any cross-cultural psychotherapeutic concept, which is to be effective even where little rational or conscious content remains, must necessarily originate from these unconscious images. Even in the most extreme chaos, the aim is to try to find fragments of narrations which could prove to be the puzzle pieces of potential psychological life. Such work with spontaneous images can never be predetermined by the therapist, but must always come directly from the affected person. What psychologists can do, and what it ultimately comes down to in Expressive Sandwork, is nothing more than to provide the adequate conditions. Astonishingly, even in extreme situations, this provided frame of conditions rarely remains empty and unused. In some cases we might believe we do not understand what is shown within the frame, when in reality we just cannot bear it.

The importance of images has been proven in trauma research. Imaginative methods have become integral in treating posttraumatic disorders. Neuroscience has confirmed that traumatic experiences are located in the right hemisphere of the brain, where imaginative, non-verbal content is processed. This explains why, for instance, some people simply *cannot* talk about wartime experiences: those specific memories were not stored in form of words and sentences. The dreaded flashbacks these people often experience are psycho-physical states of being, connected to mental images. Psychological intervention relying entirely on verbal expression would never be able to reach the emotions connected with such experiences. A form of intervention on a more 'primitive' level of expression (e.g. image rather than language) can, however, initiate a process of assimilation.

Let us return, now, to problems in settings of chronic social destitution. We have realized how difficult any form of psychological intervention is in these cases, because the collective is affected by pathological behaviour. Homicide, sexual abuse, addiction and depravity are considered normal. There are hardly any alternatives to be seen as role models for children. Even if they do exist, they are not taken notice of. Unschooled helpers, hoping to be useful in some way, will initially feel rejected because the people (including the children) are primarily deficient in their capability for relationship. We realize again that helpers would require a minimum of crisis-proof psychological methods to allow them to act competently within these given limitations. This minimum of therapeutic tools is crucial, just as carrying a bush knife in the jungle could decide whether one will survive or not. How are we to envision such a minimal offer of therapy?

Let us consider, under this aspect, the situation of a small child suffering chronic neglect. Such a child will not be capable of interacting with other children. He might be sitting absent-mindedly in a circle of talking children, or still staring fixedly at his piece of paper while the other children have already begun drawing. The child's body language alone will convey how utterly distant his emotional condition is from any state a healthy person could possibly imagine. Friendly prompting on the part of the facilitators has no effect. This child does not even register their presence. A psychological defence system is making sure that anything even remotely suspected of rousing emotions is systematically, pre-emptively faded out. This is the ultimate measure the psyche can take, once a threat has become too great and lasted too long. Since fear was threatening to exceed the level any person can bear, a mechanism has set which filters out emotional sensations.[8] Consciousness is granted almost no more access to a large part of emotional life, though it still continues to exist, somewhere. A well-meant offer of relationship will not be of much help to a child in such a state. Since all feelings have been blocked, even the *feeling of being* has got lost. The child needs help re-establishing contact with his very own resources that have been buried deep inside, and this must happen in an individual way, and in the child's own time. The setting of Expressive Sandwork is an offer of help in this direction. Initially, and for the first few sessions, the same child might do nothing more than sit passively at his sandtray. But the child will realize that even in doing nothing, nothing else seems to be expected, and he can still feel he is part of the group. After this experience of 'simply being allowed *to be*' has relaxed his body, the child might eventually unclench a fist in order to touch the sand. A form of contact has taken place. Not between two people – that would not be possible at this stage – but between two levels of existence, one material and one symbolic. The relationship on offer here could not be more elemental: the sandtray's enclosing frame, and the sand's solid-fluid consistency. Now the child might have taken some of the sand in his hand and is holding it tightly. The simple act of holding the sand *himself* can begin to activate an innate, elementary pattern of holding, and also of being held, in the child's psyche. Though he may have lost all emotional footholds within his inner universe and cannot trust in being held by anybody, the child can still draw on an inner memory of a primordial form of 'being held'. In the language of analytical psychology one speaks of an archetypal pattern of behaviour being formed. This is comparable, on a physical level, to instincts being activated and functioning, even though they have never been explicitly learnt. But this archetypal formation of psychological patterns of survival requires very precise conditions. The central principle of Expressive Sandwork is to provide these conditions.

Our question, now, is whether an adult without specific psychotherapeutic training could provide these basic conditions as well? In the described case, all the helper needed to do was to be present with his own personality and bear the child's inner world emotionally. He himself had to experience and actually share the physical feeling of how the child's hand first touched the sand. He had to be part of everything that was happening as immediately as was the child himself. This emotional participation on the part of the therapist acts like a resonating body, intensifying the child's experience. The psyche of a child in need is highly sensitized to the slightest offer of help: if one can provide even a fraction of what is required for healthy development, then that will be immediately sucked up like water by a dry sponge. But – and this is the point – even this minimal offer still needs to be adequate. It has to be offered in a form that can be received. The reader might interject that this is precisely the difficulty in the matter: a lay helper with minimal training will not have learnt what children are capable of assimilating in which situations. For the moment this concern can be appeased. The child is only being offered the protected setting, within which his own psyche can produce what it needs to heal itself. C.G. Jung calls this the self-regulation of the psyche.[9]

But before we go into detail, let us make just a short detour to see how psychotherapy is learnt in the first place. This in turn might help us assess the possibility of a reduced training for volunteer helpers. As is widely known, the essence of psychotherapeutic training – compared to disciplines in the natural sciences – lies in something very specific: students are treated with the very methods they are learning. They learn the principles of treatment through dealing with their own problems. The emotional world of aspiring doctors might never even be touched during ten years of studying medicine, but this is different in psychotherapy. During the course of their study years, the way in which students perceive other people and themselves, physically and emotionally, begins to change. Even the main psychotherapy textbooks, seen in this light, do not merely convey scientific knowledge, but aim at shifting their readers' perceptions. This could be seen as making pre-Socratic demands on an educational text. In this sense, psychotherapy is not an objective science, but partly subjective experience. A student of psychotherapy must learn to perceive another person's – the patient's – thoughts and feelings in a differentiated way, while simultaneously observing changes in his own thoughts and feelings. The student then tries to relate these two experiences, and communicate them to the patient. If possible, he should use the patient's own words, which he has previously learnt through listening. Schools of thought on depth psychology, especially, cannot help but assume that the therapist's own personality is indeed the instrument of therapy. Sandplay is such a method from the field of depth psychology. But it has one very specific addition: the very concrete and quite elaborate instruments involved – the sandtray and miniature figures.

Now let us return to our question about lay therapists or volunteer facilitators. If a person's psychological health is sound enough to loan, as it were, his personality to the patient, then a satisfactory outcome of the therapy can be expected. In addition to the therapist's personality, we have seen that sandplay makes use of very *literal* instruments that further stimulate the formation of symbols. (This has its advantages but also bears risks, as I have described elsewhere.)[10] In sandplay one can create three-dimensional structures, indeed whole worlds, in miniature. This makes optimal use of the psyche's nature of creating spontaneous images. Sandplay allows the patient to display psychological content, such as states of being, emotions, thoughts and fantasies concretely and in three dimensions, without having to learn special creative techniques. From the beginning, the patient is openly encouraged to make use of his own powers, more so than with many other psychotherapeutic methods. In sandplay, nothing is predetermined with regards to content and there is no protocol describing the process. The choice of what to create is left entirely to the patient's intuition. The assumption is that, in a free and protected space, the psyche will produce precisely what it needs to regulate itself. This principle corresponds very much to that of natural remedies compared to conventional western medicine. One does not try to cure the symptoms, but to create the right conditions for the body to mobilize its own immune response. The whole thing can also be seen as a cultural process. New worlds are created inside and out, a new story is told that is capable of taking previously incompatible differences to a new level.[11]

We are a little closer to answering the question of how volunteer facilitators, even without psychotherapeutic training, could use sandplay in precarious situations. The elaborate, actual instruments of sandplay (the sandtray and the miniature figures) shift the weight of the treatment toward the patients themselves. In all cases in which an intact potential of development has merely been buried through trauma, a volunteer facilitator, providing the right therapeutic setting,[12] is all it takes to initiate an autonomous process. As this process gains momentum and takes its course, children or juveniles are able to free themselves from their pathogenic memory.

As we have seen, the more severe the precarious situation, the more efficient body and mind become in trying to make the most out of the least they have. Even watery soup can still save a person from starvation, as long as it is edible. Offering something that cannot be assimilated is probably worse than offering nothing at all. Disappointed expectations cause feelings of guilt, powerlessness and aggression in the victim *and* in the helper. Psychological methods need to be practised with great care – especially, and somewhat paradoxically so, those with definite step-by-step procedures. In Expressive Sandwork, trust is largely placed in the facilitator's personality. Nevertheless, volunteers often ask for exact instructions and step-by-step measures. But fear of making mistakes weakens their most valuable basic equipment: their individual perceptual capacity. Explaining to the volunteers, however, that sandwork is primarily a matter of consciously accompanying a process that basically has a life of its own, might unsettle the volunteers at first, but will also soon make them relieved, curious and freshly motivated.

In one the courtyards of the juvenile detention centre in Bosasa (Johannesburg), six 17-year-old youths approach the sandtrays which have been prepared for them. The heavily armed guards keep a respectful distance. These youths' files are shocking to read: repeated breaking and entering, drug possession and trafficking, manslaughter, wilful murder. On top of this, there are the social worker's notes: 'makes an unmotivated impression', 'is disoriented', 'has no prospect of his own future', 'has no comprehension of his current situation'. The therapist and the social workers explain:

> Today you don't have to do anything in particular. This isn't a test or a task. You don't have to prove anything, and nobody is going to lecture you afterwards. You can create something in the sand with these materials – if you want to.

At first the youths stand somewhat helplessly before their sandtrays, but they don't seem mistrustful. They have a good enough understanding of human nature to realize that they are not being manipulated in this situation. This seemingly unpedagogic proposal, without any apparent goal or purpose, is different from everything they have experienced so far. They won't receive anything, and nothing in particular is demanded of them either. But the fact that six adults went to the trouble of bringing six sandtrays and all this play material to the prison awakens the adolescents' interest.

One of the youths begins, as if by habit, by pondering the play material's potential usefulness as a weapon: 'Can I keep these shells when I'm finished?' Another takes an animal figure and places it somewhere in his sandtray, and a third starts smoothing the surface of the sand. Nobody ever suggested to these youths that they could depict a scene out of their own lives. By the end of the session, however, when each of them is given the opportunity to explain what he has depicted, every single one of them has shown his current situation and wants to describe it in words as well:

'Here I am, enclosed on all sides. I am cut off from all of the good things that I once had, but from the bad things as well.'

'I am on this narrow strip of land. I have almost no room to move. The only way out is over that bridge with crocodiles underneath it. There is a path on the other side of the bridge. If one can reach it (there is a zebra standing on the path), then one will be able to distinguish between good and bad. But I am still back here.'

(See plate section: p. 1, Plate 2.)

'This group of terrorists over here: I don't even want to say anything about them. They are attacking the people in the centre. I wanted to protect the people with a circle, but I didn't have enough glass marbles to finish it.'

(See plate section: p. 2, Plate 3.)

These explanations are so clear that no further comment on the part of the therapists is required. Through sandwork each youth was able to discover something new about himself. Each one of them became more clearly aware about a piece of his own past or present.

What takes place on a psychological level between the adults and the adolescents could also be described as 'recognition'. Not recognition of specific achievements, but an anticipatory, existential form of recognition. Through the fact that no detailed instructions were given before sandplay, the therapists implicitly assumed that the youths must have the necessary competence. This advance of recognition up front (even if it *only* pertains to constructing miniature worlds) awakens in the youths a different way of perceiving themselves, which may have been a new experience for some of them.

This is analogous to what happens when parents are expecting their first child: it is probably instinct that parents behave from the beginning as if there was no doubt that their child would turn out to be a healthy, intelligent, friendly being. Already in the first few weeks and months of life, these positive expectations allow the child to establish a feeling of self, which can later develop into a feeling of self-esteem. Children from precarious backgrounds usually don't experience such an advance of positive fantasies which they can grow into. To make up for this deficit, they must develop an identity out of their fight against a hostile world. An adult who provides a sandtray to such a youth, within a therapeutic framework, behaves very much like the parents with their 'as if' fantasies: the adult assumes that even the most apathetic of adolescents will still have a diverse inner world, which can be depicted in the sand and which aims at change. This attitude, as well as that of parents, is by all means realistic. It allows an infant to develop in a healthy way, and it is one of the basic requirements for psycho-therapy. This attitude of 'positive expectation' must not, however, be mistaken with personal beliefs, for example the notion that 'deep down, every person is good at heart', or the religious stance that 'every sinner can be redeemed', or the assumption that 'every person is an artist provided he has access to the proper material'. The assisting adult will either have such personal beliefs or not, and he or she will have to exclude them from the therapy situation as well as possible. The attitude of 'positive expectation' that we are talking about here only pertains to the assumption that every person has an inner world, which can be portrayed and therefore can also be changed. If other beliefs and convictions were to play a role in sandwork, the whole undertaking would take on ideological, missionary and narcissistic aspects, and would no longer have anything to do with psychotherapy.

At this point, the reader might interject that the concepts of Sandplay Therapy and Expressive Sandwork cannot always be clearly distinguished, no matter how hard we try. At a first glance the procedure looks similar in both cases, but the difference lies in the therapist's training or, more to the point, in the lack of psychotherapeutic training in the volunteer facilitators and social workers.

Sandplay Therapy is a depth-psychological method in individual psycho-therapy, while Expressive Sandwork takes place in groups and limits itself to the provision of a free and protected space. It can also be described as 'therapeutic care'. This means that the therapist neither tries to extract a little more information from a child by means of the sand image, nor imparts his or her personal thoughts and feelings to the child unasked for. If this also leads to any verbal form of communication, is left open in each individual case.

This book is intended as a handbook for Expressive Sandwork. I have largely tried to refrain from using technical terms. If the readers, however, are expecting a technical instruction manual, they will likely be disappointed. Since the central aspect of the matter is precisely what the psyche is able to produce from within itself, the aim will primarily be to promote an attitude of greatest possible openness in the assisting adult.

The case studies and sand images pictured in this book, taken from three different cultural, social and political environments, are primarily intended to help sharpen the perceptual capacity.

Chapter 5

Trauma and 'newly contained time'

'At the time, newly contained . . .' Thus begins the last paragraph of a poem by the French poet René Char,[1] with which he finally ends the silence of blocked creativity into which he fell after the sudden death of his friend Albert Camus on 4 January 1960.[2] By the time he manages to write these lines in April, 'time has been contained once more', which means as much as that it has been reined in, or brought back under control. It is as if one has now regained one's own 'countenance' and is no longer stunned in the face of the experience.

To lose a loved person, such as happened to René Char when his close friend Albert Camus died in a car crash, can be seen as a traumatic event, but it is an experience that a person in good psychological health is able to overcome. In these lines, Char describes – with the intuitive precision typical of poets – the moment in which he comes back *out* of his traumatized state. This state seems to have been located in an existential void, beyond time and space. Only when 'time has been contained once more', once subjectively perceived time has started to pass again, does the affected person appear to notice that time had been *un*leashed *before* and that it had *not* been passing the way it should. What is more, there had hardly been any pain *before*. Only now that he feels the 'full weight of this enigma' – the burden of so many arising questions – 'does the pain suddenly begin; [the pain] which the archer, this time, will not pierce.' It is, as René Char points out, a pain of a very certain kind: one 'from companion to companion'.[3] Not a deaf pain, but one that has to do with relationship. This means that a possibility for duality now exists again for the affected person, whereas no dialogue would have been possible in his previous state of seclusion and timelessness. And 'pain suddenly begins' precisely because the capacity for relationship has begun to exist again: one only realizes the full extent of one's loss once one has regained composure – 're-contained oneself' – at least somewhat.

After three months – according to the poet's portrayal – time, space and the capacity for relationship have returned. 'Re-contained time' apparently returned by itself. Or maybe Char helped to rein it in sooner, *because* he had been able to put his experience into words.

On no account does this mean that writers are better able to protect themselves against the long-term consequences of severe traumas. This has been proven by the life stories of Primo Levi, Jean Améry and many others who became victims of collective traumas. Years and decades may have passed since the Holocaust and left nothing but an endless row of 'uncontained hours' without sense or context.

The term 'psychological trauma' is frequently used today. There is an abundance of literature on the definitions and genesis of trauma, on its cultural and socio-political parameters, on the criteria for its diagnosis and on the methods of its treatment. Ground-breaking discoveries were made in neurobiology over the past decades, which triggered new, interdisciplinary discussions on this topic.[4]

Today we realize that there are innate and culturally learned dispositions that govern whether events are experienced as being traumatic or not. The earlier the occurrence in childhood of such events, triggering a subjective experience of total vulnerability and threat to one's life, the more serious the psychological and physical consequences, with which one must reckon, will be. We are aware that these consequences become ever harder to treat, the longer a person is exposed to a traumatic state and the later treatment is begun.

Finally, we also know that there are events that can emotionally destroy a human life in any of its stages. Instead of leading to assimilation and closure, flashbacks and nightmares continually reproduce the situation of perceived helplessness anew, thereby causing further traumatization. On the physiological level, neurobiological and biochemical circuits prevent the psyche's designed attempts at psychological self-healing from working. A comparison with immune diseases suggests itself: the body attacks itself 'by mistake', as it were, and triggers the systematic destruction of its own cell tissue.

From a neurobiological approach, trauma is also described as an illness of neuronal plasticity.[5] One can envision this disorder as the 'opposite of learning',[6] as a process in which synaptic connections – which would normally react to different stimuli with the function of improving an individual's ability to react to new situations – become impoverished. They now react to every outside stimulus by invariably activating the same regulatory circuits, thereby reproducing the traumatic experience. Chances of mental representation and assimilation decrease little by little.

The discussion as to whether a traumatic episode differs qualitatively from other harmful, psychological experiences, or whether the severity of traumatic experience lies along continuous gradient,[7] is far from over. The differences already begin with the definition of trauma. What is certain is that every traumatic event sets in unexpectedly at first, and that the affected person is subjected to an experience of powerlessness faced with a – subjectively perceived or objective – threat to one's physical or mental integrity.

Renos Papadopoulos notes that

> from a solely psychological angle, traumatic responses do not always need to be classified as psychiatric 'disorders' (which is what the PTSD stands for). [. . .] In other words, we can either perceive it as an abnormal reaction or as a normal reaction to abnormal circumstances.[8]

Apart from all of these psychoanalytical, neurobiological and sociological descriptions, it is always important to keep in mind that the 'opposite of learning' mentioned above – the state of standstill in a single fragment of time where the terrible experience is repeated eternally – has, on the other hand, also taken on magnificent, cultural forms in the history of humanity, which go beyond the single individual and even beyond a whole people or epoch. Its function of creating meaning was never lost in the process.

Examples of such incomparable documents, in which traumatic petrification and rhythmic repetition have taken on a poetic form, are the *Florentine Codex* or the *Anales de Tlatelolco*. These works describe the arrival of the Spaniards in the New World, and the struggle of the individual Aztec cultures until they were ultimately defeated by such a small number of Spaniards under the leadership of Hernán Cortés. The *Florentine Codex* was compiled by the Franciscan monk Bernardino de Sahagún between 1540 and 1585 and consists largely of eye-witness reports in the indigenous language Nahuatl. It was later published in Spanish under the title *Historia general de las cosas de la Nueva España* ('General History of the Things of New Spain').

What is exceptional about these texts is not the description of a war: the Aztecs were a warrior people and it was a matter of fact to them that victories can be followed by defeats, and that neither death nor survival can occur without the other. Dying in war, even being subjugated as an entire people, were not inconceivable in the way of their world and therefore would not really have been traumatic.

The appearance of the Spaniards meant something else to the Aztecs. Their arrival from the East, from the sea, had been prophesied and therefore they were awaited like gods. This explains the lengthy hesitation of Montezuma, the king of the Aztecs. He had already received proof a hundred times over of the Spaniards' entirely ungodly behaviour, of how ugly they were, how unjust, greedy and bloodthirsty, and especially of how disrespectful they were of all spiritual ceremonies – and yet he hesitated: it was as if he were paralysed in his decision making. To be betrayed by one's gods is the worst trauma one can imagine. In fact it *cannot* be imagined, which is why Montezuma allowed himself to be taken prisoner will-lessly, and opened the way for his people's annihilation.

The detailed descriptions of this defeat, the rhythmic repetitions and the enumeration of apparently inconsequential details almost hypnotize readers and draw them into the account of these inconceivable, unprecedented acts: not deeds between warriors, or that warriors committed against their enemy's wives and children, but acts of perverse gods who destroyed their own sanctity. One can cite almost any passage in the text at random:

> Those who sang the holy songs walked naked without any clothes. They wore nothing but their shells, their turquoise stones, their lip ornaments, necklaces and feathered headdresses, their shoes of deer leather. Those who played the drums, the dear little old ones, who had with them their cymbals made of

pumpkins as well as the smaller pumpkins for their tobacco, they were the first to be attacked by the Spaniards down there. They hit them on their hands. On their heads did they hit them. They died in the same moment. All of them who had sung the songs, all of them who had been there, all of them were killed there. They attacked them for three endless hours. They killed the people in the courtyard of the temple. Then they entered the temple and spread death everywhere: those who carried water, those who carried food for the horses, those who ground the corn, those who swept the floor, those standing guard, all of them lost their lives.[9]

And from the *Anales de Tlatelolco*:

And all of this happened to us. We saw it; we suffered it. Fear caught up to us in this saddest of fates. Along the roads lie the broken lances, hair is strewn, houses are roofless. They are coloured red, the houses.[10]

One must consider that the Aztecs – warriors though they were – knew neither guns nor horses until this point. In all its terror, the following description also has something dream-like about it: it is a desperate attempt to compare this over-whelming invasion to something that had already existed before in their own world; an attempt to establish a connection to something familiar. This explains the comparison with the elements fire and water. The recurring 'as if' is a brave but helpless attempt to describe the unfathomable.

Their lances of iron, it was as if they set things afire. And their spades of steel waved like sea foam. It was as if they clanged their vests of steel, their helmets of iron. And others come, all equally covered with iron.[11]

The repetitions occur throughout the entire text.[12] The eye witnesses use them to list their miseries, but one knows that they will not bring relief. They sound like the tones of a broken instrument which is in the process of being tuned for an epochal expression of woe.

Oh, worthy warriors! Oh! Mexicans! Come and help! There, they are dead already, the worthy warriors have perished! They are dead, they were betrayed, they were destroyed! Oh! Mexicans! Oh! Worthy warriors![13]

The collective traumas, from which the fabric of history appears to be woven, are important for our specific, clinical understanding of trauma – precisely because they are *not* about therapy and healing. We know from analytical psychology that the desire to help and to bring healing can be a double-edged sword. Psychotherapists are well advised continuously to question their established notion of psychological health and illness.[14] Psychotherapists are superfluous in the few cultures that still have functioning cultural and religious systems for dealing with psychological trauma. Where such systems no longer exist – and unfortunately this is the case almost everywhere today – psychotherapists can by no means replace these systems. All they can do is to employ empathy for their fellow human beings in the best and most purposeful way possible. This can be learned in part, but in part it is a gift. The exceptionally gifted simply do it, the slightly less gifted – the author counts herself in this group – develop methods.

Back to our considerations, which will no longer now pertain to whole peoples but to single individuals. Trauma means 'fragmentation of meaning' in individual existences as well.

As regards therapies for posttraumatic stress disorder, there have been many discussions and especially many reservations since the 1990s. Methods that aimed at penetrating defence mechanisms, with the purpose of activating unconscious fragments in patients' memories of traumatic experiences, often had a re-traumatizing effect on those patients. Every method – no matter how resource-orientated it may be – can cause damage if it is applied incautiously. An expressive therapy in which patients are, for example, *urged* to draw their nightmares on paper can traumatize the patients anew. This happens when patients draw these pictures 'for the therapist's sake', because the therapist encourages and praises the patients – the therapist may be fascinated by the expressiveness of the patients' unconscious content, and may underestimate its danger. The patients, meanwhile, do not even realize that they feel worse and worse. This is no wonder, because this content has not been processed and its attractive effect on consciousness has even been increased. The underlying mistake is an incorrect handling of the transference and counter-transference relationship on the part of the therapist. To avoid such mistakes, it is helpful to let patients search for their own preferred forms of expression as autonomously as possible. Furthermore, one should refrain from any comments regarding aesthetic quality and, above all, one should take seriously even the slightest resistance on the part of the patient towards a therapeutic approach. Judging whether something is beneficial or harmful is precisely what a traumatized person is not able to do. In cases of disturbance early in life, and also when a traumatic experience is suspected, it is better to refrain from direct intervention and, with the greatest possible empathy, to maintain a state of 'standby'. Every individual has their own way of dealing with psychological processes and their own time for doing so.

A fundamental general distinction between two different kinds of trauma and their respective consequences can come in handy for our work: whether the traumatic experience affects an adult person who is relatively well balanced psychologically, or whether it affects a personality which is not yet completely formed, such as that of a young child. While a posttraumatic stress disorder can be triggered in the average adult or not – depending on subjective, objective and especially also culturally based circumstances – physical or psychological violence *will always* affect the development of infants and young children *severely*, often *irreversibly*. This happens because the traumatic event impacts an ego-consciousness which has not yet fully formed. There is hardly any way of processing experiences cognitively on this pre-ego level of development, because young children still lack the capacity for verbal expression and cannot yet store a connected series of images in their memory. It is common knowledge that our thinking is mainly organized linguistically and is thereby bound to language, or at least – analogously for the right hemisphere of the brain – to a sequence of images from memory. In the first few months of our lives, the body, the emotions and the people outside us to whom we most closely relate are one indistinguishable unity. There is no clear distinction between subject and object. If violence and mortal threat enter this infantile universe, they immediately fill it entirely because there is no place, no pivotal point, outside the unity described above from which things could be dealt with. The personality structure which then continues to form – because development and growth never cease – will inevitably contain the traumatic event within it, and will be affected by it. The personality can only try to develop despite, or next to, or around the unprocessed trauma, which can neither be thought about, nor formulated, nor symbolized at this stage. Thus, when we speak of trauma in early childhood, we must not imagine this as the mental representation of a certain event, a sequence of scenes that are recorded in memory and are retrievable thereafter. We are dealing with emotional structures and dispositions of perception that take hold of a person's entire mental state, and that comb through all outside information and impulses on a pre-conscious level, in order to filter out every possible suspicion of threat. The traumatic experience is deeply ingrained in the body: it can be roughly made out in sore and hardened muscles, and physiologically detected in a change of blood parameters, synaptic connections in the brain, cerebral volume and a whole row of metabolic processes which in turn are related to hormonal and endocrinological regulatory circuits. On the one hand, the describing of these frequently irreversible neurobiological damages has helped to sensitize the public to this matter and thereby to protect young children, but on the other hand it has also increased the tendency to proceed only according to a medical model, thereby overlooking psychodynamic connections and their interaction with physiological ones.

It was an important new discovery that emotions influence whether genes are activated or not,[15] and it gave back to psychotherapy a considerable degree of influence that had already been believed lost to pharmacological methods of treatment.

Donald Kalsched describes from a psychoanalytical point of view how early-childhood traumas come about.[16] He explains very descriptively how primitive defence mechanisms ensure that the otherwise quite differentiated palette of emotional perceptions is reduced. As Kalsched illustrates, these archaic mechanisms of defence form a so-called 'self care system', the purpose of which is to avoid renewed traumatization. This 'self care system' erects – as the term already suggests – a psychosomatic wall of protection around the core of the immature personality, around the 'inner, vulnerable child', which at all costs must not come into further danger. But that is not all. Now that the personality's core, the inner child, is isolated in its fortress from the outside world and also from the emotional world, and therefore cannot experience anything new, the self care system starts, as it were, to 'tell it stories'. Depending on the severity of the disorder, these inner acts of fantasizing are known as daydreams or as hallucinations. Their underlying purpose seems to be the ineradicable human desire to connect fragments of meaning to one another, even in an extremely restricted existence.

While the various psychotherapeutic approaches agree in the point that severe trauma partly or even entirely destroys the capacity for relationship in those affected by it, Kalsched points out that not only do relationships take place on an inter*personal* level, but also the role of 'you' can be taken, if need be, by nature, by animals or by a certain activity if need be.

An example may be found in the following childhood account.

A young woman lived the first years of her life in Russian-occupied Estonia with her taciturn grandmother (the grandfather had taken his own life). The child was left entirely to her own devices. Apart from the grandmother's house and a few pets, there was nothing but fields and forests for kilometres around. No toys, no other adults or children, barely enough to eat. Instead of regressing, the girl let herself be adopted by nature as if by some maternal entity. She began to talk to the grass, the trees, the wind, and she walked many kilometres a day, either alone or with her dog. Sometimes the girl moved very far away from the house, to the outermost limit of her world: a guarded military area around a factory in which uranium was processed. Only later, as an adult, did she realize that this area was not even marked on any official maps. Despite the many conceivable threats that a girl could be exposed to at that age, she never really put herself in any danger. The notion that nature and the animals would protect her was deeply rooted in the little girl. The decisive factor was that she had probably taken this unspoken notion from her monosyllabic grandmother. This girl – as an adult – later explained that her grandmother would never have spoken about nature or paid any particular attention to animals. On the contrary, she saw both pets and wild animals as being there for her use. Above all, the girl remembered the calm, trusting look in her grandmother's face when she looked to the sky. In this girl's case it was enough to have a human role model who could provide even a minimum of security. This activated an innate disposition towards behaviour that was directed at survival and establishing relationships.[17]

The situation is different when small children, on top of living in squalor, are also manipulated psychologically or experience direct physical violence: the children can neither defend themselves nor establish a context for what is happening.

The following account may illustrate to what extents the psyche and its defence mechanisms are capable of explaining the world. It is left to the reader to decide whether these mechanisms are ultimately of any help in life or not.

A 60-year-old retired nurse telephoned to ask for a psychotherapy session to help her 'proceed on her spiritual path and be better able to communicate with the inhabitants of other planets'. When the therapist saw the patient for the first time, she was struck by her physical appearance of neglect. It was clear that this woman lived in a fantasy world and perceived her physical needs only peripherally. The therapist asked her how she had come by the idea that she would like to have increased contact with alien creatures, and the woman began to tell her story. Even as a small child, she had always been full of generosity and love, and had always wanted to help other people. The aliens were very similar to herself: full of light, goodness and love. When she was 3 years old, she remembered having healed a neighbour, who came to visit her in the afternoons when she was alone at home. She believed he had some kind of deformity in his lower body, and so each time she readily gave him the cure he asked her for. While the patient was describing this case of sexual abuse with an inadequate emotional reaction, her body meanwhile was telling the story in a very different version that seemed to be disconnected from her consciousness: while she spoke, her face and neck had turned bright red, she had begun to sweat heavily, and seemed to be having trouble breathing. She held her arms closely wrapped around her, as if she needed to keep herself together with all her might. Thus, her body not only betrayed the detached emotion but also revealed this fantasy's underlying function, namely to keep her personality together, which otherwise would have broken apart. When the woman came to speak of the aliens once more, her body began to relax.

In order to endure the brutality of earth's inhabitants – there were enough reasons to believe that previous abuse had originally come from her own family – this woman met with alien beings within herself. Her psyche had made a decision: rather than never being able to fulfil her innate desire for love and relationship, she had invented or created suitable objects inside herself.

The numerous websites on the internet devoted to aliens demonstrate that this woman is not alone in having found this 'solution'. On the contrary, we are dealing with a collective, archetypal fantasy. Quite insightful in this connection is also C.G. Jung's text on unidentified flying objects (UFOs).[18]

If, as in the case described, a traumatic event impacts upon a child's psyche so early in life, then important psychological functions, especially pertaining to the ego-complex, are impaired. Just as when lightning hits a tree, the trunk is hollowed out but the roots remain intact. Even if the trunk – which is an allegory for the conscious ego – is no longer the centre of growth, it can occur, as we see in a painting by the Italian painter Lorenzo Lotto (1480–1557), that a smaller tree starts to grow out of the damaged trunk.[19] The roots which supply it are the same ones that had nourished the original tree. We can assume that psychic life can continue its development in more ways than through one single, coherent ego-consciousness alone.

I hope to have shown that the questions posed by trauma are not so much of a treatment-technical nature, but rather of an existential one – just like every phenomenon that leads us to crossing borders. And as always in a no man's land, be it an inner psychic or an interpersonal void, opposites repel each other, because there are no conventions that keep them together: no ritual, no prayer, no book of rules.

Trauma either brings us to the brink of despair because we simply cannot bear it, or it allows us to believe, in a kind of idealizing optimism, that with psychological techniques we could heal something that in truth lies beyond our control.

Chapter 6

Expressive Sandwork

The sand picture that is produced by the child can be understood as a three-dimensional representation of some aspect of his psychic situation.[1]

An apparatus, therefore, which will give a child power to express his ideas and feelings, must be independent of knowledge or skill, must be capable of the representation of thought simultaneously in several planes at once, must allow of representation of movement, and yet sufficiently circumscribed to make a complete whole, must combine elements of touch and sensation, as well as of sight, and be entirely free from a necessary relation to reality.[2]

Expressive Sandwork is an adaptation of the World Technique and of Sandplay Therapy, for situations in which individual psychotherapy is impossible. It is used today in various public and private institutions in Asia, South Africa and Latin America. Expressive Sandwork mostly takes place in groups. Nevertheless, individual care is ensured during the entire process. Each child works at one sandtray, and one adult accompanies and observes each child's play. The main difference to psychotherapeutic treatment is that these adults are not psychotherapists, but teachers, students of psychology or pedagogy, social workers and volunteers, who have received a short training.[3] The aim is to be able to offer a maximum of therapeutic intervention with a minimum of training. This attempt at making something seemingly impossible possible is conceivable only because the medium, sandplay itself, is so perfectly suited to a child's requirements. Children require neither special skills nor command of language to construct a miniature world in the sand. Sandplay ties in precisely where children have been expressing themselves spontaneously and individually from the earliest ages onwards: in play. The elaborate equipment involved – the sandtray and miniature figures – helps reduce the lay therapist's influence as much as possible. The lay therapist's task limits itself to creating the external requirements for a self-regulating process to take place within the child's psyche. No psychotherapeutic intervention is expected of the facilitator, nor any interpretation or verbalization of problems. It is enough for lay therapists to participate in the play process with their thoughts and feelings. Thus, it does not even matter whether they understand complex psychodynamic or symbolic connections or not. We will see why.

Expressive Sandwork makes very precise use of at least two phenomena that are naturally common to all human societies: children's innate desire to play, and the fact that humans are social beings.

The importance of play

'there is a connection between the play of children and the life of adult men'.[4]

Sandplay makes use of an innate behaviour, common to all cultures, with which children react spontaneously to difficulty, insecurity or fear, but also to new impressions and exciting experiences: play. Play belongs to a child's healthy behavioural repertoire and is the child's very own innermost way of approaching the world and internalizing it. Play is also always a process of mental assimilation. With its help, emotions can be converted into cognitive processes, into understanding. One could say that being a child and playing are one and the same thing.

Play lies in the border area between reality and imagination, which Donald Winnicott describes as *transitional space*.[5] Within this special area, psychological substance is shapeable, and is thus capable of regulating itself when disturbed. Play induces effortless change that serves psychological development and emotional differentiation. Bad experiences are replayed as often as is required for their emotional load to be weakened. In the world of play, new behavioural strategies are refined and rehearsed until a better adaptation to the outside world is achieved. There is a direct connection between children's free play and their relationship to their environment. Apart from the pure joy of experimenting, play has the simple function of increasing healthy children's vitality. Children growing up in supportive environments will take delight in discovering themselves in infinite variants of play.

If, however, children's psychological development is inhibited by adverse circumstances, play will automatically put itself in the service of development. The themes of play will revolve around the unconscious or conscious conflicts. Children illustrate what is wrong or amiss in ever new and often dramatic variations. They describe how things would be if it were not for the blockage. Mental energy is mobilized to approach an inner obstruction from different sides. Again and again the conflict is represented in play using different means. If no help appears from outside, these representations become increasingly dramatic, chaotic and cryptic to the observer. If the child's entire psychological development cannot progress, his or her play will take place within ever smaller boundaries, mirroring the child's inner hopelessness. Variations will become fewer while repetition increases until all that is left is disinterest, and play ceases altogether. In such cases a child might do nothing more than destroy objects. If this behaviour lasts for too long, the child's psychological stability is seriously threatened. When children cannot play any more, they have ceased being themselves. In other words, they have lost their very own way of experiencing the world.

As soon as a detrimental environment has changed even just slightly, as soon as even a minimal existential space has opened up for a child, his or her psychological potential for development will be activated. The child will immediately start trying out possibilities of catching up what has been missed. In this case, symbols often start to occur in play, which mark the beginning of the very level of development that had been skipped. Thereby the child's personal development is freed of its blockage. The most common symptoms that occur when children find themselves in a detrimental environment are a developmental standstill and regressions. This can be plainly seen in many small children in orphanages. This example of a 4-year-old girl in an orphanage in southern China should illustrate how Expressive Sandwork can help these children to catch up in their psychological development.

During one sandwork session, the girl takes a small, red plastic bottle in her hand and begins to fill it with sand. She takes some sand in the palm of her hand and lets it run down the neck of the bottle. She repeats this procedure patiently and in utter concentration until the bottle is full of sand to the very top. Then she pours even more sand on top, although it is plain to see that the bottle can't hold any more. Next, the girl takes another bottle, this time a yellow one. She fills this as well, in the same way. Next in turn is a glass. The glass is a lot easier to fill because the opening is wider. Again, she pours sand on top even when the glass is already completely full. A thought comes to the observer's mind that, with this action, the child must be trying to fill an inner emptiness. Next, she takes a cup. Then she chooses a chest of drawers for a doll's house and fills each drawer individually with sand. A fridge, an oven: every possible opening in every conceivable object is filled with sand. In the end, once all sorts of objects have been completely filled with sand, even objects that were never meant for such a purpose, a definite feeling of fullness and satiation is noticeable. This feeling is further confirmed by the girl's facial expression, which seems content and relaxed. Something that had been empty before has now been filled. Something that easily runs through ones fingers has been collected, contained, and given a solid form. The girl hardly glanced at her facilitator during the whole session; only occasionally and very briefly, as if to reassure herself that someone is there with her.

With this elementary act, the girl, who had been abandoned shortly after her birth, nourished herself emotionally as it were, and thereby made up for the mental and physical feeling of 'not getting enough', which she had had for so many years. She will repeat this simple auto-therapeutical act as often as she needs to; provided she can count on the same external conditions being offered continuously. This means, the same adult has to be present during the next sessions as well, and must continue to follow her play with the same interest, even if it repeats itself without variations.

Children whose early lives were affected by desertion and insufficient care can thereby find their own way back to an innately healthy behaviour. They can nourish themselves in play. They are able to induce a feeling of fullness, as it were, in themselves. They make up on a symbolic level for what they were lacking in their development. The psyche regulates itself.

The group

Sandplay, which takes place in a free and protected space in the presence of a witness, is different and has a much deeper effect than plain, free playing. Likewise, the group in which sandplay takes place is no 'normal' group. The children are not prompted to interact with each other. On the contrary, there is no talking during sandplay, and no playing together. In a way one could call this a 'regressive' group: one is allowed to take without giving. Within this unusual form of togetherness one is allowed to feel protected and supported by the others' presence, while also being allowed to behave as if one were all alone – provided one does not disturb the others in their equal right to this same feeling.

Today we know that the human brain is geared towards, and dependent on, being in contact with fellow human beings. Like all mammals, humans are exceptionally social beings. This means that our psychophysical equilibrium depends on whether, and how, we interact with the people around us. In the animal world as well, the group has many stress factors to handle. This can be observed in the greeting rituals of many wild animals. Each time a lion returns to its pride after having been away, it rubs along the bodies of the other lions. The returning animal's movements, which had initially been agitated and excited, slowly match the calmer movements of its welcoming pride. This interaction, which involves all sensory organs, signals to the brain that the previous hunting or defensive behaviour is finished, and that the corresponding hormones should now be metabolized. Within seconds a state of relaxation sets in, which the animal would never have been able to achieve as quickly and completely without its pride.

Likewise one can imagine what it must mean for children who are exposed to severe psychological stress, to be part of a group in which they do not have to expend energy to assert their position; a group in which it is not even possible to be rewarded or punished, because these otherwise usual social interactions do not exist. There is just silence. All the members are absorbed on their own work, everybody has been given their own space, which can be neither lost, nor expanded at a cost to others. Under these specific conditions, the group takes on the function of an archaic, sensual-corporal sanctuary. This works on the condition that the multifaceted potential for communication, which is normally emphasized in group therapies, is intentionally, temporarily done without. This situation is not about learning social skills, it is only about experiencing the feeling of protection and security. This creates the paradox situation of a group, consisting largely of children in psychological distress, which nevertheless forms an encompassing secure and protective space for each and every one of them. The more precisely these basic conditions are adhered to, and the more solid the facilitators' personalities are, the greater the effect.

Another of this group's aspects pertains to the adults. They also feel supported by the presence of the other adults. New volunteers can learn from more experienced ones, even without many words being exchanged. The attentive presence of each one of them is perceived by all the others at all sensory levels.

Expressing psychological content already means changing it

> An unconscious problem is played out in the sand box, just like a drama. The conflict is transferred from the inner world to the outer world and is made visible. This game of fantasy influences the dynamics of the unconscious in the child and thus moves his psyche.[6]

Depicting psychological content already means changing it. This can be summarized as one of the central axioms along which sandplay has orientated itself since its very beginnings. It corresponds with experience gained to date in depth psychology-orientated psychotherapy with children, and is further supported by results in neuroscience. Play is spontaneous psychological assimilation. As has already been mentioned, all important experiences and all forms of behaviour, which are copied from adults, are incorporated into children's play in some form or other.

But it is not only external impressions that are processed. Content and impulses that aim at future steps of psychological development impose themselves on a child from the inside as well. In free play, children test new forms of behaviour, which they have not learnt from anyone else, but which come from their fantasy worlds or from their dreams. These inner images and processes, which are discovered by and by, run parallel to the potential for development. We can assume that certain unconscious, psychological content always imposes itself on consciousness very intensely, whenever a next step of development is imminent. Children's development takes place in phases. Children seem to know that steps of psychological maturing are coupled with physical development, and that they must therefore take place within certain age limits: otherwise they are no longer possible in direct form. To an adult, coming to a standstill in development means only that time passes unused. To a child, however, it can possibly mean irreversible psychological damage. This is why disturbances in childhood years are always dramatic.

Many children in need of psychotherapy can no longer play: they have lost this innate capacity for psychological self-regulation. They must first indirectly be brought to regain trust in their gestures, images and ideas. In sandplay, children are provided with a free and protected space in the presence of an adult, in which they can describe their worlds. This depiction does not – as is often supposed – serve only a diagnostic purpose; this depiction already *is* a change to the situation.

There is no standard protocol according to which sandwork should proceed. There are, however, models of understanding that enable the adult to experience what is happening in play on as many levels as possible. Through the accompanying adult's undivided attention, emotional participation and attempt at understanding, importance is lent to the play process, without anything needing to be expressed in words. Children take this as an advance of trust for their own actions and discover things in play that they might not have found alone. The adult's presence, even without this person saying a word, enables the child to create new approaches to his or her own emotional structures.

For Expressive Sandwork to become effective as a therapeutic method in the way described, the basic principles of a psychotherapeutic approach must nevertheless be respected. Free play is good for children in any case. But if play takes place within a framework of precise conditions, its effect is greatly magnified – just as a rise in temperature will increase the inner pressure within a sealed container.

Symptoms

> A child does not think linearly as the adult is capable of doing: thought, feeling, sensations, concept and memory are all intricably interwoven. A child's thought is fluid and movement can take place on several planes at once. A child's feeling is absolute in that any emotion, while it is present, holds the whole field of consciousness.[7]

A child has been hitting and biting other children without apparent reason. The teacher asks the child why he is doing this. No answer. If a doctor were to ask a child with high fever, why he has the fever, we would surely lose faith in the doctor's art. The child knows neither why his body is reacting in this way, nor to what purpose. Fever indicates that there is an ongoing battle between the body's immune system and certain viruses or bacteria. If the immune response wins the encounter, the fever will disappear. If the bacterial infection wins the upper hand, the fever's consequences could lastingly destroy the body. Good doctors not only try to lower the fever, but also cooperate with the fever, as it were, and prescribe medicine that helps to combat the bacteria. The fever is not the cause of the illness, but the body's response to a disturbance. It is a similar story with psychological symptoms. One can interpret abnormal behaviour in childhood years as the expression of a psychological immune system, trying to defend itself against destructive environmental influences, which threaten a child's development: neglect, desertion, violence, excessive demands. We speak of abuse whenever an adult *uses* a child for a certain purpose, as opposed to *relating* to the child. Relating means that the adult realizes that the child has certain requirements at every age, and that the child's continued development depends on the fulfilment of these needs. A child's strongest instinctive drive is to grow physically and mentally. A lazy child, an aggressive child, a withdrawn or hyperactive child: these are all just parts of the whole story of a frustrated child's unfulfilled, instinctive needs; like the desire to experience the world, to engage in it, to love it. Curiosity and compassion are innate behavioural dispositions. Simply to forbid or even punish a child's disturbing behaviour will only make matters worse. Even if a symptom might disappear temporarily due to punishment, it will appear again in a different form. The symptom must be understood as the distress signal of a child caught in an inner conflict. This conflict can be summed up in one dramatic question: am I allowed to grow and develop my talents in peace, or are my surroundings so threatening and overwhelming that I am left only with the choice of either withdrawing into myself, or taking a forward escape and matching my environment in violence as soon as possible. In either case, an instinctive, innate desire for autonomy and creative expression must first be suppressed. This suppression, above all, is the energetic source for the development of psychological and psychosomatic symptoms. The energy that would normally be used for experiencing the world is now caught in the symptom. This forces the child to tread a senseless, repetitive path of destructive behavioural patterns. It creates a vicious circle and prevents the child from reaching the next phase of development. The child becomes less and less capable of adapting to his or her surroundings, while feelings of insecurity increase all the while. The child is trapped, just as the fairy-tale characters Hansel and Gretel are trapped in the witch's house. They are subjected to pathological behaviour. This pathology can be either an individual neurosis in a family or a collective mania, as in countries that have experienced generations of war. The children are completely at this pathology's mercy and cannot develop emotionally.

Let us, with the help of the fairy tale, try to understand a possible way out of this situation. It is not a major offensive against evil that leads to the desired positive ending, nor a pre-emptive attack, but a patient process of self-discipline, during which observation and the biding of time are exercised. Sometimes, even apparent cooperation with the destructive forces are called for. At the right moment, a cunning ruse is employed to turn the situation around. The evil forces perish, a prey to their own uncontrolled impulses. This fairy tale shows inner psychological structures, which can become effective in the conflict with a pathological environment. If psychotherapy is successful, then it activates a child's own creative possibilities of experiencing and acting. The majority of fairy tales have a positive ending because they describe models of development. One hardly need add that reality is sadly often very different.

The sandtray

The equipment for the World Technique is a metal tray approximately 75 × 50 × 7 centimetres half filled with sand, for use on tables of differing height ... water should be near at hand; implements for use with the sand such as shovels, funnels, moulds, a sieve.[8]

I use a sand box with dimensions 28.5 × 19.5 × 3 inches. This size confines the player's imagination and thus acts as a regulating, protecting factor.[9]

The basic requirements for Sandplay Therapy (D. Kalff) are two sandtrays with the inner dimensions mentioned above. One is filled with dry sand and the other with moist fine-grained sand. For practical reasons, only one sandtray is used in Expressive Sandwork, which is filled with slightly moist sand.

The insides of sandtrays are painted with waterproof, light blue paint. This allows for the depiction of bodies of water in the sand, for instance a river or a lake, while the light blue sides create the illusion of a distant horizon.

The sandtrays' height should be adjustable to the age of each child, and they should ideally be on wheels that can be locked. If the sandtrays are situated in a school, it is useful to include covers: that way they can be used as a surface or tables when not in use. Another advantage is that a completed sandtray image, which has not yet been photographed, can temporarily be covered safely. If possible, sandtrays should not be left standing open in the hallways in schools and kindergartens. If just anybody could play with the sand in passing, the special atmosphere that goes with this non-everyday activity would be lost. The same goes for the collection of miniatures. They should be safely kept in a cupboard, and made accessible only during sessions. This strengthens the feeling for both children and adults that this activity somehow stands outside everyday time and space.

The sand

Why is sand the chosen material? Damp sand enables a wide scope of creative possibilities in three dimensions without any special manual skills being required. Dry sand need be touched only lightly, and already traces are left behind, which never seem clumsy or unskilful – even if one draws only a few random lines with one's fingers. The precision with which the grains of sand react to the slightest movement or rearrangement creates an atmosphere of attentiveness. Sand behaves like a very sensitive receiving device that records the slightest influence with total accuracy, as if a million grains of sand were ready and 'listening'. Little by little, sand players' gestures become noticeably in tune with this mood of alertness.

Furthermore, sand offers adaptation and resistance in equal measures. Sand occurring in nature has been ground by wind and water in an infinitely slow process into miniature particles that are barely discernible to the human eye. Grains of sea and desert sand are rounded, while industrially produced sand, like quartz sand, consists of sharp edged particles. Grains of sand – like liquids – have a tendency to try to fill every available space. This can be seen as an analogy: in matters of the mind, one also tries to confront and engage in events, to resist passing empty spaces by, without exploring their depths. If one shakes a container filled with sand again and again, it will follow the pull of gravity and increasingly settle until there are almost no gaps of air left between the grains and they become a solid, rock-hard block. Sand is solid matter, but in a loose state. As a Japanese colleague once put it, 'sand is more watery than water'. He meant that, in addition to the physical qualities of a liquid, there is also a symbolic quality. This solid-liquid consistency makes it ideally suited for making psychological processes visible.

Sand can represent opposites and polarities clearly and simply. Depending on how much water is mixed with it, sand can be dry and light as dust, or else wet and heavy. Sand can seem pure and clean, and be associated with order: every grain in its place. But, equally, sand can appear muddy and dirty, representing chaos. Sand can be used to build things, and then, in the form of quicksand, it can undermine all things solid. Sand can get aggravatingly stuck between the fingers, and then again it can pleasantly cool the palms. At times a friendly face can seem to look up at one from the sand, and another time the sandtray can be like a consuming maelstrom, into which one fears to be drawn. Sometimes the fine texture of sand brings to mind the feel of skin, in which case it is gently caressed. On other occasions whole mountains, valleys, rivers or deserts are formed with just a few movements of the hand: places where no living person has ever been before, which nevertheless seem intimately familiar. Sand formations are easily changed; every destruction automatically leads to new creation. Nothing need be discarded because it is always the same sand, transforming itself over and over again. The sand itself cannot be destroyed, because it already consists of the smallest of particles.

The miniatures

Miniature play figures of about 3–5 cm in size are placed on shelves, tables or even on the floor. The figures should correspond to the child's cultural milieu: familiar objects the child knows from his or her environment, and also a few unknown objects. There should be enough objects to allow whole worlds to be created in miniature. Some of the basic requirements are stones, wood and plants, shells, fish, reptiles, insects, birds and – pursuing phylogeny up through to higher mammals – people of different ages and professions. The collection should further include different dwellings for both animals and people (from caves to sky scrapers), interior furnishings including dishes for cooking and eating, as well as food. A sufficient amount of war toys is important, as are different means of transport: from wheelbarrows to aeroplanes. Police cars and ambulances are essential: they are often used to describe danger – something that could harm the child emotionally – and at the same time show if and how the child is able to react to this danger. Ambulances can be used in their usual function, for instance while coming to the rescue of an injured person, or they can occur randomly among many different types of vehicles, without any obvious purpose. In these cases, children are not consciously aware of their own need for help. They cannot yet articulate their call for help clearly enough. The ambulance occurring in play is only a first, indirect clue to a child's need for help. Other essential objects are ones that symbolize sinister things like death or the underworld: skeletons, coffins, rats, or grotesque fantasy figures such as monsters, ghosts, witches or magicians. If these sorts of figures are missing in the collection, as is often the case in Asiatic cultures, this influences children in two ways. First, they have fewer ways of illustrating their own disturbing feelings, like fears or nightmares. Second, they feel the adult's unconscious, one-sided expectations for children to portray something 'nice and positive'; after all, the adult provided only 'nice and positive' miniatures. In Asia, adults do not always easily accept that children should be allowed to depict evil, hideous or atrocious things in the sand. This is a complete contradiction to violent computer games and films, which are easily accessible for most children and young people. The difference between a computer game in which violent acts are committed and sandwork could not be greater. In the first case, violent behaviour is veritably instilled in children, and increases the more they play. In the latter case, violence is processed psychologically and decreases in a child's behaviour as a consequence.

Figures from world religions are also important, as are the cult objects of various cultures, for instance the totems of North American Indians, figures of Buddha, or Christian symbols such as the cross, angels or saints.

A 7-year-old boy was once absorbed in play in my practice and was searching the shelves of miniature figures for a long time, apparently without finding the one he wanted. When I asked if he needed something specific, he replied by asking, 'Have you got God?' When he realized that I also did not have a particularly clear notion of what God might look like, he didn't hesitate any further and instead took a figure of Saint Francis.

It is interesting to observe how often, and in which context, children who have no association to the Christian religion, for instance Chinese orphans, use the figure of the crucified Christ in sandwork. Often he is simply used to symbolize a suffering person, whose pain is intended to be seen by all. But often children will intuitively use a figure from a different culture or time *correctly*, without knowing its actual meaning. An American child might comment on a Mexican god of rain by saying, 'This figure makes the fields grow.' Or a Colombian child might surround the figure of Anubis, the ancient Egyptian god of death, with skulls and parts of skeletons.

Because one can never include every single object a child might conceivably need, it is also handy to provide some material for free creative use. Wooden tongue depressors, such as are used by doctors, are especially popular with children from chaotic family situations. They were used in Colombia again and again to create borders, or to show order or protection. Colourful paper, meanwhile, was cut into little pieces to depict food, which was then cooked in dolls' pans. It was important for the young girls and boys, who lived in squalid conditions, to create their own food.

But it is also possible to get by with very simple material: bits of wood and metal, corks from bottles, branches and bark, glass marbles, shells and a few figures of people and animals. The following experience from South Africa shows how sandwork can even be inhibited precisely by too large and foreign a collection of miniatures. Children from the shanty towns were offered only wood, wire, stones, shells, corks, bark and a few figures of people made from banana leaves for their sandwork sessions, because nothing else was available. Thanks to a generous donation from Europe, sandplay figures were eventually sent to South Africa: animals, people, houses, war toys, and so on. When the children saw these figures for the first time they were fascinated, but their play behaviour also changed. They started to quarrel over the figures, wanted to keep them, even stole them or destroyed them. The possibility for symbolic expression had disappeared from one moment to the next. Sandplay had become an object of consumption and had lost its symbolic quality.

In private therapeutic practices, the sandwork figures are sorted according to themes so that their characteristics are better accentuated. If they are placed individually, as opposed to all being offered in a basket, they appear more alive and inviting. Naturally, this is not possible in all situations where sandwork needs to be mobile. In Africa, where the play material needed to be transported along with the sandtrays and sand, all play material was packed in jute bags. It was important that the objects be robust and have no material or monetary value. There were nevertheless situations where the older children, once the signal for play to begin had been given, all rushed to the table with the play material at once, and grabbed as much as they possibly could. One boy carried a huge pile of building blocks back to his sandtray, another took all the pieces of metal, and a third one had all the figures of people. The smaller children began to collect from the floor what little the older children had dropped in their haste. In these cases it was necessary to start everything again from the beginning, and to explain to the children that they could take back to their sandtray only as much play material as they needed each time. But it was especially important to provide a sufficient amount of each material so that, from the beginning, the children could experience the calming and often hitherto unknown feeling that 'there is also enough for me'.

In all cases where the sandwork material is permanently in one location, it is always good to keep the same figures in the same spots on the shelf. This is not only helpful to the children, but it also gives the whole situation a stronger feeling of order and clarity. Often, children will come to a session with a certain idea in their minds and might even express this, 'Today I'm going to build a city.' Or, 'Where are the aeroplanes?' If there are neither houses nor aeroplanes in the collection, this is not a problem. One can always find something with which a house or an aeroplane can be depicted symbolically.

Free and protected space

> And so I made it my task to create a free and, at the same time, protected space for the child within our relationship during therapy.[10]

The room where sandwork takes place must be quiet and undisturbed. No other children or adults are allowed to enter the room by mistake, no telephones are allowed to ring and, above all, the facilitator is not allowed to leave unexpectedly, whether physically by leaving the room for a moment, or mentally, for instance by reading a text message on a mobile phone. The adult's disappearance, even for very practical reasons, gives the child a sense of insecurity and could even cause the child to panic. An interdependency is created: because the space is protected, the child can open up; and because the child has opened up, the room must remain protected. One makes neither photos nor films during sandwork itself.

At the beginning of a sandwork session the children are shown the sandtray and play material, and are told that they are allowed to make use of everything they see. If Expressive Sandwork takes place in a group, it is helpful to explain two basic rules to the children. They are not allowed to throw sand out of the sandtray, and they should remain silent during the session. If a child is not able to adhere to these two basic rules, this must be taken seriously. The practical consequences are that the child cannot remain in the group. The child's behaviour indicates that he or she is not able to appreciate and make use of the free and protected space at the moment, and that the child requires a different sort of therapeutic intervention.

To begin with, the facilitator should give neither promptings nor suggestions, unless the child asks a question. The adult should sit at a distance from the sandtray that feels comfortable and should keep this same place throughout the following sessions. There should be room for the child to walk around the sandtray if he or she chooses to do so. As we have said, the session should proceed in silence, but each child is allowed to speak softly with the facilitator. Everyone has their own place, space and time. Even very restless children will be surprised by this special atmosphere, which they might never have experienced before, in which nothing else seems to be important except they themselves.

Particularly towards the end of the hour, the symbolic space, which was created during the session, can run the risk of becoming permeable due to carelessness. Some children might already have started to explain the stories behind their sand image to their facilitators. This should happen discreetly, so that the other children can complete their work in peace. But sometimes a child who has already finished might nevertheless bustle up to another sandtray and try to listen to that child's comments. This cannot be permitted, as it would compromise each child's individual protected space. Parents often arrive too early to pick up their children and knock at the door to the sandplay room, because they just want to discuss something briefly. These are all serious disturbances and could ruin the result of the whole session. Therefore it is essential that the symbolic space remain free and protected from outside influences until the end. Because this situation, like every therapy situation, is artificially created, there is a certain risk of it collapsing entirely within seconds. All withheld needs – especially those normally associated with group dynamics – then come crashing in as if to suddenly fill a vacuum. And that is in fact the case: this special container, which is formed on the one hand by the actual room, and on the other hand by the manner of the accompanying adults, is filled by an extraordinary atmosphere. As with all rituals, the transition back to normality must be made consciously and gradually. Otherwise, progress that was hard to come by could be suddenly destroyed in a matter of minutes. This could happen, for instance, if a child makes a derogatory remark about another child's sandplay image. One must therefore pay careful attention that each individual's sandplay session is treated as a kind of sacral activity; a private space and state which nobody from outside is allowed to enter. Some children would actually like to show their sandplay image to the others. Especially children in single sessions might eagerly ask if they can show their parents. In the interest of the protected space, the answer to this question must be in the negative, but it should be formulated in a way that emphasizes this aspect. It is better to allow a little less, than to risk the potential consequences of the child's revealing his inner life: consequences the child himself cannot yet properly judge. The child must be able to leave the room and close the door, leaving his sandplay image – which nobody has changed either materially or by commenting on it – behind him. This is a crucial moment. This alone ensures that what was newly discovered and experienced during sandplay can be preserved within, and can develop until the next session.

Free and protected time

> It is essential for the proper understanding of the nature and use of this technique that no interpretation be given by the therapist to the child.[11]

> It is not necessary to communicate the therapist's insights to the child in words, as we are dealing with the experience of the symbol in the free and sheltered space.[12]

It is important to set a length for sandwork and to keep to it. Ideally, sessions take place once a week and are ensured a continuity of some months or a whole school year. Single sessions last one hour; for a group session with twelve children, one should count a good two hours. If after a few sessions, or even after the first session, a child clearly says that he or she does not want to play any more, this must be respected. One must consider that the unconscious images that are activated by sandwork have a very strong effect and are not always indicated in every situation. One must absolutely refrain from actively urging the child to continue and especially from promising rewards. Play must be voluntary. If a child does not want to join in one day, drawing material, paints or play dough can be offered instead. Young children are mostly happy enough to play on the floor with one or two toys. This can be permitted as long as it does not disturb the other children. There are various reasons why a child might not want to play with the sand. The previous session might already have set so much in motion on the inside that the new contents still have to be assimilated emotionally, and that a greater distance in time is necessary before the next session. Another reason could be that frightening contents appeared. No new images can or should be made when things are still in turmoil on the inside. Adults should deal with this situation in a natural and matter of fact way, so that the child not feel excluded if he does not want to use the sandtray.

In individual child psychotherapy we have many possibilities for dealing with such phases. We will primarily try to understand what happened in the previous sandwork session. What the adult understands mostly has an immediate effect on the child's mood, even if no words are exchanged on the matter. It is not always possible to understand what is currently brewing in a child's psyche. In Expressive Sandwork it suffices to wait and see, and to keep an eye on the child's needs.

It can be helpful if the facilitator not only is consciously aware of his or her own thoughts and feelings, but also reflects on them as well. Once, in a group of children in an orphanage in China, a few of the children did not want to play with the sand, but preferred to sit on the floor at some distance from the rest of the group. One can easily understand that each of their therapists felt somewhat abandoned and superfluous, as they were sitting alone at the empty sandtrays. One can try to attach a meaning to that feeling, a meaning that has to do with the dynamics of relationship. One can, for instance, imagine that the child is trying to impart to the therapist, and actually make the therapist experience, what it is like to feel alone and useless. Experiencing this feeling personally enables the therapist better to relate and adjust to the child. Such observations and considerations, however, already lead us deeper into psychoanalysis and are not absolutely necessary in Expressive Sandwork. But they do make things more interesting for the adult and can therefore be advantageous to the child. Some children do not find the set length of time sufficient and try to prolong it either consciously or unintentionally. Five minutes before the end they might suddenly have a brilliant idea; just one minute before the end a handful of marbles might suddenly be tipped into the sand. These children are trying to express that they find it hard to leave this inner play world, and that it even feels angry. They can express this anger only indirectly and are not subjectively aware of it. The children could also be trying to express that they do not want to part from the facilitator. So the adult is given some extra homework – retrieving all the marbles from the sand after the session is over, whereby the adult is involved with the child for a little longer. Despite all this, it is important to keep to the agreed time. Prolonging the session would only postpone separation and would make it harder in the long run. But it can be helpful to remark on the child's feelings: 'A pity that our time is going to be up soon.' Likewise it can be a help to point out the end of the session about ten minutes beforehand. The children will thereby become aware of the time limit and, at the same time, realize that they would actually rather exceed it. But as the sessions pass, the children will understand more and more clearly that stopping does not mean that everything will disappear forever. They will come to realize that there is a continuity in their own inner world that can be relied on. Sometimes children ask if their sand image could be saved until the next time. For practical reasons alone, this question must be answered with a 'No'. But one can reassure all the more that the image will not be forgotten, for instance because the adult has written the story down, or because the image has been photographed. Writing things down gives some children a sense of being taken seriously, and they even ask why the adult is not taking notes today, if the facilitator has not started the session with notebook already in hand. On the other hand there are children who feel inhibited and cannot play freely when notes are taken. One and the same child might even have phases where she wants things to be written down, and others where she would find it distracting or disturbing. It is up to the adult's sensibility to find the suitable behaviour for each situation.

Especially when the sandwork session did not seem long enough, one might expect children to continue at home what they have started in the sand. This, however, is mostly not the case. Children may play more at home than they used to, but not in the same way as during sandwork. Certain themes seem possible only during a sandwork session. These themes start to become activated in the children as they enter the free and protected space, and practically vanish from consciousness as soon as the children close the room's door behind them when leaving.

The way children deal with this limitation of time can also be quite revealing. Some children drop everything at the first indication of a time limit – for instance when they are reminded that there are only ten minutes left in the session. They appear used to being interrupted in their activities, and do not even try to offer resistance. They cannot yet imagine a period of transition in which play fades out slowly. They find it so hard to accept a time limit that they would rather leave everything immediately. If this is the case, one must also try to help the child to take this step gradually. Turning away from sandplay too quickly could devalue it inwardly, could annul its healing effect and could even produce the opposite effect.

It is worth thinking about the way we feel when we are interrupted during a concentrated activity. Our reaction will very often be one of irritation or anger. Children who are generally slower at perceiving and thinking experience their activities being abruptly interrupted countless times a day. Often these activities would be important emotional processes, but by being terminated again and again they become devalued in the child's experience. Very young children, especially, are often not given the time to bring their actions to a natural close. The constant interrupting of emotional processes, once initiated, has been proven to increase stress and aggression.

Some children grow so accustomed to being interrupted that they actually regularly interrupt themselves during sandplay and become distracted by new thoughts and impulses. Much is begun, but nothing is finished. This can provoke a sense of restlessness in the facilitator, or even of constant failure.

A further dilemma the facilitator might encounter is the way that children make use of their time. A child might build a complicated construction in the eager anticipation of being able to play with it afterwards. But some kind of perfectionism always leads to there being some small detail still not quite right once the time has already run out. The adult realizes anxiously that another session is coming to an end, during which the child has once again undermined his or her own chance to play. Even if it may seem obvious to intervene at this point by saying, 'If you don't hurry up, you'll run out of time to play again', this is not appropriate on principle. This would be a pedagogic intervention, aiming at changing a form of behaviour. But we have already mentioned that the aim of sandwork is not to change single patterns of behaviour, but to allow problematic behaviour to show itself precisely the way it is. By never being able to play, children show precisely what is happening to them in real life. The information disclosed is: 'I never seem to get as far as doing what I really want to do.' If this message can be conveyed and is understood by the adult, the children will begin to find their own ways to change the problem in play. Thus, it is more important to follow the child's very specific path attentively, even if it may appear absurd, circuitous or pointless, than to intervene with regulations or corrections. Every correction could prevent an important part of the message from being conveyed.

One could say a certain kind of learning based on personal experience is intended. If adults feel frustration, sadness or irritation, faced with the impossibility of the undertaking, they are empathetically close to the children. The adult physically experiences and feels what the child is faced with many times a day. It is not necessary to express this feeling verbally; it could even disturb the process. If such behaviour persists over many sessions without changing, the adult might consider making a constructively formulated comment, such as, 'It's important for you that everything is very exact.' Whereupon the child one day might answer, 'Today it is good enough as it is', and thereby distance himself a little from his compulsive behaviour.

The facilitator's attitude

> This free space occurs in this therapeutic setting when the therapist is fully able to accept the child so that the therapist, as a person, is as much a part of everything going on in the room as is the child himself.[13]

Since play is securely framed by the borders of the sandtray, basically anything is allowed to happen within that space. The adult's manner must be such that children dare to play. Children must be able to rely on the fact that what they are about to create is allowed to exist. Being unbiased and free of judgement is an important precondition. Children with problems are very sensitive to any form of judgement by adults. They sense if an adult approves of something or objects to it. Even if the adult has not yet spoken a word, children will sense if their current actions are desired or not. Simply not *uttering* judgemental comments does not suffice: it is essential that one not even *think* them. Is this even possible? Let us suppose a child patiently builds an entire sand city every session, and then has it destroyed by a hurricane. People and animals are brutally killed. It seems as if the only purpose of building the city in such minute detail was to make its destruction by the storm all the more spectacular. How can we not perceive and judge such play as being destructive?

As observers we are, however, able to separate our spontaneous perception from our judgement of the situation, simply by adhering to our principle that *every* form of expression in this free and protected space makes sense and is helpful for children. That was our premise. In the setting of sandwork, we do not aspire to teach children anything. We assume that every child has an inner instinct that takes control during play. Everything that has accumulated in the child's inner world without being properly assimilated is a burden. New experiences cannot be integrated until previous traumatic ones have been processed. Children will portray everything that confuses, overwhelms or burdens them as soon as a free and protected space is provided. But the images' themes can also remain the same over a long period of time. A particular scene may be created and played through time and again, with variations occurring only slowly. This portrayal in play is *in itself* already liberating for most children, as we shall see in due time. It is possible that an adult is so shocked by the content of a child's play, that the adult believes it cannot be good for the child to portray so much destruction. Perhaps it would be better after all to show the child that there are also more peaceful solutions than having soldiers slaughter each other down to the last person. But, as was already mentioned, this would be a pedagogic attitude and is not called for in this context. It would not only be superfluous, but also prohibit the self-regulatory process. If these terrible things, laden with conflict and frightening as they are, cannot find expression with all its necessary repetitions, they will remain sealed away from consciousness. Repetitive portrayal of seemingly insoluble problems is an important step that precedes their assimilation. The facilitator needs patience, perseverance and, above all, confidence in the process. From a therapeutic perspective, every manipulative intervention could be a betrayal of all that a genuinely free and protected space promises. And so the adult simply follows the events of play without intervening and without commenting. The adult is there and just observes. This creates an atmosphere of interest in everything that might appear:[14] order, chaos, slowness, clumsiness, destruction, even boredom. Comments that children might make on their play are listened to; the same goes for stories that don't appear to have anything to do with play. Incomprehensible things can remain, so unfinished things or objects buried in the sand can be left unfinished or buried. If children share their feelings or thoughts with the adult, it is clear that the latter responds casually. Within the framework of play, children do not require adults who intervene of their own accord, but adults who are 'on emotional hold', who always provide just as much of their presence as the children need.

Many educators and kindergarten teachers need not worry about finding this correct manner; they might even be happy for once not to have to intervene pedagogically. But they might wonder, 'Is it really enough merely to be present?' It cannot be repeated often enough: precisely by refraining from intervening, the adult allows the child to experience something the child normally never would in everyday life. Within the small world of sandwork, children are allowed to be grown up and to try practising everything they want, as often as they want, and for as long as is necessary. The spatial and temporal borders towards the outside world enable children to be completely free on the inside, and to take command over their own space and time. Children are allowed to be offender and victim, creator and destroyer and undisputed sovereign of their own small world, always in the knowledge that it is only in play. In this intermediate area between reality and imagination, important experiences and steps of learning take place.

Precisely in this transitional space, described by Donald Winnicott,[15] a toy stuffed animal need not simply be a toy stuffed animal but can also become a real protective being, which can, for instance, take on the role of a mother. Thanks to fantasy, children can change objective reality in such a way that new steps of adaptation become possible. Children can fall asleep with the toy animal, without their mother having to be present. Thus, they have reached a small degree of autonomy. What happens during sandwork is similar. Whatever is confusing, threatening or simply happens too fast in the real world, children can test at their own pace in the small world of sandwork. For once the child is the central figure, since there are no manipulative actions coming from the adult. One could describe the facilitator's manner as if he or she were observing an artist at work. The child is the artist. The observing adult knows nothing about the artwork, might not even understand much of it, but relies on the fact that the artist's decisions and touches will lead to an eventual goal, even if the artist apparently keeps discarding ideas along the way. The adult presumes that every action is part of a process, which he or she must try to understand.

The child is master of his or her own play and the adult is the child's assistant. Does this not manoeuvre the child into an artificial position of importance? Isn't the adult's 'servant' manner, as Arno Stern calls it,[16] in constant danger of spoiling the child and risking that the child begin to feel almighty? This is a central question. Such a non-judgemental, permissive, even servile attitude towards children would surely be harmful outside the situation of therapy. It can be justified only if it remains strictly within specific borders. The space within the sandtray is not like outside, concrete reality. It is a reality being put to the test; it is 'as if'. That is why children are allowed to act as if they were almighty within the limitations of their sandwork. The sand itself sets natural, physical limits to the extent that feelings of omnipotence can arise: one can build with sand, but when the tower gets to be too high, it will collapse by itself. Sand offers the possibility of creating a temporary world in which the child is the one who decides and forms. The aim is to enable children to access their feeling of self. The servile attitude described above can also be misunderstood and could transform the therapeutic effect to its opposite. To serve by no way implies a physical, concrete action, like giving in to a child's demands to 'build me a mountain!' If the therapist were to give in to such requests, the free and protected space would collapse in onto itself. The adult would no longer have just an accompanying role, but would turn into a sort of opponent, which would result in completely different dynamics.

When regarding the sand images, we assume that no detail, however small, is without a meaning. Even if a process is not fully understood, we must assume that it is currently the best possible expression of an unknown content, and we must take it seriously. The expectation that every detail of play must have a sense and a purpose can also create pressure. This happens when the adult expects an orderly course of actions. Sometimes children storm into the sandplay room and know exactly what they want to create: 'Today I'm going to make a zoo.' Another time they might sit in a chair with dangling legs and say, 'I don't know what I want to make today.' On other occasions yet again they might look up and down the shelves for a long time, but nothing seems right: 'Don't you have anything new?' With this question, the child could mean that one phase has been completed, but that the next has not yet been initiated. That a new phase would be expected to take the form of a new object on the shelf can seem logical within the situation of play. 'No, I don't have anything new. But maybe you'll spot something you hadn't noticed before.' By answering this way, the accompanying adult can direct children's psychological energy towards a feeling of expectancy. Children are prepared to let themselves be surprised by an inner gestalt, which can take on a different form on the outside and is therefore not absorbed by a concrete, outside object. If there were indeed new figures every session, sandwork would quickly lose its symbolic dimension. After all, one of the values of play is that children can be surprised by their own ideas and impulses. And the adult's own feeling of surprise is also an indicator that something new has really been produced. As neuroscience has proven, being surprised is a precondition for a change in brain structure.

Even in really young children, one can observe how much they already seem to know about what it is they require. The following is an example of a child therapy session in the USA, which a colleague has kindly provided me with.

A 3-year-old boy had not yet begun to speak, although his hearing was intact and his cognitive abilities normal for his age. In the first sandplay session, the boy took two plastic cups and began pouring sand from one to the other. He repeated this procedure over the course of many sessions, without taking much notice of the therapist. The therapist either spoke to the child or watched in silence. Either way, the therapist made it clear that nothing more was expected of the boy than what he was already doing, and that his actions were being perceived and reflected upon by another person – sometimes also verbally returned. After a few sessions, the boy began to look up at the therapist more frequently, and eye contact became longer and longer as the sessions progressed. The sandplay sessions continued, but the central theme of play – pouring sand from one container to another – remained the same. After three months, the boy began to speak and never had a relapse.

The meaning of this action in play is easy to comprehend. It is a strikingly simple symbol for communication. In order for something to be able to move from one person to another, this movement first had to be tested physically, by hand. It is as if, bit by bit, the boy first needed to assure himself of the fact that a flow of communication, a back-and-forth between two individuals, can indeed even be possible. Whatever the reasons for the delay in the boy's development had been, he first learned the function of speaking through the help of sandplay, and was able to practise it on a pre-lingual level. No symptom-oriented strategy was used in this case, and no attempt was actively made to seek out the underlying psychological reasons for the symptom. All the therapist really did during the sandplay sessions was to provide a free and protected space, and to put his own personality at the boy's disposal, in the sense of an offer of relationship. The boy could then calmly, and at his own pace, assure himself of the fact that it is indeed possible for things to pass between one and another: first sand from one plastic cup to the other, then eye contact from one human being to another, and finally the spoken word. Once he had experienced this, he was ready to speak.

Talking with the parents

To understand the role of parents or other figures of trust in a child's surrounding, one must first be clear about what sandwork provokes in children. Through sandwork, children receive special attention. One can say this gives children a boost of additional energy. It excites children's sensitivity towards themselves and towards the way they perceive their own feelings. Through the sandwork sessions, children begin to perceive themselves more clearly. For this to happen without disturbances, it is important that persons in the individual child's environment know that the child is in treatment. The reason is that, during the process, the child will dare to try out new and emotionally more risky patterns of behaviour. Day after day, the child will also test if the outside conditions are ready for this.

Children who have experienced many negative situations early in their lives develop a defensive system against emotional sensations, which protects them from further harm. The psyche then from the start filters out sensations that it has learnt to associate with harm. Children who have been systematically traumatized for a long time have a cool, dull, often adult-like facial expression. Their psychological defence system reliably ensures that the original, child-like sensibility remains deeply locked away. A psychotherapist can determine the nature and the time of a psychological injury on the basis of the type and the strength of the defensive system. Sandwork shows very quickly if children will even allow an offer of help in opening up to be brought forward, or not. If they do not, the children will not be very interested in sandwork, or might even show a clear aversion. If children are fascinated by the offer of sand and/or figures, the process of granting access has already begun.

A consequence of what has already been said is that the offer of sandwork should be made to children only once the acute outside crisis situation has passed. But sandwork can nevertheless be employed very early on in trauma therapy, as long as continuity in the sessions is ensured, both in time and in terms of the facilitator. If sessions take place with different adults, as was for instance the case after the Sichuan earthquake in 2008 for the simple reason that volunteers were there for only two to three weeks, this needs to be taken into account during the planning process. Precisely because communication takes place on a non-verbal level, Expressive Sandwork requires an intense and profound form of relationship. Therefore, it is important for children to know exactly that they will have a certain number of sandwork sessions with one single adult. Even if a child clearly requires further sessions after that, but the facilitator is no longer available, it is better to wait and let a few weeks or months pass, than to continue sandwork with a new adult.

Conversations with parents should be planned regularly when Expressive Sandwork takes place in kindergartens. But what is important in these talks? Here, again, I will give only a few guidelines because, after all, we are not talking about psychotherapy. Not only the children, but also the parents learn in this model. If we want parents to listen and pay attention to their children, it is important that we first listen to the parents. We must grant them time and space to describe their problems, let downs, worries and fears, without having to fear judgement. It is not helpful to give advice for specific situations, because the problem is usually not due to parents' isolated patterns of behaviour, but due to their basic attitude towards their children. The parents' own childhood experiences play an important role in this largely unconscious attitude. Parents mostly repeat precisely what they experienced in their own upbringing, even if they might be consciously trying to do just the opposite. Comments are helpful only when they are able to change a person's perception.

A mother once asked for a strategy for protecting her 6-year-old son from her own outbursts of rage. She explained how her good will did not seem to be enough. She would still find herself scolding the boy and yelling at him when he was not making progress with his homework. The woman was intelligent and educated, and she was also aware of the connection between her sudden outbursts and her own childhood history. Nevertheless, she was not able to control her emotions, even though she also realized that she was harming her son. The boy had developed a tic and suffered from anxiety and sleep disorders. The therapist asked the mother to describe her son's facial expression in situations when she yelled at him. The mother could not answer the question. She didn't know. This made her realize that she was no longer even able to see her child's face when she lost control of her temper. Her literal blind rage severed the relationship to her son on the level of body language. The therapist and the mother agreed that, when she next lost her temper, the mother would try to do nothing else than remember to look at her son. Basically, the aim of the task was to keep a channel of perception open, despite her fit of rage. When this mother saw the fright and despair in her child's face for the first time, she herself was horrified. Her outbursts of rage quickly ceased. The woman learnt to register her son's feelings with heightened perception.

Many disputes escalate because one cannot correctly read the facial expressions and body language of the other person, one's dialogue partner. Never-ending arguments on the phone are literally never-ending, because one cannot see the hurt one causes. The counterpart's voice often does not offer enough feedback.

Sometimes a description of how their child behaves in kindergarten can also be helpful for parents. One can assume that parents generally see in their child only what their own psychological state allows them to see. If, for instance, a child is suffering in a way that exceeds the parents' threshold of suffering, they simply will not be aware of their child's pain. They deny it, which means they effectively do not even feel it, and naturally cannot help the child either. If a child has a natural talent that surpasses the parents' creativity and fantasy, they, in turn, might find it difficult to promote this talent. It is out of the ordinary and unsettlingly unexpected in their eyes. Luckily, talents often prevail despite unfavourable environments.

It is easy to sum up what children need: structures that give a sense of security, a model to imitate and adults, who show that they trust in the children's developing personalities. Neuroscience confirms today what popular wisdom has always known: children learn from actions, not from words. Children imitate the personalities of the adults they live with, from their body language, all the way down to habits that they actually imagine they are keeping secret from the children, and that the children thereby should not even have been able to observe. Wherever possible – and this is the advantage of extended families – they will, with infallible instinct, choose the healthiest adult the family has to offer. Something in children seems to know that this will further their psychological development and increase their life potential. The smaller the family circle, the more limited are the possibilities of learning from different models. Chronic disputes between children and adults occur mostly in small families. Children in these situations seem to be fighting in vain against being exposed to only a single aspect.

A conversation with the parents can also aim at trying to understand what types of one-sidedness are present in the child's upbringing. Are the parents too strict, too indulgent, too negligent, or do they pressure the child with expectations that are too high? A psychologist does not primarily find out these things from what parents explain, because parents often unintentionally describe the exact opposite of their domestic situation. In their endeavour to escape a diffuse feeling of guilt, parents often, in good faith, describe their efforts and their behaviour towards their child in the way they would like to see themselves. The psychologist mostly has to deduce the actual facts indirectly from the parents' descriptions. Direct questions mostly do not lead to much.

So how does one speak to parents without running the risk of misunderstanding things and then giving the wrong advice? Once again, the answer has to do with sensibility of perception.

A special form of perception, which does however require considerable knowledge of oneself, is illustrated by the following cases.

During a conversation with the parents, a counsellor has the unique opportunity to experience how the child must feel with these parents. The counsellor's precise, subjective perception of the feelings these parents stir in him, gives him a direct clue as to how exactly the child is suffering. It is possible that particularly friendly and obliging parents, who are seemingly prepared to do anything for their child and who trust the counsellor blindly, start to induce a feeling in the counsellor, the longer the conversation lasts, that too much is expected of him. If he manages to grasp this feeling consciously, then he has gained valuable information. He has experienced with his own senses how the child must feel with these parents. He can safely assume that these parents' positive and idealizing expectations are too much for their child. He can further assume that they are probably also overburdening themselves with excessive demands. If the psychologist can succeed in directing the conversation to this issue, and in showing the parents what role this problem of overburdening expectation plays in their lives, then much has already been achieved on the child's behalf, without its having even yet been directly spoken about.

In the case of another set of parents, the listener might feel constantly torn between two opinions, or might feel the urge to come to the defence of one or the other parent. The child probably always feels at home just what the psychologist feels in his brief conversation with the parents. Some parents, whose children do badly at school, have such an intensely unsettling effect that even the psychologist suddenly may find it hard to express himself properly, or makes a mistake when calculating the bill. Such reactions in the therapist are valuable, because they are a very direct way of detecting problems in relationships. The psychologist will then try to find the right words to describe to the parents how their child might be feeling. By doing this, he is simply trying to expand their awareness, for one can change whatever one is aware of in oneself. People mostly inflict emotional pain on each other only when they do not realize that the other person is suffering. Every experienced educator uses such instruments of psychotherapy completely intuitively; they are nothing new.

Another important intervention in conversations with parents is asking about memories of their own childhood. Often this suddenly makes parents realize that they are able to put themselves in the child's position. By appealing to the former child in the parent, and by taking him or her seriously, the psychologist can bring about another important emotional step. Common reactions are, 'I was just the same as a child!', or 'I was the complete opposite.' In the memory of how things felt back then lies a new path to understanding.

As to the sandwork sessions, one rule must be observed absolutely: the content of play, everything that the child expresses either verbally or non-verbally during the sessions, must be protected even from the parents. As we have seen, children open up their utmost vulnerability in the special protected space of sandwork, and we have no guarantee that parents will be able to acknowledge and respect this vulnerability. On the contrary: if they could, their child would probably not be in therapy in the first place. No information the accompanying adult may deduce from sandwork must be allowed to reach the outside, at least not in the form in which the child expressed it.

It would be a serious breach of a child's trust if the therapist were, for example, to tell the mother her child had played war again today, or had fed lots of little animals, or was altogether at a loss what to do today. The process takes place in a protected space, which absolutely must remain sealed from the outside. Information which the accompanying adult has deduced indirectly from play, or which the child has entrusted to him or her directly, must also be handled very delicately. One must never forget that the 'place' in which this information was entrusted to the adult is an artificially created space, and that this was therefore no ordinary form of communication. If a child imparts sensitive information to an adult only within this protected space, but conceals it outside, this is likely to be for very specific reasons. The entrusted problem was not noticed in the child's environment, and even now would not be taken seriously, if it were treated as simple information and disclosed to the parents directly. But, through sandwork, children also learn to communicate better with their surroundings.

An 8-year-old boy who was born prematurely and had spent a long time in an incubator, once said to his mother when she came to pick him up from his sandplay session, 'Now I need a hug.' He had never expressed anything like that before. Sandplay had enabled him to verbalize his need to make up for a lack of physical contact in his infancy. Until then, this could have been surmised only indirectly from the fears that had brought him to therapy.

The situation is more complicated when information appears in sandwork that indicates an acute danger for the child. Sandplay that was accompanied by a lay therapist must never be used as evidence or be the sole motive for initiating action with respect to the child. What is depicted in play is psychological reality, which sometimes also corresponds to material reality. If the facilitator believes he or she can deduce information about the child and the parents from sandwork, this must first be very discreetly verified through other information about the child's everyday life. Such information can come from the child's behaviour toward other children, behaviour in play outside of the sandwork situation, verbal comments or physical symptoms. With time, the sandwork therapist can mostly tell if a child is depicting a concrete outside situation, or if the child is busy processing a psychological trauma that happened in the past. Generally, what looks like brute force does not actually depict the worst. Things that cause really serious harm are mostly implied indirectly, as if in passing.

A nervous 6-year-old boy once created a peaceful world in sandplay, in which various animals had made themselves homes. Every family had their own home; a hitherto unknown atmosphere of calm and security filled his play. Suddenly, a tornado shattered this scene – the boy used an upside-down fir tree to depict the tornado. The boy laughed loudly and joked as the whirlwind raged through the little houses and destroyed everything. From the therapist's point of view, the boy's play became more and more brutal, but the child seemed to be enjoying it all the more. The therapist felt torn between the child's cajoling and his pity with the animals, whose homes were being destroyed. What made the child's message so dramatic was that he had become an aggressor himself. The boy's father was an alcoholic, who often included his son in his rough, loud and inappropriate activities. Often he would wake the boy in the middle of the night to play. And then he would disappear for weeks. The boy had no choice but to go along with all this, if he did not want to lose his father's attention. In sandplay he now had the opportunity to become consciously aware of both aspects: the frightened animals, who had lost their homes, represented his own homelessness, while his outright sadistic exuberance, which he was beginning to take over from his father, had the purpose of covering up his suffering. This play enabled the therapist to point out clearly to the father what he was inflicting on the boy, without actually mentioning the content of play itself. After a few sessions the boy was able to talk about his father, and he deplored for the first time that he actually found much of his father's behaviour not funny at all, that he was often afraid of his father's loud, raucous laughter, and that he would often prefer to hide when his father came home.

Content of children's play

In the following, the contents of various sandplays from psychotherapeutic practices will be described. The reader should acquire a feeling for how play can be understood as the expression of a child's emotional state. This is not about interpreting individual sand images; the aim is to illustrate how psychological processes can express themselves in play and how they are connected with the child's moods and feelings.

Sandplay therapists have observed a connection between a child's play and the therapist's ability to understand the inner-psychological dynamics involved.[17] This understanding on the part of the therapist, which takes place not only on a rational, logical and analytical level but also on a more intuitive and emotional one, influences the course of play and also its emotional intensity. The more clearly the adult is able to see the relationship between children's play and their psychological state, the more deeply the children will become involved in depicting their inner world and conflicts. But if the therapist is distracted and remains concentrated on his or her own thoughts, the types and contents of play will become more like how children would normally play if they were alone.

A good observer is always one who knows a great deal, but who is still impartial enough to be easily surprised by something new.

Fighting scenes

Animals, teams or soldiers are set up either singly or in groups. Then the fight begins. Setting up the two opposing units often requires a lot of time and is done very precisely. The balance of strength can by all means be quite equal even if the two armies are from different historic epochs, for example Native Americans on horses fighting against technologically equipped soldiers. It is often the case – especially when such battles take place for the first time in a sandplay session – that one fighter from each side valiantly survives all the individual fights and battles, only to die as well at the very end.

If the therapist then asks the superfluous question, 'So they're all dead now?', the answer will often be a somewhat impatient 'Of course, you can see that.' The child might indeed feel a certain ambivalence – like an author who has to let one of the characters die – but the child seems to know that the story has its own unchangeable dynamics. Trying to influence its course, for example to create a happy end, would mean a loss of authenticity. The child needs to find an ally in the therapist, someone whose desire to find out how the real story continues – even if it be hard to take – is stronger than a wish to see it end happily. The therapist's presence should facilitate the expression of precisely these conflictive issues.

Scenes of war, which are frequently drawn out over many sessions, often represent a conflict between opposing impulses, wishes and drives that cannot be solved at the moment. Different variations will be integrated by and by. One can assume that any change in play content or behaviour always has a corresponding change in the child's real world.

The parents of Marco, a 7-year-old single child, were strict but insecure at the same time. He had often been sick during the first years of his life and had had to endure numerous operations during long stays in hospital. Therefore Marco was weaker than other children his age, and he had never been allowed to partake in sports lessons. What is more, he had inhibitions to express his own will and ideas. He was hardly able to assert himself against other children his age, because he not only looked younger than his age but also, like a young deer, made the impression of being in need of protection. In a holiday camp he had once fallen victim to sexual assaults by a boy three years older than him. In school he hung out with a group of very aggressive boys, who molested and threatened other children. If there was something he didn't want, he was incapable of saying so even at home: he would agree to everything and then secretly destroy a valuable object later, as if out of compensation. He had difficulty with his homework, and so he would often hide his books or tear out pages to conceal the fact that he had homework to do. The parents' punishments were demeaning and did not improve matters. Eventually they decided to have their child treated by a psychotherapist.

Initially Marco was very shy. But, like many inhibited children, he was openly interested in the sandtray and the miniature figures from the beginning. He had understood quickly that this was not going to be a situation like in school; he was not going to be judged or graded. He began working in the sand as if there had been no one else in the room. I tried to be as 'invisible' as possible and sought no verbal communication, because I sensed clearly that I was more of a disturbing factor than anything else.

Very purposefully, Marco began creating a moonscape. It was as if he wanted to convey how estranged he felt in that moment – and maybe his entire life long. Something that interested him could take place only far away from daily reality: on the moon. Only there could his fantasy be free enough, and not be burdened with inhibitive associations. Astronauts had come from earth and were engaged in a battle with lunar aliens. Marco made the appropriate fighting noises, but the whole scene was nevertheless confusing, because everyone appeared to be fighting everyone else and there was no apparent aim or purpose. I found it hard to concentrate and my thoughts kept drifting off. The child had learned to keep adults out of his world. It was easy to forget Marco even in his own presence. He didn't give me the feeling that he needed me.

All life forms on the moon were dead by the end of his play. Even the spaceship had exploded after being hit by a meteorite, but none of this seemed to stir any particular emotions. The child could not have staged his emotional detachment in a more effective way: the empty, white moonscape and the pointless battle. After about half an hour, Marco asked if he could go to the toilet. He made it understood that it was going to be 'a number two'. Possibly something in his autonomic nervous system had been set in motion and had relaxed. Apparently he had been able to rid himself of something.

In the following session Marco began again to set up a lunar landscape. But after a few minutes he cleared it away again and said: 'I've changed my mind'. It was the first time he established contact verbally. From then on I was invited to partake in the action. I was apparently supposed to witness that he was able to change something. This time Marco created a prehistoric scene. He was now able to deal with a dimension that was closer to reality (on the earth instead of the moon): this was huge progress. What had been a distance in space was now a distance in time. This ancient landscape was inhabited by frightening, carnivorous plants and vicious, voracious dinosaurs. Larger life forms ate smaller ones after just a brief struggle – and with obvious satisfaction. This behaviour was repeated not only during the one session, but also over the next few sessions. It was always clear what would come next. He depicted single body parts being devoured in such sadistic detail that it was often hard to watch. It felt like being in a cold-hearted world where only one law counted: big eats small. I began to doubt if this play was even good for Marco, or if he were immersing himself too far into experiencing violence for violence's sake. My attempts at talking to him about this were of no avail whatsoever: play continued in the same way. Finally, a new variation showed itself in one of the next sessions. This time there was a small dinosaur that was more intelligent and playful than the rest. The little dinosaur kept managing to escape the attacks of Tyrannosaurus, Brontosaurus and Stegosaurus through all kinds of cunning ploys: a new behaviour which I hoped would prevail. Sadly, at the end of the session this likeable little fellow also disappeared down the throat of a Tyrannosaurus rex, the mightiest of all reptiles – but not before inflicting a mortal wound on his aggressor. This friendly little dinosaur must have been a potential of Marco's. Feelings, talents, humour and a capacity for relationship: all of them qualities which had so far fallen victim to psychic drives and to violent assaults from the outside. These qualities had finally been able to make an appearance in his play. Marco was able to see them in action and I, the therapist, was his witness. He had kept a close eye on how I reacted to his play. He knew that I had found the little dinosaur as likeable as he had. And so we consoled ourselves in knowing that the little dinosaur had at least achieved something in his death. This completely changed the way that Marco played in the next session.

A very different kind of fight took place this time: between a dragon guarding a pearl and some soldiers. The dragon – a mythological variant of the dinosaur – still represents primitive impulses of power, but on a new, allegorical level. The figure of the dragon appears in legends and narratives, which makes it, culturally, a creative figure. In the reality of the outside world, Marco had so far compensated for his weakness by choosing to associate with stronger boys – he had accepted the world of the dinosaurs. The soldiers in this sand image represented a controllable form of aggressive power. They defeated the dragon and won its pearl. This fight was not just for bare survival, there was also something precious to be gained. The pearl can stand for inner wholeness, for aesthetic values that actually have more to do with female principles.

In the following session Marco set up four large armies with great patience and precision, one at each edge of the sandtray. There was symmetry, clarity and order. Each army had a leader and its own colour and flag. They rehearsed different strategies against one another. In the end, after long and fair individual combats, one soldier fighting against another and either falling or standing his ground, one of the armies was victorious.

After this sandplay session, Marco's parents reported that he had talked to them about problems with his classmates for the first time. Apparently he had been more open and cheerful over the past weeks. He needed only half as much time as previously to do his homework. His psychological powers had begun to structure and discipline themselves, and were thus available to the ego to confront not only the inner conflicts but also those in the outside world. In the next session Marco said: 'Today I need people – normal people, not soldiers.' He seemed to have progressed even further: he was now able to create something constructive instead of just fighting. His image told a story that revolved around the construction of a castle, which Marco built out of moist sand. It had a grand entrance gate, colourful glass mosaic pieces formed the windows, and the roof was made of a large crystal. The castle was inhabited. It can be seen as a representation of Marco's personality: he felt strengthened, and his inner steadfastness and self-esteem had increased. He was able to conciliate his inner and outer worlds. This was indicated by the windows, which Marco had made with great care, and of which he was particularly proud.

Marco continued to make good progress. His parents were encouraged to listen to him more attentively, to trust him, and to refrain from punishment. During the sessions Marco had never spoken about anything other than what he was creating in his play at the time.

Although this was an example of individual psychotherapy, taking place every fourteen days over the course of fifteen sessions, one can easily imagine how such a process could also take place in a setting of Expressive Sandwork with an adult who is not trained in psychotherapy.

The child did not only *get by* without verbal communication: most likely this would even have distracted him from his self-healing process, which took place in the presence of an adult and yet almost completely autonomously.

Movement

Many different means of transport occur in sand images. These can be buses, aeroplanes, cable cars or ships. At times they encounter obstacles, at others they race around in circles as if they were fleeing from something. Sometimes they are simply placed next to each other in the sand, but so many and so densely packed that they cannot move. Sand images showing such traffic jams were remarkably common in the orphanage of Guangzhou, China. Because cars greatly expand our range of individual movement and therefore bring to mind a feeling of independence, they often symbolize psychological energy. One can assume that many of these children do not receive enough outside incentive to unfold their feelings, thoughts and ideas. Sandwork itself, as well as the increased individual attention the child receives, are enough to set things back in motion: the vehicles pave their own ways through the sand image or combine to form geometric shapes.

Hiding and finding

Children of all ages play different variations of hide and seek in the sand. Sometimes animals, people or cars are repeatedly buried and unearthed again.

In one child's play, cars kept disappearing in a great, 'car-ivorous' mountain of sand. The boy's dyslexia had not yet been recognized although he had consistently failed in school from the first class onwards. Shortly before the end of the session the boy retrieved the cars one by one. This was accompanied by loud cheers every time he unearthed another car, almost as if they were being born again. A desire in the boy for autonomy must have been frustrated every day, because he kept failing at school and in his social surroundings. Unearthing the cars was equivalent to regaining confidence in his own abilities and proficiencies.

If, on the other hand, buried objects remain buried at the end of the session, this is an indication of things that the child cannot confront at the moment. But it means a lot to the child that someone else knows and has witnessed that there is *something* buried under the sand. Sometimes this is the real core of a child's personality, the child's true self, which must remain hidden so as not to be harmed any more by a pathological environment.

Destruction

Whenever houses, castles, cities or gardens are destroyed, the question arises: 'What in the child's life is it that needs to be destroyed?' Is it peaceful order which is being attacked? Or is it an unyielding world which can be changed only through destruction? Often the destruction seen in sandplay is the repetition of a situation that the child has actually experienced. This can be violence on the part of adults or the child's own failure faced with excessive expectations. Whatever happens in sandplay, it is always reality in respect to the child's inner world. Certain elements of a child's play can shock an adult, because they can most certainly pertain to physical or psychological violence that the child has experienced in his or her surroundings. It is possible that the child will talk about these elements at a later point in time and that their initial non-verbal depiction was meant more as a test question: 'Is there anyone who cares for me?'

The depiction of destruction is also always a first expression of personal initiative. It is a sign that depression and traumatic petrification, which would paralyse the expression of psychological content, have not yet set in. But what does one do when destruction assumes such proportions that large quantities of sand are thrown out of the tray or objects are wilfully destroyed without being part of any particular depiction?

When arms and legs were torn off play figures in China to illustrate the victims of the earthquake, this was counted as part of the children's symbolic expression and was therefore allowed. It was a borderline situation when a little girl in an orphanage tore off a doll's head and threw the doll to the floor without wanting to continue with play on that day.

There are cases where sandplay is inadequate and other forms of intervention should be sought, that act more clearly on the level of the ego and do not directly stimulate unconscious content. Learning a musical instrument or a handicraft not only is more effective in such cases, but also presents no risk of re-traumatization through therapy.

Preparing food and feeding

Preparing food and feeding it to animals or children is a game that girls and boys alike can play with great dedication.

A 5-year-old girl was suffering from fits of rage due to her fears of abandonment (her mother was about to leave her father, who didn't want the separation). In the first sandplay session she began placing animals in the sand, and asked the therapist what each of the animals liked to eat. It meant a lot to the girl that each animal receive its specific food: the rabbits were given grass, the fish algae, the dogs meat and so on. These questions were repeated over numerous sessions as if the girl kept forgetting which food went with which animal. Again and again, each animal was given a sufficient amount of its own food. One could tell how play progressed on the basis of the animals' phylogeny. She had started with fish, then came wild mammals, then cats and dogs, and finally a farm where many different kinds of domestic animal were given their food. Even the farmer himself and his copiously filled storeroom appeared in one of the last sessions. The girl's infantile needs had been nourished and satisfied through this almost ritual act. Her fits of rage abated, because she was able to express to her parents more clearly what she needed and what frightened her.

Threats

A number of families – humans and animals – live in different homes in harmony. In the evening they eat, and then the children are laid to bed and the animal families go back to their huts. At night, a huge snake and other animals from the underworld creep up on this idyllic scene. This was what Carmen, an 8-year-old girl whose parents fought most of the time, depicted in her sand image. She was very pretty and intelligent but suffered from secondary enuresis and a deficit of healthy aggression. The father was an alcoholic and the mother too weak to assert her children's and her own needs. Carmen's classmates made fun of her at school and she thought herself ugly and stupid. It was plain to see in this sandplay session that the therapy room was not yet protected enough for her: she played with her back to me, avoided eye contact and spoke so quietly that the content of her play was barely intelligible at first. But she did explain it later when I asked if she would like to. Somehow the peaceful world with its many children and small animals was always saved from the looming threat of the snake. Someone always woke up at the last minute, saw the snake and warned all the others. Each time, the snake had to concede defeat.

On the one hand, the conflict between the frightening aggressors and the cosy, infantile world could mean that Carmen wanted to remain in an infantile world herself. On the other hand, she might already have realized that other, 'snake-like' properties are also often called for in life and in interpersonal relationships. The snake and the other chthonic animals not only represented her fears, but also concealed an imminent step in the girl's development: it would eventually become necessary for her to resort to cunning and emotional coldness in order to gain respect among her classmates and to oppose her father's excesses. She would have to integrate a degree of evil in her personality to assert her own will.

Beauty

We often underestimate children's extraordinary sense of beauty. Educators and kindergarten teachers, who are accustomed to taking notice of such things, are full of enthusiasm for the sophisticated perceptivity displayed by even very little children: they are able to distinguish the slightest differences in colour and texture of objects. Music teachers and therapists using expressive methods both agree that working material (colours and paper) and musical instruments for young children need to be of exceptional quality.

In difficult moments especially, children have a desire to create something beautiful. They use glass marbles, flowers, shells and stones to create symmetrical patterns, either round or square or a combination of both. When children ask adults if they find something beautiful, the children might be seeking confirmation for their way of feeling and perceiving the world. Am I doing this right? Do I feel this properly? Responding by asking whether the child finds it beautiful is a respectful reaction as long as it does not happen mechanically. It also reduces the risk in the next sessions of the children only wanting to make things that are to the adult's liking, and that distract them from the way they themselves feel about them. Sometimes a child can be surprised by something beautiful that has appeared in the sand. In this case the child's question might not be due to insecurity but because the child would like to share this experience of something beautiful with another person. Children who live in chaotic and violent environments have a clear desire to create beautiful and orderly things – maybe not only to compensate for the squalor in their lives, but also because 'beauty' may, on an archetypal level, correspond to 'goodness'.[18]

Chapter 7

Expressive Sandwork in South Africa

It takes a whole village to raise a child.

(African saying)

When driving along the bumpy streets of Munsieville, a township near Johannesburg, one cannot help but notice the shoes dangling at regular intervals from wires strung high across the road. Tennis shoes, boots, children's shoes of various sizes, single ones or pairs – a surreal sight. What are those perfectly good shoes doing up there? Who in this poor neighbourhood can do without shoes, and even go to the trouble of hanging them way up there? Our driver's explanation silences all cheerful attempts at guessing the answer: the shoes mark the borders between territories that are controlled by different drug gangs. They are a warning to those who do not follow the gangs' laws: you won't be needing your shoes any longer.

Expressive Sandwork was conducted at the Munsieville elementary school in August 2007 with children between the ages of 6 and 10. The school is located at the edge of the slum area which is a few square kilometres in size. Food is distributed at the school twice a week by a private relief organization. Many of the classrooms consist of containers without heating or ventilation, into which up to 60 children sit crammed together for their lessons. Every now and then a head will sag to the table, because its owner did not get enough sleep at home. The teachers are overworked. Every one of these children really require individual attention, the majority have behavioural disorders, and many have untreated physical illnesses. The main problems, from which these children suffer, are neglect, hunger, sexual abuse, family or neighbourhood violence, as well as having to cope with alcohol and drug addiction in adults. Many children who live in Munsieville do not even have family any more. When their last relatives die, these children hide, because they do not know what will become of them. Often, elder siblings care for their younger brothers and sisters.

The teachers of the Munsieville elementary school had chosen children who had shown conspicuous behaviour during the previous months. Emotional withdrawal and a sudden drop in performance are indicators of an acute, traumatic experience. The information about the children was limited to their approximate ages and the problematic behaviour the teachers described. If siblings or neighbouring children also attended the school, we were able to compare and verify some information. The children themselves were always least talkative when their bodies showed clear signs of violent physical abuse. Organizing home visits by social workers was possible in theory, but came with a high risk in reality. I was told that children would disappear shortly before the visit, or the social workers would be threatened, and were not prepared to visit the family again. They were intimidated not only by the families themselves, but also by the families' neighbours. The adults' behaviour is governed by fear of the criminal organizations that control their neighbourhoods.

One of the fears among the children of the shanty towns is to be taken by a 'sangoma', the original, general term for medicine men in the tribal communities. The number of criminal sangomas has increased alarmingly since the 1990s (the end of apartheid) in the urban areas of the townships, and especially in the shanty towns. They lucratively promote the belief that having sexual intercourse with a virgin cures AIDS: an atrocious business with young girls. Those involved in these hideous crimes care little that the girls are also infected with AIDS after the rape. It is very hard to find explanations for such shocking behaviour; poverty cannot be reason enough. The people in the traditional tribal communities were also poor, but never did such 'magical' practices develop, in which children fell victim to the egoism of single pathological individuals. The offspring of a people are that people's future. In a healthy society, children enjoy a special status of protection by the adults: if children lose their parents, other adults will care for them. Harming children in any way is condemned in every human society. Apart from this cultural, moral inhibition, humans and most other mammals also have a special instinctive inhibition, which has been described by ethologists.[1] Neither of these two inhibitions seems to remain effective in the misery of the shanty towns. The children of one ethnic group are not precious offspring in need of protection, but a kind of fair game for the adults of another group. They can be abused – and killed. An increase in such perverse behaviour is one of the long-term consequences of the collapse of traditional tribal units following centuries of colonial rule.

After the end of apartheid in 1994, South Africa experienced a rapid increase in immigration from its poorer and politically torn neighbouring countries. The first years of the new state were characterized by openness and tolerance; everybody was happy that the transition had been managed without bloodshed, and nobody considered it particularly necessary to control immigration. But quite soon the city centres and the townships were crowded with people who had immigrated and were without a job. Around the cities, sheet metal and cardboard shacks grew to vast slums, in which squalor and crime assumed inconceivable proportions, and where police cars strayed no longer. The flow of millions of people, who wanted to reach the South, wealthy and free South Africa, did not cease. The results are shanty towns like Soul City near Johannesburg, where 20,000 people from up to

15 different ethnic groups have to share just a few wells. The children who grow up here find themselves in a threatening situation. There is no community of adults offering them protection, because no such community ever formed in this randomly thrown together settlement of helpless people.[2]

The brutality with which young people of different ethnic groups, all living in the same wretched shanty town, attacked each other with knives and sticks in May 2008,[3] speaks for itself: these young people *would have been* the future of their individual ethnic groups, but in truth they did not have a future, because nobody was interested in their courage or intelligence. The determination they showed as they turned every random object into a weapon against 'the others' – those who in reality were nothing but a reflection of their own miserable selves – suggested an underlying suicidal aspect to the undertaking. This common, unconscious goal, if nothing else, united the two sides in the end: at least to add a heroic aspect to one's own downfall.

The following pages describe sandwork sessions with children of different ages.[4] The therapeutic procedure is very different from anything we already know from private psychotherapy practices – often quite the opposite. In private practice, it is not even possible to treat a child whose parents are not involved in the therapy process. Normally, child psychotherapy begins with a talk with the parents and an amanuensis, which produces a clinical diagnosis. Sandplay can help verify or correct this diagnosis, but its main purpose is for the child to confront the problem with his or her own resources. In the cases described here, a further purpose of sandwork, even before any psychological examination of problems, is to provide a concrete picture of the child's daily life situation. The assisting adult will be put to the test time and again in having to distinguish between reality and the child's fantasy.

It is self-evident from what has been said so far that sandwork sessions are in no way limited to a diagnostic purpose. Nor do they aim merely at improved communication between children and adults: these are just positive side effects. In the following examples, we will see that the considerably more important and far-reaching result is a different one: with the help of sandwork, the children are able to become aware of their own life situations – seen both objectively from the outside, and subjectively from the inside. This active engagement with one's own difficult life situation activates reserves of energy, which might until then have been blocked by a defensive, passive or suppressive attitude.

Far, far away

Unlike all the other children, 8-year-old Baito had said from the start that he did not want to play in a sandbox. The group sessions were taking place outdoors at the time, and there were no individual sandtrays available, just long boxes filled with sand in which the children played next to each other, each in their own allotted space. There were far fewer facilitators than children at the time, so the children could not be individually cared for.

It might seem surprising at first that all the instructions for sandwork, which were described in previous chapters, are not really properly applied in this example. But this exception from the rule can help sharpen our appreciation for what really counts in sandwork.

This lack of organization suited Baito quite well: unnoticed, he took a few of the figures from the table as it was being prepared, and moved away from the group without saying a word. After a while, Imme Thom, who was leading the sandwork project, found him next to a couple of rubbish bins, absorbed in play. She observed him for a long time. He noticed her presence, but did not even turn around when he began to explain: these were his parents (Picture 5).

After a long shared silence she asked him where his parents were, upon which he answered, 'Far, far away'. It turned out that Baito had been living all alone in a shack for some months, and that he ate only when his neighbours occasionally brought him some food. For fear and shame he would never have disclosed this information of his own accord, but he had described his situation in play, and after that he was also able to talk about it in words.

It was important for Baito to establish a sort of connection to his parents: he did not even know if they were dead, or if they would one day return.

Picture 5

He had to find them again in his memory, and in order to do this he had to distance himself from the group. That the place he chose to play happened to be 'aside' from all the rest, where there were no other witnesses apart from two rubbish bins, was part of a kind of stage setting. At that point Baito could not *depict* his life situation with figures in a sandtray; instead he first had to *enact* it in the first person. Above all, it was important for the therapist to come to find him, just as he had set himself the task of finding his parents on a symbolic level.

The fact that Baito had known from the start what he would need for his play suggests that his relationship with his parents, while they were still with him, had been positive and stable. On this solid emotional basis, he had recreated the image of his parents inside him. He was also able to find a phenomenological explanation for their disappearance: his parents still exist, of that there is no doubt, but they are far, far away. Being able to show his play to the therapist had two effects for Baito. On a concrete, practical level, people began taking care of him: he was accepted into the 'Shongololo children's home' in Munsieville. On a psychological level, a positive parent *function* activated itself inside him. That day, Baito's parents, wherever they were, moved a lot closer to him in his emotional world. And, through the therapist's mediation, he himself returned at least partly out of his isolation back into a community.

The preconditions for this were free play in a protected environment and an adult who understood the contextual relationships.

I'm running to get the police

The two sandwork processes described in the following, those of 11-year-old Chlony and of 9-year-old Tumi, seem to have much in common at first. In their initial settings, both boys depict their own homes; in the one case the father is standing in front of the entrance, in the other case it is the stepfather, but each of them is threatening the mother with a stick. Both children describe the action with similar words, but the ways in which they have each depicted it are distinctly different. We will soon see which details already indicated in the very first session that these two stories would end up running very different courses (Picture 6).

Chlony had made his sand image quickly, without much hesitation, and then explained: 'My father is beating my mother. I'm running to get the police.' The message is shocking, but the image appears well laid out and impressively clear. There is a house in the top part, with a wall around it. In front of the door, one figure is holding a stick raised menacingly above another figure. A third figure is running through an opening in the wall to a different house in the lower left corner of the sandbox – the corner where Chlony

Picture 6

himself was standing as he made this image. He has portrayed his family situation. He obviously needs help. But the image's clear structure, along with Chlony's explanation and the fact that he portrayed himself running to the police, all indicate his inner strength. He is able to react, and he also knows the concept of a police force that can really help. This does not go without saying in Chlony's township. The 'police' in his image could therefore also have a symbolic meaning. Maybe being allowed to take part in sandwork gave Chlony hope that he would be protected by the therapist. If this was so, he was to be proven right. As a consequence, a social worker visited the family at home, and his parents were prepared to accept help. For Chlony, sandwork was a unique opportunity to express convincingly what it was that grieved him, without needing to use words. In his case, the therapist decided that it was more urgent to deal with outer reality immediately, rather than wait for development in further sandwork sessions. It is not always easy to make this judgement. Such decisions can never be made by the therapist alone, but only in cooperation with people who know the child's environment, and the cultural customs of the respective ethnic group.

The next two sand images were made by 9-year-old Tumi. When he describes his first picture, we could initially believe we are hearing Chlony's description again: 'My stepfather is drunk. He is beating my mother. He says he will kill her. Mother goes over to the neighbours for help. I am playing with my animals.' It is the same scene of family violence, but the boy's description is much more dramatic. Furthermore, in Tumi's situation, it is his stepfather and not his own father. He must have been very afraid that his mother could really be killed. The image itself conveys a completely different message from Chlony's. The boys' age difference alone is not a sufficient explanation for this difference (*see* plate section: p. 2, Plate 4).

Two homes are visible in the top half of the picture. In front of the house on the right, there is a figure with raised arms holding a stick, and a second figure turned away from the first: Tumi's drunken stepfather and his mother. There are some animals in the upper left corner of the picture. This is where Tumi says he is playing. The neighbours' house is in the middle of the picture, although they do not seem to play any particular role in the scene. The whole sand image, especially the rough, unlevelled sand, makes an impression of disorder and disharmony. The houses are like caves that are separated from one another by walls. The top left corner, to which Tumi has retreated with his animals, can be seen as a symbolic place of regression. It shows that Tumi would rather stay in a fantasy world. It is his emotional retreat from a situation, with which he is in no way able to cope. The fact that he hasn't depicted himself with a figure is a further indication of his extreme helplessness: it is as if he doesn't even want to appear in this scene. Tumi can't imagine any possible way out of his situation. Playing with animals could allude to his basic ability to create symbols. But this creative ability is not well established in his real life – it is even separated by walls. At any time, the boy himself could become a victim of his stepfather's violence.

Imme Thom was alarmed by this sand image. She visited the family and confirmed what Tumi had depicted in his sandwork. His mother was being maltreated by his stepfather, who repeatedly threatened to kill her. She was offered police protection, which, however, she declined. Tumi's fears were soon to be proved terribly true: there was no way out. Three days after he had made this sand image his mother was dead – beaten to death by her husband in a drunken rage. Six children were made half-orphans and the stepfather went to prison. Tumi was first brought to live with an aunt, but he wasn't happy there. The aunt had only very reluctantly agreed to take care of the children.

On the day of his mother's funeral, Tumi made another sand image (see plate section: p. 3, Plate 5). He explained that the mound with the cross was his mother's grave. It is at the top of the picture, in the centre. Beside this, separated by a ditch and a wall, is the aunt's house. He depicts himself in the middle of the picture, sitting at a river with a friend. Below them is a crocodile. Tumi says he is playing with this crocodile.

Depicting his mother's grave is a huge psychological achievement. Tumi is not pushing his grief aside, but is beginning to process it. Paradoxically, because the very worst he could have imagined has already happened, he is now relieved of his fear. Not only does he depict himself in the image this time, but also he even takes a central position. What is more, there is now also a friend, who is very close to him. He is separated from the grave and from his aunt by a wall. The figure of the friend can also be seen as an increase in his own emotional strength: through his mother's sudden death he probably received a lot of attention and sympathy from other children his age. The crocodile, like every symbol, indicates a more complex connection. It symbolizes his traumatic experience. In his first sand image, Tumi had been playing with elephants and lions – mammals – whereas now he is playing with just one, cold-blooded, animal – a reptile. In terms of phylogeny, this represents a regression. On the one hand it expresses that Tumi now runs the risk of becoming 'crocodile-like' himself (i.e. aggressive and cold-blooded), on the other hand he will probably urgently need a certain degree of 'crocodile-ness' to survive in his environment. But the figure of the crocodile bears yet another quality, which is common knowledge to everyone in South Africa: female crocodiles carry their young in their mouths to protect them from harm. In case of danger, the little crocodiles swim into their mother's mouth, and lie between her rows of teeth as she glides along the surface. In Tumi's cultural environment, crocodiles therefore symbolize maternal care. We also know that the so-called 'reptilian brain' in humans plays an important role in processing traumas. So this symbol of the crocodile means that there is a potential for survival deeply rooted in the boy, an ability to extract what he most needs from his surrounding reality, even under the most adverse conditions. And this would indeed prove to be his strength: after a few weeks he was able to say that his aunt was not treating him well. He found a place first in the 'Shongololollo children's home', and then in a new adoptive family. He took part in sandwork sessions regularly and did well in school. In the following years he did not show any more signs of troubled behaviour.

Unspeakable

Refilve is 14 years old.[5] She was sent to Imme Thom by her teacher, because she had always been a good pupil, had done all her homework, but one day she had suddenly stopped making any effort for school. When asked about this, Refilve simply answered that she didn't want to do anything any more. She stopped washing herself. It was impossible to get a word out of her; her silence seemed defiant, yet sad. Imme Thom offered her a chance to take part in a sandwork session. Refilve set to work in silence – probably encouraged by the other children, who were working with the same concentration. She felt protected in the group and taken seriously, without being made the centre of attention. After she had completed her first sand image, she began to cry. She explained her picture: 'My mother is far away visiting friends. This is my house' (see plate section, p. 3, Plate 6).

In the enclosed space in the centre, Refilve is being raped by her step-father. Her stepbrother is standing guard at the door so that nobody can come in unexpectedly.

As a consequence of this sand image, Imme Thom – with Refilve's consent – spoke to the girl's mother and told her what had happened. The mother was shocked and immediately agreed to help her daughter. The stepfather was reported to the police and arrested. This mother's reaction is, surprisingly, actually quite exceptional. It is thanks to her mother's behaviour that Refilve was able to overcome her traumatic experience in the following sandwork sessions.

If such an incident is denied and the abuse continues, the following sandwork images usually look very different. If violence and abuse persist, children will often not accept the offer for therapeutic expression. Psychological defence mechanisms set in. A non-recurring trauma, in contrast, is relatively easy to treat, especially if two basic requirements are fulfilled. First, there must be a solid emotional basis, which means that the child must have experienced a positive relationship to adults in the first years of his life. And second, the traumatic event must be acknowledged as such by the child's environment and must not repeat itself.

In the second sandwork session, a week later, Refilve repeated her story. She still broke into tears. Again, we see the rape scene in the centre of the picture (see plate section: p. 4, Plate 7).

Obviously it still plays a central role in her life. In the upper left corner, the mother is visiting her friends again, and is therefore not at home. In the front left, close to where Refilve herself was standing, she created a scene that shows her as a little child, being protected under an umbrella by her mother in a red dress.

This expresses the possibility of protection, which Refilve is now able to perceive, because the adults reacted properly in her situation. It means that there can be a protecting mother, even when her actual mother was not really present. This important step in psychological development normally occurs in early childhood. In this case, it was apparently necessary for Refilve to return to that phase, which she had surely already passed once in her development. Psychologically speaking, she returned to being a small child and needed to reassure herself that there is indeed an outer and an inner protective maternal function. This inner function was probably reacti-vated by therapy, because sandwork made it possible for the child to talk, and for the violence to be stopped.

Refilve took a very long time with the third sand image (see plate section: p. 4, Plate 8). She spent the whole afternoon burying the evil man in the tunnel-like structure in the left part of the picture. Her mother is sitting and drinking tea with her friends on the right. In the bottom part of the picture, Refilve made four elephant enclosures. In South Africa, these animals are often associated with women and can be seen as an expression of female strength. Considering the girl's age, this burial of the evil man is definitely an adequate form of processing her trauma. It needs to be buried and forgotten at least until puberty, so that she can live the rest of her childhood in peace. It is possible that the problem will be processed again, differently, at a later stage in life. For the moment, the harm inflicted by the violence is no longer effective, physically or psychologically. It was plain to see that the girl already felt better after this third session (see plate section: p. 5, Plate 9).

After making her fourth sand image, she explained: 'I am feeling better. This is where I work,' – there is a shop in the far right corner of the picture – 'and this is where I play.' She has shown herself playing with a friend at the lower right and has created a play room at the lower left. 'Up here on the left are my mother, my aunt and my grandmother. They are drinking tea.'

With this image, Refilve expressed in many ways that life can go on. There is no sign and no more talk of the evil man. In the coming years, it will be important for her to strengthen her feminine energy so that she can assert herself in later life in the world of men. This is possibly already expressed by the group of women sitting at the round table drinking tea.

Before the description of the next sandwork process, let us make another short comment on the play material itself. The reader will have noticed that the sandwork miniatures in South Africa are different from the ones normally used in sandplay. They consist only of bits of wood, scraps of metal, bottle caps, some plant material, shells and a few glass marbles. The human figures are made from banana leaves or bits of metal. This gives the images a very special aesthetic attractiveness. It also puts a greater emphasis on the children's creativity than if the miniatures were already fully formed. When Imme Thom began her work with children in Africa, she chose only material from the children's surroundings as a matter of course. Once, after a trip to Germany, she brought back the plastic play figures and miniatures considered normal there. When she offered these to the children (as we have already mentioned), something unexpected happened: for the children, sandplay was suddenly reduced to a mere *playing in the sand*.

> The children were no longer able to attach symbolic qualities to the fully formed toys. They were no longer creating expressive images of their unconscious, but began to actively play with each other. It was chaos. The children fought over the figures, and even broke some of them.[6]

Imme Thom realized that these children had not grown up with toys.

No father or mother ever paid money for something one can only play with. Toys are the last item on any list of survival. In the Tswana, Xhosa and Pondo cultures, the traditional toys are animal figures, which are made from clay, bones or grass.[7]

Thom returned to her original method and used only objects that fulfilled the following three criteria: they needed to be durable, they needed to come from the children's daily surroundings, and they were not allowed to have any material or monetary value. These simple figures also proved to be perfect for juveniles, who might normally consider toys too childish.

The sangomas

We now come to a further terrible episode, which not only pertains to South Africa but also concerns many countries on the African continent. I am aware that I am expecting a lot of the reader with this account. African tribal communities have, and always have had, traditional healers (herbalists), who treat illnesses and maintain a spiritual connection to the transcendent world and to the ancestors. In remote areas they are an important alternative to medical services, and they are also consulted by wealthier people from the cities. These healers first listen to a sick person's symptoms and then induce a state of trance through song, prayer and beating drums, whereby the cause of the illness is revealed to them. The cure mostly involves a combination of remedies made from plants, minerals and animal parts, as well as ritual acts, such as paying tribute to a neglected ancestor. The long discussions between sick people and their family members and ancestors, which used to be common in many cultures, are becoming lost under the increasing influence of modern ways of life.

These healers, who are integrated into the village communities and widely respected, are in no way to be confused with another figure, the 'sangoma', who deals with occult magic for the purpose of power. Sangomas promise sexual potency, the possibility of inflicting illness and misfortune on one's enemies, and general superiority – in former times in battle, and nowadays in business affairs and politics. Sangomas were never integrated into village communities. They have always acted in secrecy, and often moved from place to place. They draw their power from people's fear of them.

In a shanty town most people have no work and are therefore psychologically weakened. Their confidence in life and in themselves is generally shaken. The ritual and social bonds, which normally protect an individual from depression, anxiety and moral waywardness, are lost. This is fertile ground for superstition and the desire for magical assistance, and it plays perfectly into the hands of the sangomas. They are as feared in today's shanty towns as they have always been in rural areas, but now there is one fatal difference: it is no longer possible to keep a sangoma at a safe distance and thereby limit his influence. Nowadays a sangoma can move into the shack next door unchallenged. This would never have been conceivable even in the poorest villages. The practices of these criminal sangomas are beyond anything one can imagine, certainly beyond any form of anthropological classification. It is psychopathy at its most extreme: they make their magic potions not just from plants and animal parts, but primarily from human organs, which are extracted from their victims – mostly children – while they are still alive, because the effectiveness is supposedly thus greater. They are rarely criminally prosecuted because everyone, including the police and judiciary, fears their magical powers. A sangoma also lends money, sells drugs, and usually keeps a child as an apprentice, who was surrendered to him by indebted parents. Both men and women can be sangomas. One sangoma was successfully reported and arrested in direct consequence of a series of sandwork images, which were made by a boy who felt that the sangoma was following him. What sounds like a medieval horror story is reality for thousands of people. Dr Ogbu Kalu, a historian of religion, confirmed to me in a personal communication how even successful business people and politicians wear their 'medicine' in the form of an amulet under their suits and ties, and know – and at the same time try to forget – that it is not made only from plants.

Of course there have always been criminal practices in all societies, but they have also always been condemned by the community and were thereby limited. In no traditional society has a child ever been allowed to be killed for the gain of a single individual. The ritual child sacrifices of some pre-Columbian Central and South American cultures had a symbolic function for the good of the whole community. The word 'sacrifice' in Latin – *sacrificium*, derived from 'sacrum facere' meaning 'to perform something holy' – describes the purpose of these sacrifices: an offering to a certain deity, a ritually defined exchange with the transcendent world. When isolated psychopathic behaviour becomes so widespread in a society that children must fear it in their everyday lives, one speaks of collective perversion. Adult individuals are psychologically infected and find it hard to offer resistance. In consequence, the perversion can come to be considered as inevitable or even normal.

The sand image in Picture 13 was made by a 12-year-old girl named Lina, who took part in only two of the four planned sandwork sessions, because her mother would not allow her to attend the last two. This is her second sandplay image. Lina worked on it slowly and precisely. The image has various separate parts. The tavern (mostly a place of prostitution and drug dealing) takes up a large space to the bottom right of the sandtray. The top right area is her own family's house. There is a church at the upper left, with a garden next to it. The setting corresponds to the girl's actual living situation. The tavern is indeed right next to her hut, and presents a real danger in her life. In the lower left corner she has depicted a seated sangoma. Towards the end of the session, Lina worked for a very long time on the diagonally opposite corner of the sandtray, the little space behind the outer wall of her own hut. It seemed as if this was an important place, which was,

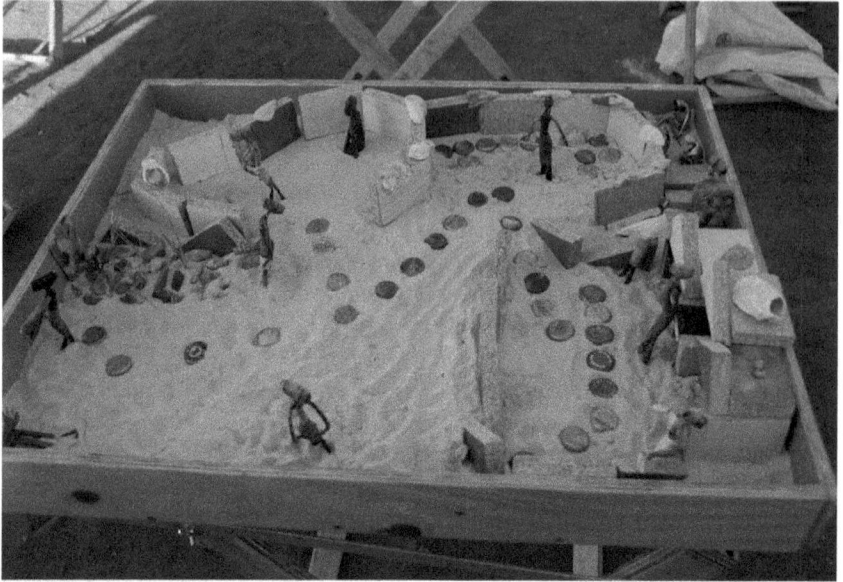

Picture 13

however, difficult to get right. She went to a lot of trouble, patiently making lots of little steps; she kept rearranging the figures that were intended for this corner. At the end of the session, once she had finally achieved more or less what she intended, she seemed greatly relieved. As she explained her sandwork image, she did not mention one word about the tiny corner at the top. When asked about it, she answered that this was the school. A conflict becomes apparent: the school is crammed into a tiny space in a distant corner, yet the amount of time Lina spent working on the school was exceptionally long. The school lies diametrically opposite the sangoma and appears to be the only place – apart from the church – where Lina can learn other things than those she learns through her family.

In their final report to the teacher, the therapists made it clear how important attending school was for the girl – without mentioning the content of her sandwork directly. Even if Lina's achievements at school were not particularly good, and though she did not seem very motivated to learn, her sand image made clear what a vitally important lifeline school was for her, amidst all the irrationality and destructiveness of the adult world around her.

The video camera

Jeremy is 13 years old, has four siblings and lives with his grandmother. His parents are dead. Apart from their English name, children in South Africa also have an African name. Children of mixed heritage, however, have only an English name, and the other children often make fun of them because of this. The African name always has a meaning with a connection to events and circumstances at the child's birth. Jeremy's African name, for instance, means 'rain', because there was a rain storm on the day of his birth. Jeremy is a lively and intelligent child. The reason he took part in the sandwork group was because he had recently become very fearful. His grandmother explained how he was afraid of a man who had moved in to the hut next door. Jeremy claimed that this man hated children, and would even beat them.

In his first sand image, the boy depicted the situation shown in Picture 14. In the centre of the image stands his own house – an indication of a solid feeling of security. The evil man actually appears twice in the right half of the picture, which adds to the sense of his unpredictability. In the lower right corner he is asleep in his house. Jeremy often heard him snoring at night. Above that, one sees the man threatening two other people with a stick: Jeremy himself and his friend. It appears that this man is an ominous presence in Jeremy's life, by both day and night. The left half of the image shows Jeremy's grandmother and his aunt. A water pump is visible as well. There is a conspicuous detail in the top left corner, which seemed to mean a lot to Jeremy: the screw is meant to be a video camera.

In his next image (Picture 15) Jeremy explains that the school is in the middle of the picture. His own house is in the far right corner, and once again there is a video camera, this time on the roof of his house, 'in order to see exactly everything that happens'. His animals are on the right, and behind the fence in the lower left of the image is a playground. 'When we

Picture 14

Picture 15

are at school, playing in the school yard, the man watches us from behind the fence. The camera takes pictures of everything.'

Imme Thom, who has known such situations for decades, took the opportunity to speak to the boy's grandmother, who confirmed that the new neighbour was a sangoma. She then urgently advised Jeremy to steer clear of the man wherever possible. With the grandmother's consent, Imme Thom informed the school and spoke to the police.

In the third sand image (Picture 16), the sense of imminent danger has become more acute. Jeremy's own house and that of the menacing neighbour are now built adjoining each other, and are separated only by a see-through fence. The two figures in the left house are his grandmother and his friend. In the adjoining house, the sangoma can be seen attacking Jeremy as he was playing ball. Jeremy said that the man wanted to beat him, but then an older friend came to help him.

Imme Thom could not be sure if this had actually happened, or if it only expressed the boy's increased fear. Even if the latter was the case, she considered the situation to be very dangerous. She found that the video

Picture 16

camera, which the boy seemed to insist on in play, gave the whole thing an especially real quality – as if the boy felt he needed to prove something. She spoke to the police a second time and requested protection for the boy. Since the police had also received information from other families in the mean time, they were able to conduct a search of the sangoma's house. The man was arrested on the spot: they had found parts of corpses under his bed. There was a human hand buried in his garden, attracting future victims with a beckoning index finger. The boy was spared these macabre details.

Jeremy described his fourth sand image (Picture 17): 'The police took the man away. I am still afraid. Here, I am playing in the park with my friends. The evil man is no longer in his house.' In the far right corner of the image, one sees the sangoma being taken away by the police. A big iron chain separates the picture in two parts. There are animals in the right hand part. It appears that the boy's fear is still very present. The big chain is an attempt to separate his play world, in which he can just be the child he is, from the rest of the world. In this play world, Jeremy can enjoy himself with his friends and rest assured that the video camera, which has grown even bigger and apparently even more important in the mean time, is still recording everything.

Picture 17

Jeremy's fear decreased only gradually, once he could really believe that there was no longer any danger. With the help of his sandwork images, a murderer, who intended to commit further crimes, could be removed from the lives of these families. All this is far too great a burden for a child. A lot of time must still pass before Jeremy can one day be proud of his story and will have processed it inwardly. Above all – as his last image shows – he must be allowed simply to be a child again, without acute danger or threats.

In chains

This brief description of a 7-year-old boy's first sand image, on the other hand, shows us what inner resources children can have, and what an amount of psychological work they can achieve all by themselves, without any intervention having even been attempted on the part of the adults.

Thabi made a cave-like house in which, he said, three children lived (Picture 18). When the therapist asked if anybody else lived in the house, he shook his head. In response to the next question, whether he himself lived this way with his siblings, Thabi nodded. He lived with a younger and an older brother, and without a single adult to look after them. But that was not all: the older brother drank and often beat him. Thabi feared for his younger brother. The older brother is depicted in the sand image with a heavy chain around his neck. The chain is the alcohol, Thabi explained. His brother may feel strong, but in reality he is a slave (Picture 19).

Plate 1

Plate 2

Plate 3

Plate 4

Plate 5

Plate 6

Plate 7

Plate 8

Plate 9

Plate 10

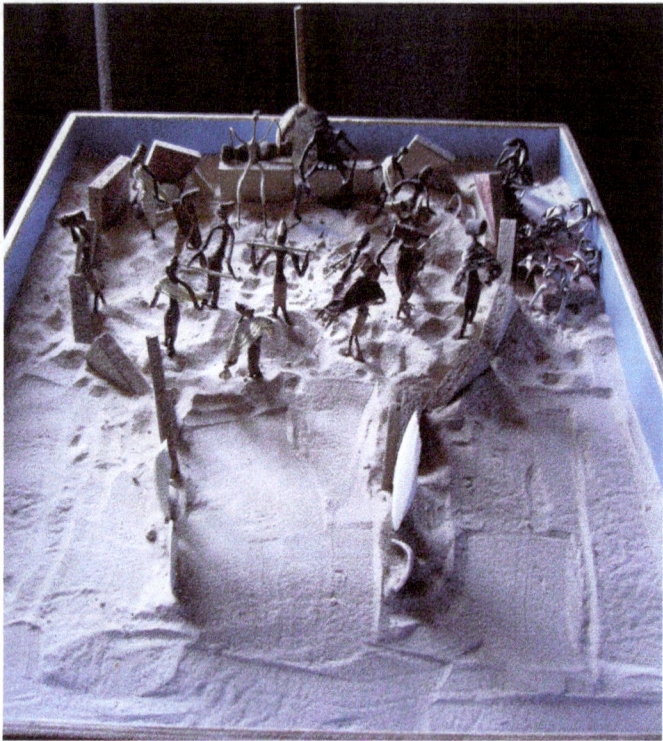

Plate 11

Plate 12

Plate 13

Plate 14

Plate 15

Plate 16

Plate 17

Plate 18

Plate 19

Plate 20

Plate 21

Plate 22

Plate 23

Plate 24

Plate 25

Plate 26

Plate 27

Plate 28

Plate 29

Plate 30

Plate 31

Plate 32

Picture 18

Picture 19

Sandwork not only had enabled Thabi to draw attention to his situation, but also was a remarkable attempt at making himself aware of the potential danger posed by his brother.

A safe place

Now we come to a more difficult situation. It is more difficult because violence played a big role in this girl's life from earliest childhood onwards. What is more, at the time of the sandwork sessions, it was not yet clear if the girl was safe from violence. Sand images are more complicated in such cases. It is often precisely this perplexity of the image, as well as the physical feeling of discomfort in the observer, that indicate that one is now dealing with serious pathologies: not necessarily the child's own pathologies, but ones to be found in the child's environment.

Mapule was 6 years old and appeared to be a very fearful child. The teacher's notes on the girl contained the comment: 'recently sexually abused by an old man'. There was no mention of who had reported this. The social worker had planned a home visit, but her plan never materialized. The mother's stepfather – Mapule's grandfather – had let her know that she should stay away if she valued her life.

Mapule herself did not speak. She was an exceptionally pretty child. During the first sandwork session she tried her best to be invisible. She kept hiding between the other children, or underneath the table on which the play figures were laid out. For the longest time her sandtray remained untouched. By the time half the session was over, she had barely collected a few blocks of wood, some plants and some shells. She proceeded to lay out one piece of wood after the next, and then the shells and the plants, as if she were acting in slow motion. It appeared as if every movement were a huge effort. By the end of the session she had actually completed a sand image (Picture 20). When asked if she wanted to explain anything in the picture, her answer was barely audible. The blocks of wood were 'a house'. It was not clear if the human figures represented anybody in particular. 'That is my mother,' she answered when the therapist asked about a certain figure. 'That is me,' she answered to another question. 'My sister, our mother ... that is me ...' It was unclear who was where. The same figure could be a different person every time the therapist asked. Mapule herself appeared in different places in the image. No male figures were named. The whole image makes the impression of having been ravaged by a storm, while, at the same time, appearing as static as a recurring pattern on wallpaper. There are no spaces that are in any way separated from each other. The 'houses' have no roofs; nothing relates to anything else in particular.

Mapule's behaviour was similar in the second session. She even disappeared from the classroom for a while without anyone noticing. Again,

Picture 20

she worked very slowly, but she seemed a little more confident (Picture 21).

There are two walls at a right angle in the right half of the picture. This is precisely where Mapule chose to place herself. It is a sort of pre-stage to a building. This time the human figures are named. The large, dominating figure in the centre is the grandmother. To her right is the mother. The grandfather is sitting behind these two figures on a white bench, and even further in the background is a figure made of dark wood – an uncle. Children call almost any male relative or neighbour 'uncle'. Next to this figure, another figure has been pushed into the sand and buried: obviously something that cannot be spoken about at the moment. The girl has also placed the figure representing herself far away from all the other figures. We know from experience in trauma therapy how important it is to find a stable outside and inside place, where one feels safe from danger. The two walls that the girl has erected next to herself could indicate a desire for such a place. The grandmother seems to play a central role in the girl's life. In real life, it was the grandmother who had tried to protect the child. We could not know that three months later the grandfather would severely injure this

Picture 21

grandmother with a knife, while she was trying to prevent him from returning to her household, where Mapule lived.

In the third picture, a clearly demarcated space, separated in two parts, is visible: Mapule's house (Picture 22). She explains: 'I don't have a father. My father died. He was stung by a bee. I miss him.' The insect that killed the father can be seen in the top left corner. The girl herself is once again positioned in the top part of the sandtray. This time an aunt is not far from her. She explains that the right hand, empty part of the house is the kitchen, and that her mother and father are in bed in the left part. We do not know if her father is really dead, or if he has just disappeared. Many fatherless children prefer the first version, for shame and anger at having been abandoned. The fact that Mapule can now express how much she misses her father, shows how much trust she has gained in her therapist.

Surely a lot is depicted in this sand image, which we cannot yet understand. The metal figure on the right, for example, is not named. If a child's body language signals that questions, like 'And what is this? And that?', are not wanted, this is respected without exceptions. It means that what has been depicted cannot yet be fully grasped and expressed. One must never forget that Expressive Sandwork is

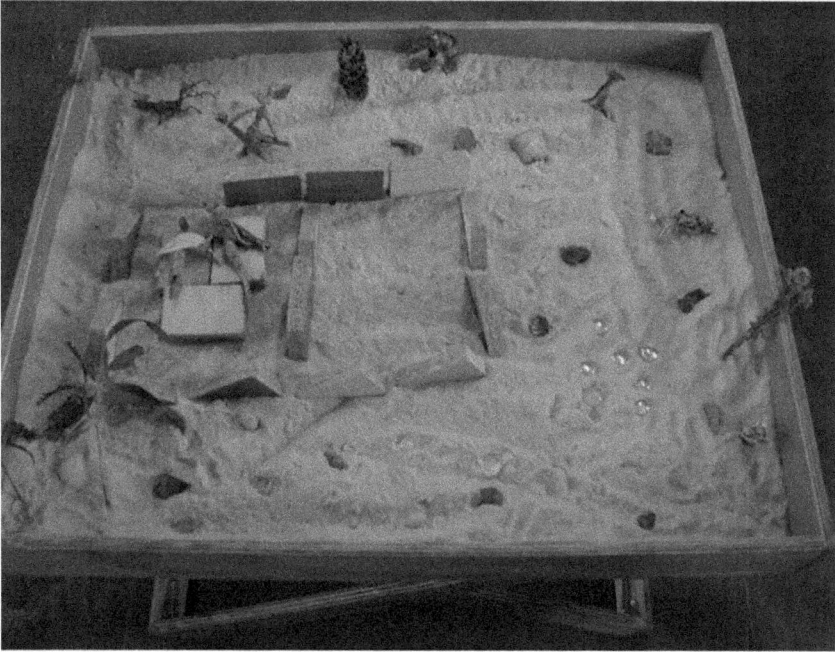

Picture 22

not psychotherapy. The assisting adult is in no way supposed to encourage children to open up more than they are already doing of their own accord. We restrict our work to that which the children express by themselves, regardless of whether we can already understand it or not. In any case, we assume that representation and depiction are in themselves already the first stage of psychological assimilation. One thing we can say for certain is that the third picture is the first in which an enclosed space appears, a story is told, and a concrete feeling is expressed. The feeling of confusion, chaos and redundancy, which the first picture had left behind, is no longer present.

A further important step is achieved with the fourth sand image (Picture 23). The straw, tree-like structure in the lower right corner is a tree house, in which Mapule says one can hide. There is another enclosed space on the left, which she calls the 'house of worms'. She says she likes the worms and enjoys playing with them. Even the therapist, who had grown up in a shanty town himself, found this strange. He did, however, believe it possible that Mapule might actually play with real worms, just like other children play with dolls. In either case, the important fact is that Mapule was now able to create a protective space for herself. She was able to overcome a chaotic

Picture 23

inner state in just four sessions, despite extreme outer conditions. This is an astounding psychological effort. To allow for the consolidation of this new achievement, everything possible was done to allow Mapule to work with the same therapist once a week for the next few months. She continued to make sand images. It was during this time that the grandmother was badly injured by her former husband. Shortly afterwards, Mapule made a sand image, which shows three separate rooms. It is an indication of the fact that she was now also able to make inner distinctions, and that the initial chaos did not return, despite a new act of violence. She even assimilates what happened: there is a small child in the lower right corner. The child is as far away as is possible from a man in the upper left corner. There are visitors near the child, who are praying for the injured grandmother. This image shows again that Mapule (the little child) has inner resources, which are related to her grandmother. The grandmother may be sick, but she has other helpful adults around her.

Unfortunately the photos of this sand image and the following ones were lost when technical equipment was stolen from Imme Thom's house. At the end of the school year, Mapule's aunt took her to live in a distant city. Two years later, we heard that she was still living with her aunt, and that she was doing well.

Soul City

A further Expressive Sandwork project was carried out in August 2007 with twelve adolescents in Soul City, a shanty town near Johannesburg. Many of the adolescents living in Soul City did not grow up there. They originally came from the country, where they were raised by their grandparents in great poverty, and were full of hope when they came to the city to find work at age 15 or 16. Often they left a whole village back at home waiting for their return and fantasizing about the wealth they would bring with them. Jo'burg still counts as *the* city of gold diggers and diamond hunters. But for many of these young people from the country, Soul City is the first and the last stop. They are ashamed not to have made it in the city, and would rather slowly decay there themselves than return and disappoint those they left behind.

Any half-hearted attempt at intervention in such a conglomerate of corrugated metal shacks, in which everyone mistrusts everyone else, can be helpful to some and harmful to others at the same time. Occasionally, campaigning politicians suddenly decide that it is important to bring electricity to these shanty towns. From the point of view of the children, this is an advantage, because they freeze less in winter. But for many it also creates a new problem – one that many children have described again and again in sandplay: with the arrival of electricity, there also comes inescapable, loud music blaring from loudspeakers all night long. The children and adolescents do in fact go to school, but they already know that this will not help them find work. The biggest problem is drug abuse. Alcohol is too expensive, which is why other, highly toxic mixtures have been invented, for instance beer brewed in old car batteries. The remaining battery fluid gives this brew its extra kick. The drink costs one South African rand per litre, and makes young people who consume it regularly look ancient after just a year. In winter, the huts are usually heated with fires lit in so-called konkas, which are basically old paraffin containers with holes. Old car tyres are the most common fuel for the fires. People regularly die of asphyxiation from the toxic fumes, if they forget to put out the fire when they are drunk. Friday is a day children fear. Those men who have work receive their week's pay and spend it immediately on drink: violence and sexual abuse follow.

The young people who agreed to take part in sandwork were chosen by social workers. They were boys and girls with obvious problems, but who had already distinguished themselves through strong will power. None of them took drugs regularly, and one had already completed a withdrawal. Some had completed a computer course, a few were active in a theatre group, and others even took care of a group of younger children. The young people had been told that sandwork could help them to become aware of their own personal problems, and to confront them.

It was fascinating to observe the matter of course with which these 17 and 18 year olds, who had already had so many negative experiences and setbacks, were open to something as harmless as a sandtray, a few figures, stones, bottle corks and some bark. There was silence from the start. The low hut, into which all were crammed, was hot and dark. The therapists had difficulty taking notes and finding a good place to stand. Smaller children watched with curiosity through the only small window, laughing to see the older children playing, and trying to distract them. But the adolescents did not even seem to notice. Each one of them was deep in concentration and was making use of this time they had been given.

These young people had no future. Nobody took them seriously and nobody really cared if they disappeared today or faded away tomorrow. Fate had given them nothing but their bare lives, and they used the sandtrays as if they were new worlds, which it was up to them to create. Some of them depicted a conflict about which they spoke afterwards. Others discovered memories from their childhood. One important, and often painful, step was that the process made them more clearly aware of their current situation.

The grandfather

The following is an example of how it is not only current problematic situations that appear in sandwork, but also positive things these adolescents have experienced in their lives.

Now 16 years old, Ana had come to Soul City with her older brother when she was 14. Brother and sister had grown up in the countryside with their grandparents. When the grandfather died, they had to move to the city, where their mother was earning barely enough to survive through prostitution. Since moving there, Ana was not doing well. She was often sick and probably suffered from a chronic kidney disease. She seemed passive and her red lipstick created a sad contrast to the noticeably yellowy skin of her childlike face. Ana told how she had already been in the hospital numerous times, and that the medicine prescribed for her was expensive. In talking to her, it did not seem as if anyone really cared whether Ana actually received this medicine and took it regularly.

Ana was extremely obliging towards the other young people in the group. She would, for example, only take such play material from the table, of which there was more than enough available. If someone tried to jump the queue, she would give way.

Ana worked with great concentration, and only at the beginning exchanged glances with the girl next to her. This was obviously her friend, who was distracted a lot more easily than Ana herself. Ana described her sand image (Picture 24): the building at the top left is a tavern – a place where people get drunk and prostitutes earn their living. Her brother is sitting in front of the tavern with his head in his hands. Ana explains that he regrets having gone to the tavern. She had finished this part of the image quickly, but fell into a kind of dreamlike state while making the right hand side of the image.

Picture 24

She worked on something for a long time; even her movements became slower. It seemed to be important to her to choose exactly the right stones and flowers with which to decorate the rectangular area at the right edge of the image. Over and over, she changed another little detail, added something new, and considered it for a long time. She gave the impression of caring deeply for something.

Ana herself was not represented by a figure in the sand image, but her presence was none the less felt in the loving way she made the rectangular area at the edge of the image. It was like a ceremonial act, as if she had recalled something after a long time. When Ana explained the various parts of her image at the end of the session, she left out precisely this rectangular area on the right. The therapist commented that something very important must have happened there, upon which she said softly that this was her grandfather's grave. After a while she added that she greatly missed living in her native village. A saying in South Africa has it that one is at home in the place where one's relatives' graves are. The grave of her grandfather, with whom she had lived up until two years ago, was hundreds of kilometres away from Soul City. Maybe she had rediscovered memories from her childhood, particularly all the good things her grandparents had left her. Ana was lost in thought and preoccupied with herself after this session.

In some situations it is not easy for the therapist to put away a sand image at the end of a session. In this case it meant clearing away a grave as if it was not important (see plate section: p. 5, Plate 10 (detail)).

Ana's next sand image, a week later, showed that this action had kindled new vitality in her. Where the tavern had been now stands her own house. It consists of two separate rooms; one of which is her own, as she emphasizes. In reality, all corrugated metal huts in Soul City consist of a single room (Picture 26). Thus, her image expresses psychological differentiation as well as a desire to set herself apart from the rest. If there are two rooms as opposed to one, it is logically possible to walk from one room to the other, or, in a metaphorical sense, from one emotional state to another. There are alternatives. To the right of the house, Ana is sitting outside with a friend, reading a book. This time she talks about school. She likes to read. When asked which books she likes to read, she names a book about the personal hygiene of the female body. Ana obviously knows what is important for her. She wants to protect her body, just like her grandfather had probably protected her while he was still alive. At the same time she senses how difficult it will be to avoid all the dangers that lurk around the corners in this sickening environment, and that are a threat to a young girl like herself day after day.

The radical change from Ana's first to her second sand image shows, however, what inner resources Ana has within her. Similarly to George – the boy whose vegetable garden was described in Chapter 4 – Ana belongs to those young people,

Picture 26

who would probably profit most from financial assistance – immediately and without any further intervention.

Initiation

Samuel's light skin colour, his plaited hair and his Northern Sotho language all identified him as a Pedi. He was 21 years old and came from the Limpopo province, one of the poorest regions in South Africa. Today, 47 per cent of the people there are still without work. The Maroteng, or Pedi, settled south of the Steelport River in the second half of the seventeenth century, and preserved a strong cultural and linguistic homogeneity over a number of generations. The invasion of the Boers at the beginning of the nineteenth century marked the beginning of decades of fighting with some intermittent, futile negotiations for peace. In 1876, the Pedi population under the leadership of their king Sekhukhune was finally able to defeat the Boers. What happened next is essentially the same story as in most colonial countries. The British troops, who had benefited from the Boers' defeat, occupied the region a year later and did everything in their power to subject the Pedi. It took them two years to defeat this proud people. The Pedi's traditional ways of life have nevertheless been partly preserved in the Limpopo province.

We knew that Samuel had finished secondary school more than a year before, and that he wanted to continue studying. However, he neither had the means to do so, nor was he able to find any work. He had no idea how his life was supposed to go on. People in his native village had collected the money for his education, and their expectations that he would return as a successful man weighed heavily on his shoulders.

Samuel seemed out of place in the squalor of Soul City. His manner of working in the sand soon attracted the attention of all other people present. From the beginning Samuel worked with the purpose and determination of a builder following an exact plan. He would not, like most of the others, first place an object somewhere, simply in order to try it out, and then remove it again and try replacing it elsewhere. The next step was always clear. The damp sand took very precise shape under his hands and the resulting constructions seemed like miniature edifices of an ancient culture.

In his first picture, Samuel depicted a group of people, whom he called 'the royal family'. On the far right, one sees figures who 'are sad because they are not part of the family', as Samuel explains (see plate section: p. 6, Plate 11).

A striking feature of this image is the vase or uterus shaped border, which could be the imaginative expression of an ancient feeling of security; not a linear but a cyclic world, like the one described by Mircea Eliade.[8] It is possible that the 'sad excluded people' refer to himself, far away from his people and in a hopeless situation.

In the second image, Samuel built a round house encircled by a fence: this is the traditional African way of making houses. The foundation was so solid it appeared like cement, and its shape was a perfect circle. Samuel had, after all, spent 40 minutes working on it. Then he left the hut, in which sandwork was taking place, and disappeared for a while. He seemed pleased when he returned with an old broom head, which he proceeded to use as a roof.[9] A traditional building with a real straw roof had suddenly been created. Samuel explained that the scene showed a wedding, the way his people would traditionally celebrate them: bride, groom and friends bringing presents (see plate section: p. 6, Plate 12).

He had depicted a large, special ceremonial happening. A wedding is a significant moment, in which a man and a woman unite and a new generation begins. Symbolically, it is a moment where different, complementary life energies come together: the culmination and completion of a process of maturing comes together with the beginning of a process of renewal. Specifically, it should normally be the next big event for a young man like Samuel, if life were to take an orderly course. But, due to the obstacles of circumstance, his particular life has strayed into a dead end. No one needs his virility now, and no one cares about his inventive talent. Already after this second image it was as if the depressive mist clouding his eyes had been wiped away. In this dark and stifling corrugated metal shack in Soul City, Samuel had encountered his people, as if in a dream, and had celebrated a wedding with them in their century-old tradition – the happiest of all festivities. The other adolescents marvelled at his sand image without envy, as if they too recognized parts of it. The traditional way of building houses brought back memories of their own childhood. In a sense, Samuel had not only depicted his individual problems, but also spoken to all the others. We, the therapists, thought about this for a long time. We wondered if there was any significance to the fact that Samuel had depicted a royal family in both his images. After the third image, his therapist asked him if he came from an aristocratic family. He confirmed that this was indeed the case, and asked as if she had been able to tell this from his sand image. The therapist answered that it simply wasn't every day that royal families were depicted in sandwork.

Again, Samuel worked with professional concentration. He worked the sand with such precision that the construction – rectangular this time – seemed hewn from stone. Samuel explained that the image showed two graves, and he called it 'the death of the king'. One grave belongs to the king and the other to his servant. In front of the graves are the respective widows, crying. And behind them stand the rest of the mourners, in hierarchical order: the royal family on the one side, and the servant's family on the other (see plate section: p. 7, Plate 13).

Samuel went on to explain that when a king died, custom dictated that his servant must also die. The king represents social order. If the king dies, there is a risk of disorder, chaos and upheaval. These are times in which evil can gain the upper hand.

Samuel came from a functional social community and has ended up in a messy heap of uprooted existences. Symbolically speaking, the king has already been dead for a long time in a place like this. It is possible that this sand image helped Samuel gain a better perspective of his situation: where he is now, there is no principle creating order, no structure. However – trying to see things optimistically – after every death there is also a chance for renewal. Samuel, who came from a royal family himself, must have felt something inside calling upon him to create a new world order, at least within his own life. After the session, he told stories of the customs and ancient traditions of his people, and the other adolescents listened intently.

We were curious what Samuel would depict in his next image. Could there be any hope in his situation, or would he sink back into resignation? Samuel called his fourth and last sand image 'initiation' (see plate section: p. 7, Plate 14).

He told how he himself had experienced the traditional initiation ritual of his tribe when he was 14. This had prepared him for his traditional duties as a Pedi. He had learnt to endure hunger, cold and solitude, and how to hunt by himself. Ritually, he had become a man. After that, he had even managed to step into the modern world and successfully completed secondary schooling. What his initiation had not prepared him for, was then finding himself amidst drunken and violent adults, with neither the prospect of work nor enough money for further education. He had received no instructions on how to survive emotionally a situation like this. We do know that there is an innate predisposition of the psyche, a potential of behavioural patterns, which allows for adaptations to outer circumstances without actually having to learn them directly. Initiations are the cultural representatives of such archetypal patterns. Viewing the sand image from a forward-looking and purpose-oriented perspective, the scene of an initiation may have appeared precisely *because* Samuel's current situation is hopeless and life threatening. He now has the chance to remember that difficulties and hopeless situations can generally be overcome, even if one has never before encountered and learnt to deal with this particular form of hopelessness. In contrast to his first image, there are no sad, excluded people depicted in this last image. All of those present have come together for this martial initiation. The scene radiates energy.

The question remained whether Samuel would be able to unleash this potential within himself here in Soul City, where he was no more than one too many. Two months after completing the sandplay project, we learned that Samuel had returned to Limpopo. We cannot say if that proved to be a good decision for his future. What we *do* know is that sandplay aroused something in him, which he himself already thought he had lost: his roots, and his will to grow up.

Chapter 8

Expressive Sandwork in China

That which is to be shrunk must first be stretched out.
That which is to be weakened must first be strengthened.
That which is to be cast down must first be raised up.
That which is to be taken must first be given.
(Laozi, Tao Te Ching, Verse 36)

In Guangzhou in September 2002, at a conference for sandplay therapy, an unknown student comes up to me after my conference talk with an expectant look in her eye, as if she were seeing me again after a long time of absence. She takes my arm and talks to me insistently, with her face very close to mine: 'It is so important that we understand all of this. We have so many patients, so many . . .' She has difficulty holding back her tears. I listen to her and am somewhat concerned about her psychological stability, because most Chinese people would normally consider such a display of emotions towards a stranger embarrassing. At the same time I become aware of how great the thirst for knowledge in the humanistic disciplines must currently be in China, and how passionately willing the people are to absorb any psychological knowledge. The lunch break is over and the *discussion*, as it is announced in the conference programme, begins on time. Since I am not speaking in China for the first time, I ask myself how this term would probably be phrased in a Chinese language programme. I assume: time for questions and answers.

'What is the healing factor in psychotherapy?' is a female student's first question. As so often before, my attempts at instigating said discussion – a habit from the 1970s, when I was the same age as these students – show hardly any effect. I know that a kind of mastership is expected of me, that I have been hired to pass on a certain technique. It matters little that psychotherapy does not even belong to the objective sciences: it is more fitting to describe it as one of the hermeneutic disciplines. After a while we agree that the healing factor of psychotherapy has to do with the relationship between therapist and patient, and also generally with trying to tie up 'loose ends' in the patient's life history. Furthermore, the patient's own inner resources become activated in psychotherapy. Ultimately, the decisive healing factor lies *within* the patient.

I look into the open, friendly faces of these psychology students and consider how different my own life experience must be from theirs. In the 1960s, while we students in central Europe were sitting in occupied universities discussing the imminent revolution, such a revolution had already swept through China, over-powering millions of people. Most of the images in my memory from that time show a vast grey-blue mass of people waving countless red books under an equally red sky full of flags. That was the generation of these students' grandparents. The next generation – my students' parents – were the children of torn-apart families: during the Cultural Revolution children were raised in collectives and grew up far away from their own parents. What effect did this have on their emotional lives? What sort of family life could they later provide for their own children, who are now sitting as students before me? One could object that the Cultural Revolution lasted only ten years, from 1966 to 1976. But in these few years, all forms of cultural expression – books, millennia-old scripts, paintings, ritual objects and figures of deities, temples, monasteries, simple household objects and even whole art collections – were systematically destroyed in an historically unprecedented way. Even the ancient trees in village squares were deemed counter-revolutionary, and were chopped down by the red guards – for which Mao Zedong recruited largely under-age youths.[1]

The next student's question brings my wandering thoughts quickly back to the conference room: 'What is a psychotherapist supposed to do when a patient cries?' It seems to have taken its cue directly from my digressed thoughts. This is exactly the point: the students are searching for a norm, for a universally correct method, because, unlike what we Europeans might assume, spontaneous reaction probably often cannot be taken for granted.

I try to explain that it is not about learning rules and instructions, but, far more, that we should strive for a *basic therapeutic* disposition. I hear myself uttering these words and realize at the same time that they will not meet with much response in this room. 'Basic disposition', the students seem to be repeating behind furrowed brows, in a futile search for an image of such an abstract concept in their minds, which throughout millennia of pictographic writing have grown moulded to distinctly right-hemispheric perception. So I try to make things easier to understand with an example. I tell them about a young psychotherapist from Beijing, who for years had tried to harden himself into being a 'tough guy', because his father had pounded into him daily that life was a struggle. During the Cultural Revolution, from the age of 11, his father had had to fend for himself because his own parents had both been imprisoned for being English teachers – an intellectual profession. The young psychotherapist not only was well versed in all kinds of western behavioural therapies, but also had acquired the physique of a body-builder. Nevertheless, he suffered from a series of psychosomatic symp-toms and fears. During the course of his training in analytical psychotherapy, it had been very difficult for him to admit to his vulnerability. But his symptoms began to abate with the help of depth-oriented psychotherapy, during which he could begin to understand his father's fears, seen in the light of the past. From then on, the question of what to do when a patient cried was no longer relevant to him. He could rely on himself. He knew that, when confronted with emotional suffering, he would somehow be able to react adequately.

But the problem's roots lie deeper still, and one cannot help but delve into the matter of differences between eastern and western views of life – regardless of how homespun and obvious this might sound.

During the following seven years in which I travelled regularly to China, I was able to witness how psychology students increasingly dared to perceive and express feelings of personal vulnerability. It is no coincidence that there is no Chinese word for 'vulnerability'. The question is not simply whether traumatic experiences are assimilated differently in Chinese tradition than in the West. Far more, we need to approach an entirely different disposition that is quite foreign to us. What we call 'vulnerability' could be distantly related to the Chinese term 'losing face', 'face' being one's dignity as seen through the eyes of others. To lose one's face is equivalent to psychological death. During the years of the so-called Cultural Revolution, countless people took their own lives because they had been publicly disgraced. Personal feelings and problems from which an individual might suffer are not of primary importance in China; one does not necessarily presume that a person requires special help simply because, for example, he has suffered a tragic loss. For thousands of years difficult life situations have been assimilated emotionally through rituals: collective and individual behaviour that protects the individual from psychic illness. Thus, it is the community that is primarily responsible for processing painful experiences, and not only on a concrete, practical level: a kind of collective soul bears the fate of each and every individual. It is not really possible to fall out of this collective. There is only one exception: through 'losing face'. If this happens, there is no way back. The face is by no means just a mask: there is nothing else behind it. The face is – in western language – a person's moral, social and religious identity: the core of their being.

Now let us consider the role of the psychotherapist in China. The presence of psychotherapists is still relatively new and modern, and they are in the process of integrating themselves into a cultural context, which in turn is changing at an incredibly fast rate. The work of psychotherapists, who do after all promise a sort of wisdom, is surely influenced by traditional expectations. They are primarily seen as masters, figures of authority. Unlike our western notion, it is inconceivable for the traditional Chinese mentality that psychotherapy might be about venting suppressed emotions, or that patients can symbolically attack their own psychoanalyst in place of their parents. The fact that one does not criticize one's parents, let alone a teacher, is reason enough. Even if today's students study primarily western theories of psychology, deeply rooted traditional attitudes still influence their interpersonal relationships – all the more so, the less they are consciously aware of them.

While considering what has just been said, let us now return to the question of what a psychotherapist should do if a patient starts to cry during therapy. Bursting into tears could already be a *result* of the worst possible thing that can happen to a person in China: having lost face before a figure of authority, such as the therapist no doubt is. So the question is not so much *what* the therapist should do if a patient starts to cry, but far more *if* the therapist *can* indeed do anything at all. It took years, and a different geographic location, for this question to find a satisfactory answer.

In Nanjing in November 2009, I was instructing a new group of psychology students in sandplay. Nanjing is the old capital city of China. In 1937, a large part of the city's population was brutally murdered by the Japanese occupying forces. That was the generation of these students' great-grandparents. I wondered if any of their families still remembered these events, which occurred only a couple of generations ago. What psychological effect would that have on today's generation?

When I showed the students sand images that were made by a sexually abused child from an orphanage, they were silent for a long time. At last a young man asked, 'Can we, as therapists, allow ourselves to cry with the patient?'

Pictographic writing and the psyche

The following examples should illustrate how strongly Chinese language and pictographic depiction are interwoven, and should highlight the interconnections between Chinese pictographic characters, culture and emotional perception. Everyone who travels to China for the first time will notice the symbol shown in Figure 9.1, first on the seat belts in aeroplanes, and then on the sides of police cars.

It means 'safety': seat belt in the one combination, public safety in the other. The character shows a house with a woman inside it (Figure 9.1). Thus, safety means 'when there is a woman in a house'. One can see how the characters are not only concrete depictions of the world, but also interpretations. The Chinese character for crisis, for example, is a pre-stage to the character for creativity. An especially descriptive example is the Chinese character for what we call *psyche* – which is in itself borrowed from Greek antiquity. It is composed of two separate characters: one for heart, and one for mind (Figure 9.2). Thus, 'psyche' means an interaction of the heart and mind. On this basis, psychological concepts, such as a traumatic disturbance,[2] can be described very precisely and descriptively. If the psyche is hit by an intensely harmful experience, there is a risk that the heart or

安　　思

Figure 9.1　　　Figure 9.2

the mind might sustain damage. To protect itself from this potentially irreversible damage, the heart has no option but to fall into a state of apparent death and to remain there. The mind can now do all it can to ensure physical survival – coolly, and without emotional interference. The mind can actually perform this task much more effectively without the emotional centre's – the heart's – influence, because fear, insecurity and grief have disappeared. If this state persists – even when the initial danger has long since passed – the cleft between heart and mind will deepen. The personality's development becomes one-sided and the divided 'heart-mind-formation' remains separated – the psyche is sick. Its natural ability to heal itself is impaired, because it would require the feelings and emotions of the heart in order to do so. It needs help from the outside. More precisely, it would need to borrow another intact psyche – a complete 'heart-mind-formation' – with which it can come into resonance, with the aim of recalling its own complete function.

Sandplay has spread throughout China quickly and very successfully. While Chinese trainees often find the theories too abstract, they seem to have an exceptional talent for understanding the sand images. They are surely helped by their good memories and by the ability to orientate themselves quickly in complex pictures, which they acquire at a very young age. Children in China learn their characters very early on in life. However, Chinese sandplay trainees tend to confuse the notion of a symbol with the concept of their characters, and try to apply a fixed set of meanings to all symbols. For example, everybody in China knows that red is the colour of luck and wealth, that the number four symbolizes death, and that the dragon means spirituality.

How differently a mythological figure needs to be interpreted, however, depending on the cultural context, is best illustrated by the figure of the dragon. In China, the dragon resides in heaven and is revered as a harbinger of good fortune. In Europe, dragons hide away in caves and must be defeated by valiant knights in shining armour. It is mythologically inconceivable in China to want to kill a dragon.

It is important never to behold a sand image or its separate symbols in an isolated way, but always in a close connection to the situations within which they were created. Apart from the different geographic and cultural variants, this also includes the relationship to the therapist. It is clear that if a sandplay session were to take place in a room where a video camera had been placed in order to record every detail, then the process would be decisively influenced by this fact. The same laws are valid here as in physics: the result of an experiment is influenced by the experiment itself.

Real progress in sandplay can be achieved only on a basis of trust between two people, and this is possible only within a sufficiently protected private space.

Sandwork in kindergartens

Sandwork has been offered in some Chinese kindergartens and elementary schools since the year 2000. It is usual for children to stay in kindergarten around the clock from Monday to Friday, starting at the age of 2 years. Huge, clean dormitories with countless pink and pale-blue bunk beds lined up in row and order do not arouse, in the western visitor, quite the enthusiasm that the institute's directors might have hoped for. Many of the children suffer from fear of separation. What is more, the parents, who effectively share almost no everyday life with their child, often are not sure what to do with the child at the weekends. Single children always find it hard, in any case, to convey to their parents what they feel, what they would need for happiness in life, and what they might be suffering from. Solidarity between siblings, which can sometimes help parents to empathize with their children's world, is missing in this smallest of family units. The adult world, in which children often feel like they are strangers, is characterized by harsh competition in professional life in twenty-first-century China. Rapid social ascent is the aim, and is measured by the amount of consumer goods a person can afford. This is the same in other countries as well, and it means that family life falls by the wayside. But in China there are additional circumstances, which have to do with the country's history. When I ask how people deal with children who are afraid of going to sleep, I always get the same astounded answer: 'Well, they are told to behave.' As psychologists, we know – at least since Bruno Bettelheim – that children need stories, rituals, songs, tales and the notion of a protective entity such as a guardian angel. The many angels that are used by Chinese children in sandplay might indirectly indicate such a desire.

The hidden brother

A 6-year-old boy, Wan, disturbs the other children in kindergarten with his aggressive behaviour.[3] He bites and shoves the younger ones whenever he can. An initial talk with the parents offered no information that could help explain the boy's behaviour. His mother has a job; she seems shy and, above all, ashamed of her son. Raising children is still the mother's responsibility in modern-day China, and this is a big problem for mothers with jobs. The many behavioural problems that Chinese children develop, especially during adolescence, are attributed to these difficulties in their upbringing. Wan's father, a civil servant, was very reluctant to come to the initial talk with the psychologist. His opinion is that the boy simply ought to be punished. Both parents expect the psychologist to practise strategies with Wan through which his behaviour could be changed.

When they are told that a new form of therapy based on play will be attempted, they are sceptical at first, but agree: as long as *something* will be done. The boy is given the opportunity to have eight weeks of sandwork in a group of four children. During this time his aggressive behaviour decreases and eventually disappears entirely, as if he has forgotten it. After eight weeks, Wan is cheerful and even shows cooperative streaks in his social behaviour.

What happened? What had such a strong effect on him that he was able to replace his problematic behaviour with a manner appropriate to his age? Let us try to consider what changes can be brought about by the simple fact that a child is going to receive this specific form of help. For the parents, consenting to sandwork means that they can free themselves of the lone responsibility, of their shame and helplessness – at least for the time being. They can pass on a problem that has become insoluble in their eyes. This gives them more free space, and can lead to a higher degree of patience from their side. The child receives attention from the adult world. For the time being, the symptoms have achieved their concealed, constructive goal: to make more space for child and parents.

After a month – after the first four sand images – during which Wan has already been making progress, the sandwork therapist invites the mother to another talk. Only now does she really seem able to trust in the process. When the therapist asks her whether the boy has suffered from anything in particular in the last few years, she begins to cry. This time she tells what she had left out during the first conversation: Wan had been sent to his grandparents in the country when he was only one and a half years old, because she was pregnant again. A second child would have had serious repercussions for a civil servant like Wan's father: not only would he have had to pay a huge fine – mostly one year's salary – but also he would have lost his job. The boy was hurriedly sent to live with his grandparents, who lived a two days' journey from their home and whom Wan hardly knew. After six months his parents came to visit, and learned that he had been inconsolable and had refused food for weeks. The grandparents had not been able to win his trust. A few months later still, the parents managed to sort things out. The fine was paid, the baby was born and Wan was allowed back home. The parents hoped and assumed that all difficulties would now be past. But they hadn't reckoned with Wan's jealousy. He took every opportunity to try to make his new-born brother cry. Naturally, from Wan's point of view, it was his brother's fault that he had had to live away from home for such a long time. The parents hoped that kindergarten would bring a change for the better, but things only got worse: Wan felt shunted off all over again, and started to vent his anger and disappointment on the younger children. The therapist explains this all to the mother, who is grateful for the realization that there is a connection between her son's current behaviour and these events from the past. She is also very relieved to realize that no one is judging her. This helped her to understand her son's feelings, as opposed to just seeing them in a negative light.

Surely this change in the parents' perception of the situation contributed to Wan's positive development, at least in part. When regarding the sand images, however, we realize that this problem was also processed on another level, for which Wan alone was responsible. Every week Wan made a sand image without ever commenting on any of them verbally. But it was plain to see how much the sessions meant to him.

The chaotic traces that remained in the dry sand in the middle of the first image show how churned up Wan must still have been during the first session (Picture 31). The number 'two' appears to dominate the scene: there are two rows of plants, two blue patches, two flowers and two human figures, one of which seems to be a sort of alien. A bridge, which could be used to establish connections, has collapsed and is lying at the left edge of the picture. Just like the human figures, the bridge almost seems to be falling off the edge of the image. One could say that Wan has staged his problem around the central question of how a togetherness of two people could possibly be lived.

In the second image (Picture 32) he has, still rather awkwardly, tried to create a sense of order. The fences form an inside and an outside, and two cars drive along between the two fences. They keep colliding and eventually end up lying at the left of the picture, just like the bridge in the first image. 'Togetherness' is associated with aggression in this case. No constructive cooperation appears to be possible.

In the third image (Picture 33), the perspective view emphasizes the beginning of two roads. They seem to be beckoning the observer into the image. There is damp sand on the left side, where the collapsed bridge and

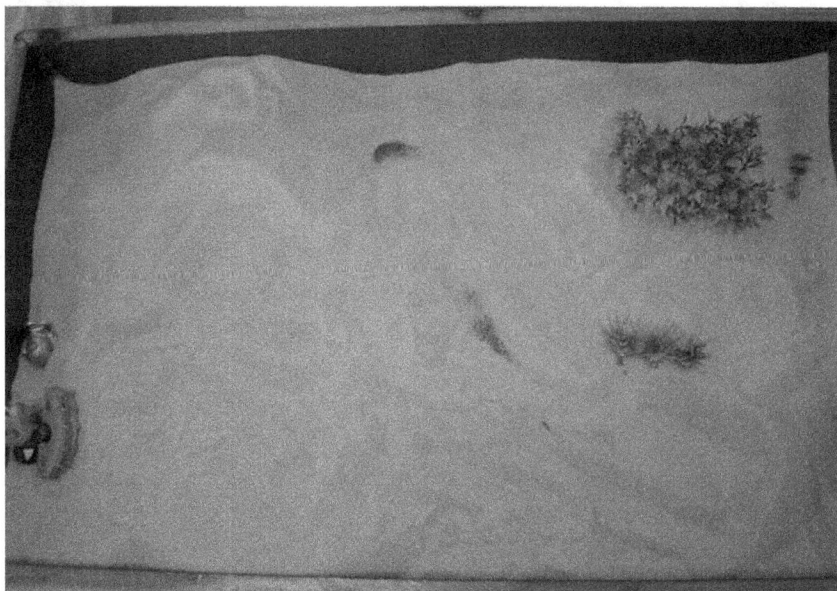

Picture 31

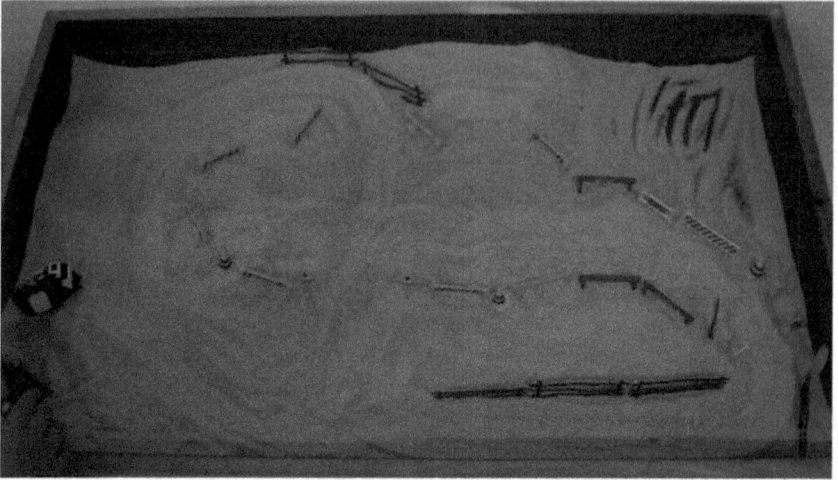

Picture 32

Picture 33

crashed cars had previously been. The purple flowers to the right have almost quadrupled in comparison to the first image. There are no more cars. Figuratively speaking, the ground is being prepared for a new mental attitude, for new behaviour. Above all, a space has been created in which fantasy and creativity can express themselves.

The theme of the two roads is repeated and varied in the next images. The penultimate image (Picture 34) is separated into two large areas and

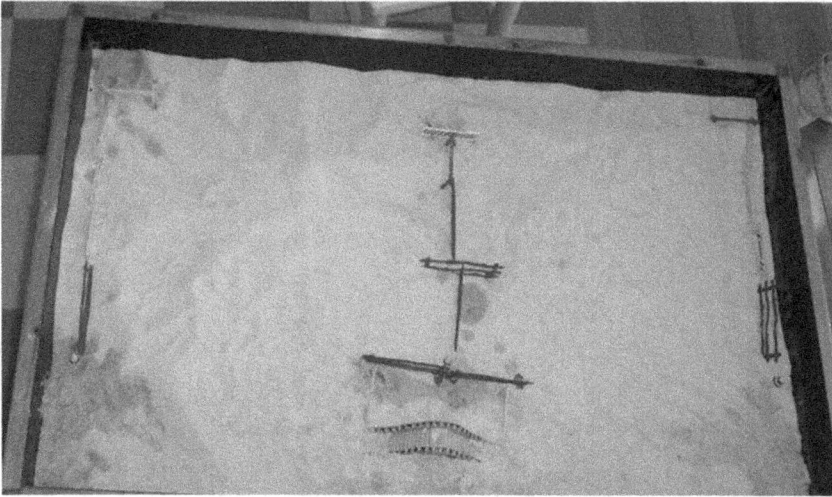

Picture 34

once more features the bridge from the first image. This time it has been given a central position and an important function: it connects the two symmetric areas. When one considers Wan's history, it is easy to understand the connecting bridge as a solution to his conflict with his brother. Wan is finally able to accept him and integrate him into his own personality as a relevant representation of 'you'.

Three corners of the sandtray have been dampened in this image, as if something has been sown. Surely enough, there are different plants growing out of each of the four corners in the last sand image (Picture 35). They are invigorating and anchor the image at the same time. The boy can now rely on an organically grown order. Four well-structured spaces – maybe for the four people in his family – have been created, and the yellow car, which could represent his newly discovered autonomy, can drive freely around them. From then on, Wan is cheerful, active, and shows no more problems in his development.

In an orphanage in Guangzhou

The term orphanage is not quite correct, because most of the children here do actually have parents, but were abandoned by them. When I casually ask how many of the 1000 children are girls, the director does not answer my question at first. We are sitting in his welcoming, simply furnished office and begin talking about other things: about the improvements that the government's financial

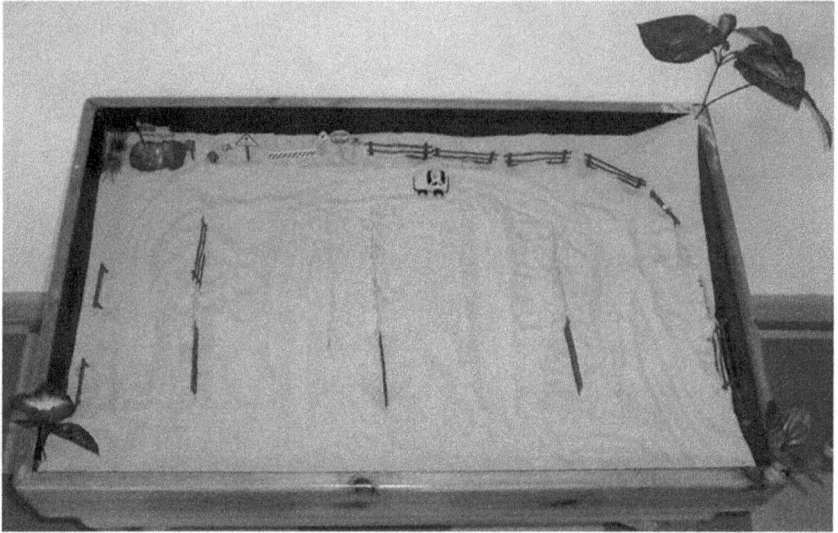

Picture 35

support has made possible in the past years, about the increase in the number of carers compared to the year before, and about the necessity for psychological training of these carers. Eventually we come back to the difficult subject. It is difficult because it is connected with a feeling of great shame: hundreds of thousands of people in China have still not given up the practice of abandoning newborn girls. This orphanage represents no exception; as in any of the 300 other orphanages, 80 per cent of the children here are girls. Of the 20 per cent that are boys, about two-thirds suffer organic diseases. The children are abandoned shortly after birth at the entrances to temples or hospitals. Sometimes they have a note attached to them, bearing their name and date of birth.

In the West, Chinese orphanages were considered the epitome of squalor up until the early 1990s. Underpaid carers had to look after 40 to 50 infants during 14-hour shifts, and could not help but neglect them. The new building, the neat garden, the cosmopolitan director and the international homepage, which organizes adoptions to other countries, are all a huge leap forward. But there are new risks as well, especially if progress happens only on a material level: merely having a large number of toys as well as colour televisions for the children to sit in front of with untrained carers is certainly not enough.

Sandplay has so far been introduced into six orphanages and into countless kindergartens and schools. Even if the guidelines, which are described here, cannot be implemented correctly in all cases, the core idea that sandplay promotes nevertheless has an important compensatory effect in a society that is changing as rapidly as China's. This core idea could be summed up as follows: play is an integral part of a child's mental health. It requires neither technological nor didactic games to stimulate children who have become arrested in a certain phase of development. They can heal themselves if they have access to a free and protected playing space within a stable relationship with an adult. Every problematic behaviour that a child might develop has not only a reason, but also an intention. It always aims at interpersonal relationship and attention, never at a mere material advantage. If one tries to intervene without having understood this intention, then the desired change will not come about.

The long journey through the desert

An 11-year-old boy, Tian, works with utmost concentration. He makes four different sand images in a single session, and after each finished scene he asks his therapist, 'Is it right like this?' She seems to play an important role, as if his feverish work were made possible only because there is someone there to share the experience of all these things that are appearing in the sand before his very eyes. Tian gives the impression of wanting to make the absolute most of this offer of therapy, as if a vast amount of unprocessed emotions had accumulated inside him over the years, of which he now feels the need to rid himself in a single session. The rapidly changing scenes have to do with aggression (wild animals, air-strikes, bombs) and abandonment (a baby alone inside a house). Tian makes no comment on the images and there are no clear story lines. When, in the fourth image, aeroplanes collide with brutal force in mid-air, the therapist clearly feels his anger and frustration. But soon his play starts to calm down. The picture that remains in the end consists of only three elements: two trucks and an excavator in the upper part of the image. Tian comments on this by saying: 'I love excavators. They have so many different functions.' Maybe he is talking about a desire to unearth his own potentials. He expresses how much he relates to his therapist not verbally, but by placing all of the figures so that they are facing her. Everything inside him is orientated towards this lifeline, which is supposed to help him catch up on his developmental deficits. Tian does not do well at school. Based on an IQ test result of 65, he was classed as a child with 'slow mental development'. The aptitude for relationships that was displayed by Tian during sandplay, which an IQ test naturally does not take into account, indicates an emotional maturity corresponding to his age.

During the second session Tian works only on a single scene. When he is finished, he says: 'This is a desert. The cars have travelled a long way. They have reached these petrol stations. Someone has planted trees and flowers, and there are ducks in a lake' (see plate section: p. 8, Plate 15).

This time a story line is described. There is talk of a long journey through a desert – possibly Tian's emotional desert since his life in the orphanage.

The petrol stations are a place where fuel – energy – can be refilled, even if they are not yet easily accessible. There are obstacles that hinder one's progress. But Tian has reached the end of his long journey (perhaps the many years after the loss of his parents) and is about to step into new territory. The appearance of the five trees, which 'someone has planted' – this is his fifth sand image – indicates his imminent psychological growth. This is further underlined by the symbolic meaning of the ducks. They can be seen as elements of transformation, because they are able to move in three of the four natural elements: earth, water and air.

During the next session, Tian requires a few attempts to complete the image he calls 'park'. It consists of one square and one circular area. Each of them is lushly overgrown with dense plants and has eight glass marbles glistening through the leaves (see plate section: p. 8, Plate 16).

It looks like an oasis, which he has just discovered in the middle of the desert. The boy, who just two weeks ago was timidly asking for reassurance that he was doing things right, now regards his image for a long time and says: 'I know that this doesn't really exist. But if it did exist, then I would love it, because it is beautiful.' With these words, Tian not only described his sand image, but also summed up the whole meaning of sandwork in a most synthetic way. It approximates Winnicott's *intermediary space*,[4] which is at the same time both real and imagined, and the new creations resulting from it, which interact in nature and culture. But the most important thing that Tian expresses is that he loves something because he finds it beautiful. It means that love can arise out of beauty, and that even a child who has experienced little parental love in his life can still produce love from within himself. Intelligence tests are not always the most reliable method of determining a child's maturity.

When Tian's therapist had to go abroad after eight months, he was told that he could continue sandplay with another therapist. He tried this for two sessions but then declined the offer disappointedly. He realized that sandplay was possible for him only within the one very specific therapeutic relationship. There followed a few weeks of aggressive and regressive behaviour. During this time, the original therapist tried to remain in contact with the boy from abroad. As time passed, Tian continued to make good progress, despite the premature end to his therapy. With all that he had achieved inwardly up until then, he was able to endure this new experience of abandonment to a certain extent. It was a help that his feelings over the loss of the therapist were understood by his environment, and that he was offered other activities. This example shows clearly how important it is to keep in mind that sandwork processes are mostly unique, and that one therapist can rarely be replaced successfully by another. This means that a therapist who begins sandwork with a child for the first time needs to be very aware of the responsibility involved. Sandwork allows such a deep relationship to form even if, or perhaps precisely because, hardly any words are exchanged.

The Barbie doll

There is no information available as to how long 6-year-old Qifei has been in the orphanage.

When Qifei enters the sandplay room for the first time, she has a sullen look on her face and trudges at a distance behind the therapist who has been assigned to her. When a passing teacher politely asks where they are going today, the child does not answer. The therapist also receives no answers to her questions. She appears not to exist in Qifei's eyes. Nevertheless, the girl is prepared to join the sandwork group and works at a sand image in silence (see plate section: p. 9, Plate 17).

Underneath a large green leaf, the girl has placed the figure of a baby – after tearing off its head. The scene also shows a group of ducks, with one duckling left behind. There is a small figure of a blonde woman, who has her back turned to everything else as if she were staring into space. The therapist is deeply concerned after seeing this image. The single duckling lagging behind the others, especially, creates a sense of grave danger. In nature a little duckling is lost if it falls behind its family.

Next, the girl takes a Barbie doll and removes one piece of clothing after the next. If the clothes do not come away easily, she rips them off the doll's body. The therapist finds this hard to watch. Then the girl tears at the doll's head until it snaps off. In the end she throws all the separate pieces on the floor (Picture 39). During the next sessions as well, the therapist needs strength to endure her unease. The abandoned duckling appears again, as do dolls with torn off heads.

Before the fourth session Qifei no longer wants to come to sandwork. As she is walking with her therapist through the garden between the living quarters and the building where sandwork takes place, Qifei suddenly sits down in the grass and makes it understood that she would like to stay there. She begins tearing out grass in a rage. The therapist lets her be and sits down next to her. The girl begins to cry, but does not want to be held. After about half an hour she has somewhat regained composure and agrees to join the other children in the sandwork room. She takes her place at the sandtray and starts creating an image as if she were in slow motion (Picture 40). A growing feeling of nausea overcomes the therapist. The countless objects in the image were not, as one might think, simply thrown into the sand, but were carefully placed exactly where they lie – one after another. The therapist almost believes she can smell the stench of a giant rubbish dump.

Countless people, animals, means of transport and household furnishings are lying around, as if discarded. There is one empty space in the form of a brown lidless teapot in almost the exact centre of the image. This is all the more striking when one has already witnessed so many other children of the

Picture 39

Picture 40

same age patiently filling every available opening and every container with sand. The only upright figure is a dwarf at the top of the image. He is facing the therapist: a glimmer of hope. The only discernible form of order, maybe the beginning of a structure, is an accumulation of household furnishings on the right hand side. There are two things that could have made it so hard for Qifei to come to the session. First, the previous sandplay images may have stirred her up because they depicted a severe trauma. And second, the child was going to be adopted by new parents in the USA some time in the following weeks. One can scarcely imagine what must go through a 6-year-old girl's head in such a situation. What is certain is that she was both afraid and enraged.

One can but speculate as to how and why the girl came to the orphanage in the first place, because there was no information on either point. Sexual abuse seems likely to have played a role, in which case the risk of a child psychosis is high. The next image is the last one Qifei made before she was picked up by her new parents (see plate section: p. 9, Plate 18).

At the lower left of the image there is a similar chaos to the one in her previous image. There are still many 'discarded' figures, but none without heads. The centre is dominated by three so-called spiritual figures: a Buddha and two angels. It is not clear if these three are communicating with the other, smaller figures. The two sailing ships to either side appear to be travelling under full sail. They let us, the therapists who must stay behind, hope that this girl's journey through life will continue under a more auspicious star than so far.

The free and protected space is disturbed

The term 'free and protected space', which was coined by Dora Kalff,[5] deserves further explanation, especially to avoid it being taken merely literally. We could also call it 'free and protected holding',[6] which emphasizes that it is not merely a matter of a certain physical expanse, but of something that needs to be created afresh at the beginning of every session. It is the precondition for sandwork's being able to fulfil its therapeutic function. It means providing conditions that allow the sand worker to find inner images and states of mind and to express them subjectively and without outside expectations, influence or judgement. Protectedness pertains to outside disturbances (for example, if an unknown person enters the sandwork room unexpectedly), and to inner disturbances (for example if the therapist's attention is distracted by a subjective emotion). Children sense this latter disturbance or inhibition very clearly, but usually cannot place its exact source. The following example should illustrate this in detail. As is well known, the easiest way to understand how a system works is often through exceptions to the system.

For six months – between November 2007 and May 2008 – a group of twelve children took part in weekly sessions of Expressive Sandwork. The assisting adults were psychology students in their third year of studies. The students regularly discussed as a team their notes and photographs of the completed sand images, as well as any problems or questions that had arisen. Their behaviour and interventions were continuously scrutinized by the other supervisors and by myself.

The events I would like to describe here took place in May 2008. I had been working with the students for a week and was soon going to visit the orphanage myself. I had thought it important to have a chance to see the students working with children, because many of their questions could be answered only after direct observation. However, I was aware that my presence during a sandwork session – especially as a non-Asian – could be a disturbance for the children. Since these children's lives were largely limited to the orphanage and school, it was safe to assume that they had probably never before seen a European. I nevertheless believed that the expected disturbance would be minor, since my presence during sandwork sessions in Africa had not been a problem. I had overlooked the fact that in this case, unlike in Africa, the group sessions had already been taking place in exactly the same way for months, which must have become a kind of fixed ritual and a basis of trust for the children.

To make matters worse, the rector of the university had taken my presence as an opportunity to attend the therapy session with two of his students. And so, with the session about to begin, I found myself in a bright, inviting room with twelve sandtrays, and shelves one metre high along the walls, on which the miniatures were sorted by theme and were easily accessible. Sitting beside me on the bench were my colleague Professor Gao Lan and the gentlemen from the university. I had a bad feeling about the whole situation. After casting a questioning look at Gao, it was clear that asking the rector and his students to leave was not an option. A first group of small children entered the room with their therapists and spread out to the various sandtrays. The children pretended not to notice us observers. Then a dark-eyed girl of 14 appeared in the doorway, cast one brief, questioning glance at us and suddenly ran through the room, holding her hand flat just above the top shelf of miniatures. As she brushed against the figures, they started to rock dangerously. A baroque porcelain doll fell loudly to the floor and shattered into a thousand pieces. The girl had reached her sandtray. It was an embarrassing situation: her therapist went to fetch a broom and dustpan, and swept up the fragments submissively. The girl had lowered her gaze but was holding back a smile. The provocation could not have been more successfully staged. Without using a single word she had clearly let us know: 'Something valuable has been broken.'

Some of the children had already begun touching the sand, while others were still at the shelves, choosing their figures. Now a new problem arose: a 6-year-old girl refused to go to her sandtray. She did not want to play today. Her sandtray was the one closest to us, the visiting strangers. Once it had been moved to the other side of the room, the child was content.

Sandwork began, the children worked in concentration, and the atmosphere appeared calm. I noticed that the smaller children were spending a long time at the shelves and had begun to play there on the floor. Their therapists were sitting at the sandtrays alone, with nothing to observe or write down. One could say that the children had abandoned their adults. It also struck me that some of the children had patiently lined up figures along the edges of the sandtrays: soldiers in one case, cars and food items in two other cases. Unmistakably, these attempts at artificially increasing the height of the sandtrays' edges gave the impression that the space within the sandtrays needed to be defended. At the same time this effort seemed movingly helpless. Worst of all, it consumed so much time and energy that there was hardly any time left to play (Picture 42 and Picture 43).

When we studied the sand images at the end of the session, and compared them to photos from the previous sessions, we made the most remarkable discovery. A regression could be made out in the work of every child. Themes that had already been processed and closed reappeared in every image. One child, who had been telling a continuous story over the past sessions, had returned to a previous behaviour of placing figures in the sandtray only briefly and then removing them again. Our presence had

Picture 42

Picture 43

clearly had a disturbing influence. There was a single child who had not shown a regression in this session. On the contrary: this 11-year-old boy had even made a leap forward in his development. From his imaginative depiction, he had managed to move on to a verbal expression. Why had he – contrary to all the others – been able to use the disturbance as a catalyst? It was as if he had secretly thought to himself: 'I'll show these strangers.' The subsequent discussion with the students brought the answer. When I asked them how they had felt with the children during this session, they began to vent their feelings. 'Uncomfortable', they said, 'controlled, criticized.' – 'I was afraid that I was sitting too close or too far away from the sandtray.' – 'I felt stiff.' – 'The child tried to grab my pen. He has never done that before. What was I supposed to do?'

It became clear that the disturbance had had an effect not only on the children, but also on the adults. The therapists had perceived my presence as a controlling interference. Thus, the children had lost their stable dialogue partner. Instead of the person who had so far always witnessed the events of play intensively and shared their experience, in this session the children had nothing but a bundle of nerves to relate to. It was no wonder that this had been answered with regression. But there was that one exception: Tian, the boy whose sandplay was described earlier in this chapter. His therapist was the only student who could speak English fluently. Like the other students, she had also sensed the tense atmosphere, but she nevertheless felt comfortable. She noticed that the boy was displaying a certain behaviour in play that he had not displayed for a while: for a long time he did nothing but bury figures in the sand and then unearth them again. The student attributed this to the visiting strangers' presence and thereby found a logical way of explaining the boy's behaviour to herself. Thus, she continued to trust in the boy's actions, and her presence continued to have a resonating, therapeutic effect for the boy: he still had a free and protected space at his disposal, just as he had had in all the previous sessions. And so it was, during this session, that he managed to perform the quantum leap of expressing visually *and* verbally what sandplay meant to him. 'I know that this doesn't really exist. But if it did exist, then I would love it, because I think it is beautiful.'

The earthquake: the pupils of Beichuan

Chengdu, Mianyang and Beichuan in August 2008, three months after the earthquake: looking out of the car window on the drive from the airport to the centre of Chengdu, one sees what appears to be an endless forest of building cranes along the highway – nothing but cranes, kilometre after kilometre. It makes one wonder that so many of them could even exist. The surroundings of Chengdu are described in every tourist guide as an area of particular scenic interest. I ask Dr Chang Lee, a professor of religious history at the University of Chengdu, who is sitting next to me in the car, if Chengdu has an historic core. As he does not respond, I specify my question: is there still a part of the city with historic buildings, like the Hutongs in Beijing or the two roads with wooden houses in Shanghai? It occurs to me too late that a direct negative answer is considered impolite in China. How many times have I been sent off on hopeless ventures after asking for directions and taking literally the friendly 'Yes', which had actually meant 'No'? Obviously I hadn't asked Dr Lee the right questions. Before I can attempt to salvage the situation at least somewhat, I do get an answer: 'We have lost our history.'

Mary, an English teacher from Hong Kong, who came to Mianyang as a volunteer after the earthquake in May 2008, is nervous because giving interviews to foreign journalists is forbidden. But we are not journalists. It is not our job to find out who might have been at fault for which parts of this terrible tragedy. We are psychologists and are only concerned with the tragedy's emotional consequences. We are standing in the provisional campus of the Beichuan school. It is already mid September and Mary is still here. After being here two months, Mary decided to stay for two years. In the first weeks after the earthquake, the children had but one single wish: 'Day after day they asked me if they could go home.'

Home, in their case, means the completely destroyed town of Beichuan in the upper valley of the Min river, 200 km away from Mianyang. This mountainous area, where the earthquake's epicentre lay, is home to the 'Qiang', one of China's 55 ethnic minorities. Up until the previous year the Qiang consisted of about 300,000 people. In the school of Beichuan alone – a middle and upper school with a connected boarding school – 1700 children and 60 teachers lost their lives. For nearly 20 hours, the surviving children dug with bare hands in search of their classmates and teachers – one whole afternoon and throughout the night. Not being able to save a person whom one has heard calling from under the rubble for hours is very hard to forget, even for an adult.

The following morning, a group of children set out on foot and reached the valley by evening. The people they encountered down there were dealing with a catastrophic situation of their own. The government had dispatched the military and provided tents and food, and international aid did not take long to get under way, but in the following months the focus was on getting the bare essentials for survival to as many people as possible. The children received medical attention, but had no opportunity to talk to anyone for weeks. They could not tell anyone about the things they had seen.

After rescue operations had been completed, the entire bottom of the Beichuan valley was enclosed with barbed wire fencing. Guards now stand in front of the large iron gates, and no one is allowed in any more. One can only look down from the mountain slope onto what used to be a modest little town nestled along the curve of the river. All that remains now are collapsed rows of houses, ruined bridges and bits of road. The earth still has gaping holes in places, and giant rocks lie strewn about. Thousands of people are still buried under all of this, including the parents of most of the children. This is why they want to go back.

The 1300 survivors of the Beichuan school, pupils and teachers, have been temporarily housed on the premises of the household appliances company Changhong. The classrooms and the teachers' apartments are made of prefabricated elements, which evidently have neither heating nor running water. The sight of 80 children crowded into each classroom, or of huge dormitories filled with bunk beds brings to mind a refugee camp. For the next few years this will be their home. Most of the teachers have lost at least one relative in the earthquake, they teach 40 hours a week and are badly paid. They would really require psychological assistance themselves, not only for having to deal with severely traumatized children every day, but also for their own grief. When pain becomes too great, it causes depression and loss of sensitivity. Depression means that one is incapable of perceiving the pain of others. This creates new injuries. Mary, who is the only outsider here, is living proof of something which is common knowledge to all helpers in disaster areas: it does the affected people good to be able to talk to someone who did not experience the catastrophe.

On 19 May, Gao Lan and her husband Heyong Shen, both professors at the Institute for Analytical Psychology at the Normal University in Guangzhou, travelled to Beichuan with six of their students. There were still aftershocks, there was a high risk of epidemics, and yet three times as many students had volunteered as they were able to take with them. The team was confronted with difficult medical and hygienic problems during their first weeks in the earthquake area. But despite this largely material emergency situation, they had taken along from the beginning miniature figures, colour pencils and notebooks: children and adults were to be given the possibility of expressing themselves without words, if they wished.

After a while, children and adults could begin to give visual expression to images that came to them in nightmares and sudden flashbacks. From their fragmented descriptions it soon became clear that they felt guilty: guilty for having survived, guilty for not having dug even longer for their friends, guilty for not having been heroes but having turned and run when the earth opened up before them and devoured a whole lake, as if someone had pulled the plug in a giant sink.

Even now 17-year-old Wu still can't drink tap water. Underground water has been poisoned in his eyes. He is startled by the tiniest of noises and his concentration is poor. But this is his graduation year. The government allowed pupils who were affected by the earthquake to attend extra lessons in the summer months. That way, in August and September, they can catch up on what they did not learn in May, because their school and their teachers no longer existed. They attend classes for ten hours a day. But can they learn anything at all in their state? Wu needs more than just lessons. He is one of those who always ask the teacher if she could take them home for just one day.

On the hundredth day after the earthquake, the day when the Chinese ritually bid farewell to their deceased, the time has finally come. Mary and four of the children set off for Beichuan. They take a bus up to the place above Beichuan where the school had once stood. Remains of walls stand like skeletons amidst a sheer endless field of rubble. Those who dare take a closer look see bits of metal from old school desks, a school bag and some clothes. Everything is covered by a thin layer of lime dust. The visitors strew flowers, lay down farewell letters, and hang photos of the children in a long row along a wooden wall. The boarding school building, where the dormitories had been, still stands unscathed with hardly a crack in its walls. If the earthquake had come at night, they would all still be alive. Before Mary can react, the boys have slipped past a barrier and have disappeared inside the building. She follows them up onto the third floor. Clothes, school books and pens and pencils are strewn all over the floor. One of the boys pauses for a long time in a corner room, then he slowly moves towards the window. When the earthquake struck, he says, he had been the last one in his classroom and had jumped out of the third floor window. Then the school collapsed. He was buried up to the waist and had broken a leg. Two days later he was treated by paramedics. Then he lay in a tent with his leg in a splint for six weeks. There were hundreds of people in the tent, but no one ever spoke to him.

The children continue walking with their teacher, past signs saying 'No Camera', down a little trail to the town of Beichuan. There they spend the afternoon and show the teacher where everything had once stood. On the other bank of the river they see a dog, the only living soul in this eerily empty city. Then 13-year-old Shu points towards a huge landslide: his parents' house is underneath it. For the first time since May, Shu cries. Mary says prayers with the children, and they hold a farewell ceremony for the dead.

Late that evening, once they have returned to Mianyang, Mary checks on the children in their dormitories once more. Shu tells her how everything seems so hopeless. 'What could you do yourself to create hope?', Mary asks. The boy looks at her and answers with a fury that he has never displayed before: 'Back at home everything was different from here. We had no televisions, no skyscrapers and no supermarkets. We would make a big fire and dance the *Solong*.'

Suddenly Mary realizes that these children are not just suffering from the loss of their parents. They grew up as part of a mountain people, with their own language and traditions, and now feel alienated in this city way of life. Mary tells the children that it depends on them if there will be another community in the future like the one they knew in the past. They are the future of a 3000-year-old people, which has lost a large part of its members. If they are diligent now and manage to accomplish something in life, then they could rebuild everything the way it had been. The boys listen to her. If Mary is proven right, the notion of 'home' in the children's fantasy moved from the past into the future on that day. This is an important step in the assimilation of traumas.

One of the symptoms of posttraumatic stress disorder is a change of the affected individual's perception of time. The past has a positive association and pertains to the time before the traumatic event. If one asks traumatized individuals about their 'present', they will only describe the terrible experience again and again; it has taken root as something eternally present. In a sense, time no longer passes since the trauma occurred. This means that the traumatic experience can never become part of the past. The notion of a future does not exist. Psychotherapy, however, can exert an influence on this inability to experience new emotions.

'We don't need psychologists,' said Liu Yuchuan, the director of the provisional Beichuan school in Mianyang, with a defensive gesture. Professor Heyong Shen and his wife Professor Gao Lan had not expected this scepticism when they offered their psychotherapeutic help at the end of June. But, as psychotherapists, they also knew not simply to take the words at face value, and so they remained seated without answering. A sense of hopelessness filled the room as the director continued: 'We will manage this by ourselves. We don't need questionnaires and psychological tests. These are healthy, strong children, who have experienced bad things. They will study and work hard, and they will get somewhere in life.' Professor Shen was silent. He was thinking of a scene which he had just witnessed out in the hallway. A volunteer had instructed an 8-year-old boy to write a letter to his mother, who had died in the earthquake. The boy managed to write half a page, because a Chinese pupil usually does what he is told, but then he handed the paper back to the volunteer and was close to tears. She took the letter, told him he would soon feel better, and then disappeared. Heyong Shen could still see the boy through the open door, sitting in the corridor as if waiting for further instructions. The volunteer had not returned. Heyong Shen asked if he could bring the boy, who was waiting out in the corridor, into the office. The director consented, they brought the boy inside, and Gao Lan sat down with him on the floor. They started to talk quietly. The two men sat opposite each other without saying a word. The sound of voices wafted up from the school yard. Midday break had started. Hundreds of pupils were being released from the tightness of their barrack-like classrooms. Director Yuchuan drew his gaze away from the window and told Heyong Shen that he had lost his wife and his son in the earthquake. He often didn't know how to continue, he added after a while. It wasn't true that they didn't need help here in this school. The pupils and the teachers all needed endless help, they just didn't know what sort. Under no circumstances would he again make the mistake of allowing strangers to come in with questionnaires, asking the children to tick how many relatives they had lost in the disaster, and how many times they woke up at night.

In the mean time the boy had pulled up his sleeve and shown Gao Lan a large cut, which so far had gone untreated. She offered to bandage it up for him and he agreed after some hesitation. Afterwards, while Gao Lan was accompanying the boy back to his dormitory, the director asked Heyong Shen: 'How do you work?'

Since August 2008, the team around Professor Heyong Shen and Professor Gao Lan has free use of a 30-square-metre room in the central row of prefabricated barracks. The room contains two sandtrays, sandplay figures, drawing material, play dough and some musical instruments. Most of the 200 children who lost both parents in the earthquake have 'dropped by' at least once. They can listen to music, read, paint, be creative, and they can sign up for a series of sandplay sessions. The same goes for the adults, who can choose between single and group sessions.

Professor Shen describes such a session, which took place just weeks after the earthquake, when the volunteers were still housed in tents.

Four men are sitting around a sandtray on the floor, with small play figures beside them to choose from. A middle-aged man has chosen a miniature house and is holding it in his hand. He wants to place it in the right hand corner of the tray, but he hesitates. Another man begins to flatten the sand for him, where the house is supposed to go. He says the ground needs to be solid, and that he doesn't find the sand hard enough. He flattens the sand for some time, while the others watch him, until his neighbour starts to compress the sand as well by flattening it. The first man is still holding the house in his hand, and when he finally finds a good place for it, he begins to cry. In that moment, his misfortune is shared by the others wordlessly.

Some of the children's first sandwork images surprised the volunteers, because they appeared so 'beautiful' (see plate section: p. 10, Plate 19). How does a path of hearts, flowers and angels appear within a reality of ruined houses, death, loss, dust and despair? Such images were often the first in a longer series of images. Apparently it was important first to conjure up precisely what had been lost in the earthquake: beauty, colour, love and protection. A child's psyche creates life even when death surrounds it. Instinctively, it seems to activate precisely what is needed in the child's life. Other children depicted the destruction from the beginning. The earthquake was recreated in the sandtray. First a whole village was patiently built up with all its details: houses, animals, people, a river – their past lives. 'This is how it had been,' the children said. Then they destroyed the whole thing, even tearing limbs off the animal and human figures, which then stuck out of the sand grotesquely. The worst of it was depicted again and again. Sometimes what had been destroyed was rebuilt again, only to be destroyed once more. During these processes, nothing else was asked of the assisting adults than to be present with their own feelings – and this was difficult enough. As has already been mentioned, the fact that the therapists came from outside, and had not experienced the earthquake themselves, was probably an advantage.

In the weeks and months after the earthquake, large groups of volunteers were trained. Experiencing sandwork personally, which is normally an essential part of sandplay training, needed to be reduced to a minimum. Each volunteer could choose a miniature, concentrate on it for a while, and then share the images, feelings and thoughts that had come to his or her mind. Everyone was allowed to touch the sand in the sandtray and explore this experience in their imagination. It goes without saying that this is not really enough. But it was nevertheless interesting and impressive for the trainees to experience themselves that, even through this extremely condensed involvement with unconscious images, it was precisely their most current fears, concerns and thoughts that came to light and could be confronted. By the end of the weekend course, the trainees had experienced at least in part what it feels like to work with depth-psychology, even if only a tiny part of their personal problematic issues had been activated.

Naturally the theoretic basics were conveyed as well, and there was plenty of room for questions. The volunteers were already in the middle of their working lives, and were mostly sacrificing their holidays. They were teachers, nurses, social workers, civil servants, mothers with grown-up children, and students. They saw the weeks that awaited them as a great opportunity in their lives. One of their common concerns was whether they would be able to do the right thing for the earthquake victims. Their questions regarding the use of sandwork were proof of their empathy, humility, and great respect for other people's suffering.

Overcoming a traumatic experience

The following eight sand images were made by Liu, an 11-year-old boy who had lost both his parents in the earthquake. In August 2008, three months after the earthquake, he did a series of sandwork sessions with Gao Lan. Liu had withdrawn, he no longer spoke to anyone and his previously excellent performance at school had become poor.

At a first glance, everything still seems to be in order in the world that he depicts in his first image. There are plants, particularly lots of colourful flowers, but also houses and animals: butterflies, turtles, rabbits and gazelles. Upon closer inspection, however, one begins to notice details that give the image a strange, unreal quality. The number four appears often: four angels, four white rabbits, four turtles, four houses, and a kind of partitioning of the whole image into four parts. Everyone in China knows that the number four signifies death, and that white is the colour of mourning. No people are depicted in the sand image, which fits Liu's behaviour. He cannot relate to other people, nor does he want to. Instead he has withdrawn into a world of plants and animals where there is no aggression. All the animals depicted here are harmless.

It is not easy to understand what it means when children who have not had a Christian upbringing use angels in their sandwork images. Angels, hearts and flowers were the most commonly used miniatures in the first weeks after the earthquake. The children would sometimes spontaneously say that the angels were the deceased people. As has already been mentioned, the therapists never ask for meanings to be explained. Only occasionally can an indirect question be in order, for instance when a child has said nothing about a particular area of the image with which he was intensely preoccupied during play. In such a situation one might go as far as asking: 'Is anything important happening there?' This shows the child that one is interested, and gives the child the opportunity to express something verbally as well, if he wishes to.

In the second image, the earthquake is re-enacted in all its destructive power, emanating upwards from the lower left corner. A mountain has fallen on a house, an aeroplane has crashed, dinosaurs and other wild animals roam the village. The turtles, which are mostly water turtles in China, are lying on dry land. One of the animals, a brown gazelle, is fleeing to the upper right corner, but a dinosaur with a fiery dorsal plate has caught it and is biting it in the back. (see plate section: p. 10, Plate 20; p. 11, Plate 21 (detail)). This unsuccessful attempt at escape appears to be blocked by the black and silver aeroplane, which is facing in the opposite direction. It appears to be only a question of time (the hourglass) before one will have to turn back and face the terrible things that have happened. This black and silver aeroplane is intact, full of energy and ready for take-off. In the cultures of antiquity, birds often represented the soul. When modern-day children use aeroplanes in play, these do not always represent a motorized means of transport of human invention, but can sometimes also be an image for anything that people have ever expected to find in the sky. Thus, this aeroplane could also be the expression of a 'higher', spiritual vitality in the boy, which is aimed at overcoming fear and confronting what has happened.

Instead of saying a word about his image, Liu took off his T-shirt once the session was finished. He showed Gao Lan a big wound on his back, which had gone untreated since the earthquake, almost three months before. Gao Lan asked why he had never shown anybody this injury. Liu answered that he was sure that his mother had suffered much greater pain when she died in the earthquake. He thought it only right that he too should endure pain. The depiction of the helpless animal which was about to be eaten by the dinosaur had enabled him to perceive his own wound differently, and to let it be treated. The therapist's attention awakened a new 'motherly' feeling within himself which freed him from his identification with a mother in pain. Overcoming feelings of guilt is often an integral part of working with trauma patients. In especially severe cases we know that it can prove to be impossible. Guilt of having survived has driven people into suicide, even decades after their initial trauma. The chances of processing feelings of guilt are greater in children, because everything inside them is instinctively geared towards development.

After this sand image, Liu apparently gained enough confidence to dare confronting the tragedy on a new level. One can tell by the fact that he uses only dry sand in his next image, and no miniatures whatsoever. What he wants to depict can apparently be better expressed in the two dimensions of a drawing. With just a few sweeps of his fingers Liu draws a grotesque face (see plate section: p. 11, Plate 22). One sometimes sees such animal masks hewn in stone at the entrance to Chinese temples. They are meant to keep away evil spirits. Eerily slanted eyes with the hair above them – a fiery mane – bristling upwards, and an evil snout below, which looks as if it were about to snap shut. Liu asks the therapist if this frightens her. He had had to stare into nature's evil face and now he wants to share his fright. He needs a warm, humane reaction. A week later, Liu uses the sand as a drawing surface once more. His swiftly drawn lines make up the top part of a face: wide eyes – this time with eyelashes and pupils – a human nose instead of an animal snout, and a small shape on the forehead which could be a crown or an angel with raised arms (see plate section: p. 12, Plate 23). The events have now become humanized for Liu, his fear has become less, and the fright can become assimilated.

When Gao Lan sees the next sand image, which Liu once again drew only in the dry sand, she thinks of her own long hair and has to smile. Compared to the previous image, the figure now has a lot more body – obviously a female body, because its breasts are emphasized – which shows that all three dimensions are slowly prevailing once more. The mouth's expression is ambivalent: a careful, maybe still somewhat sad smile. But the image expresses motherliness (see plate section: p. 12, Plate 24). Once more, one could say that Liu has managed to produce an inner motherly function within himself, to make up for the loss of his real mother. He is doing better now outside of sandplay as well: for the first time in months he took part in a football game.

In the next sessions, Liu is ready to leave the archaic level of depiction seen in his last images, and can return to daily reality. He uses miniatures once more to create a picture of the ocean, which he says he would dearly love to see sometime: we recall that he grew up in the mountains. He is now ready to explore completely new territories. The sea is symbolic of the primordial origin of all life.[7] In the lower right corner, one sees a village scene: houses, animals, people and a car – a peaceful world. The sea opens up to the left. Eight fish have formed a circle, which looks like a mandala – a symbol for wholeness. Dancing the *Solong* in a circle is something that Liu, belonging to the Qiang population, would have been used to doing. In any case, one can say that there is something more to these fish than just their 'nature'. They are not limited merely to eating and being eaten: they have created a symbolic form, have created culture. This can happen only where the fight for survival has already been won. There are four shells in the upper left corner, as well as more fish and two octopuses (see plate section: p. 13, Plate 25).

A bridge leads from the village to another area, which is apparently inhabited only by two white rabbits. We know these rabbits from Liu's first sand image. Perhaps this area represents what he has lost: a safe and cuddly children's world. There is a boy standing on the bridge looking out to sea – Liu himself, as he explains. Clinging to his back is a dark monkey, which one can easily imagine must represent his nightmares, flashbacks and terrible memories – a burden that he will still have to carry for a while. This monkey, as well as the two octopuses, could indicate a tendency toward depression, which he has not quite overcome. But there are countless turtles swimming under the bridge and out towards the sea like a river of energy. A lot could be said about the meaning of turtles, especially in Asia. Here we will limit ourselves to the most obvious context. In an earthquake area, where everyone has lost house and home, turtles are the lucky exception: they always carry their homes with them. Therefore, they represent survival, endurance, strength and a feeling of innate protection.

With this image, Liu achieved a big step towards the assimilation of his trauma. As if he wanted to take the process one step even further, he created the following moving sand image in his last session. He explained that this was his mother's grave. Since he had not been able to bury her, he made her the most beautiful grave that ever existed in the world, here in the sand (see plate section: p. 13, Plate 26).

Chapter 9

Expressive Sandwork in Colombia, Latin America

> Just so must I go away?
> Like the flowers that have wilted?
> Will nothing remain in my name?
> Nothing of my renown here on this earth?
> At least flowers, at least songs![1]
>> (Cantos de Huexotzingo, Inscription in
>> the National Museum of Anthropology,
>> Mexico City)

'This country could have everything,' says Dario, the owner of an Italian restaurant in Bogotá, and places his newest invention – gnocchi or 'noquis' made from tapioca flour – on the table. He continues:

> Colombia would have everything it takes to become the fruit and vegetable garden of all of Latin America: access to two oceans, up to five different climatic zones, good soil and enough water. But what happens? – Corruption, drug trafficking, paramilitaries and guerrillas.

Dario, who is originally from Trento, was once abducted by the FARC himself and was held hostage in the jungle for eight months. Luckily he was able to convince his abductors that he was not as wealthy as they had initially assumed. Months of negotiations resulted in a reduction of their demands for ransom from 100,000 to 10,000 dollars. During his time there, he had taught his three heavily armed guards – 16-year-old youths who changed shifts every eight hours – not only how to read and write, but also how to cook Italian food.

At the beginning of the sixteenth century, around 80 million people lived in both Americas between Alaska and Patagonia – one-fifth of the world's population at the time. It is estimated today that the indigenous population declined by 95 per cent in the first 130 years after contact with the conquerors – they were all but eliminated. Although some historians consider Henry Dobyn's estimate to be too high,[2] it is generally accepted today that a genocide of inconceivable dimensions took place in Latin America.

> Five centuries ago there were about a thousand different cultures, which means hundreds of different languages, mythologies, religions, family structures, traditional dresses, styles of architecture, rituals, sciences and ideologies. Today there are maybe still 170 independent cultures in the whole of Latin America. The others have been lost for ever.

Thus writes Roberto Gambini,[3] a Brazilian sociologist and psychoanalyst, who is trying to imagine the psychological consequences of the 'expulsion of the Indios' for the following generations.[4] The Spanish and Portuguese conquerors treated indigenous men and women in different ways. The men were enslaved and often died after just a few years – either from the consequences of their slave labour in the silver and gold mines, where quicksilver was used extensively, or through epidemics or suicide. The indigenous women passed into the ownership of the white men, who – unlike the North American invaders – had come without their own families. Thus, today's inhabitants of the southern continent have the following family constellation in their family trees: a mother who had to break with her culture and tradition and could therefore fulfil her motherly function only in a limited way, and a father who was barely interested in the many children he had conceived with different women. Even if many of these indigenous women were able to fulfil their instinctive maternal role despite their depressions, they remained inferior and defeated in the eyes of their children – particularly their sons. This is an impediment for a positive relationship. 'Children have a natural tendency to identify with success, with things that work and that deserve to be imitated.'[5] The fathers were such figures with which the children could identify, because they belonged to the ruling class. But they had mostly been involved only in conceiving the children and never developed into husbands. What is more, the children were mestizos – the fathers could not have taken their children back to Europe without feeling ashamed of them.

In his book 'Open Veins of Latin America',[6] the Uruguayan author Eduardo Galeano writes about how the consequences of this initial exploitation have never ceased to influence the entire continent.

The psychological state of the 'New World's' inhabitants has been shaped by violence, depression, powerlessness and great difficulty developing a feeling of belonging. We know from psychoanalysis that emotional structures can be passed down from generation to generation. The less this communication takes place on a cognitive level, the more direct it is. We can picture these people's collective soul – their common psychological state – like a geographical map with gaps: vast areas of something that cannot be named, thereby creating insecurity and fear.

Are traces of this still detectable in today's modern psychological life? A certain subtle form of violence which many people inflict upon themselves in modern, affluent societies could be seen as such an unconscious long-term consequence of old psychological injuries.

The book *Sin tetas no hay paraíso* ('Without Tits There is No Paradise'), which appeared in Colombia in 2008 and quickly became a best-seller,[7] describes how countless young girls habitually undergo cosmetic surgery as soon as they have saved up the necessary amount of money for their next operation. Today's 18-year-old girls do not want books or trips abroad for their birthdays, they want their noses, lips, breasts, stomachs and hips surgically corrected. This applies equally to university students as well as to women with a high income. It makes no difference if the women are of indigenous heritage or of Spanish descent or both, if they belong to the ambitious middle class or to a lower class on the brink of losing their livelihoods: the compulsiveness with which they model their bodies is always the same. Their bodies are flawed in their eyes. They need to be adjusted to match a certain pattern, otherwise they will not fulfil their purpose. Such behaviour can have deeper motivations than each single individual's conscious decision simply to want to look better. Conspicuously sexualized young women give the impression of offender and victim being united in the same person: a form of self-aggression which is, however, not perceived as such. The image of bleeding to death, which Galeano chose for the economic and political exploitation of Latin America, could also apply to this widespread South American phenomenon.

On top of this there is the absence of a fatherly figure in the children's upbringing, which is also connected with the behaviour just described. When something exceptional and very unexpected happens, people in Mexico call out 'Padre!' It is as if this word were the epitome of something that usually does not occur in daily life.

For the first sandwork project that took place in a Colombian city in September 2009, six children were chosen from a total of twenty families who were being cared for by the Comunidad de Sant'Egidio.[8] We tried to ascertain what role the fathers played in these families and found that not a single one of the almost fifty children in these families could rely on a father who lived permanently in the same household. The exception was a 5-year-old girl whose drug-addicted parents had been arrested and whose grandfather had been nominated as her guardian. This grandfather, however, had sexually abused the girl when she was 3 years old.

But what are the consequences of this absence of men in the children's upbringing? In North America a significant correlation has been established between absent fathers and criminal behaviour in sons.[9] When such a lack of a fatherly principle becomes normality, it is only a short step more towards a normality of criminal behaviour. This applies not only to the lives of individual young people, but also to society as a whole.

As always in human history there is also another side to the coin, a counter-current: the explosive force of expressiveness emerging from people who are suppressed, a force which seems to contradict whatever tragic prophecies that may have been made. The fact that Latin American writers, painters, architects, musicians and directors have not only influenced the world's art scene but actually shaped it, probably requires no further explanation. From the countless examples I would just like to mention the huge number of classical music talents currently emerging from Latin American youth orchestras.[10]

The amalgamation of different cultural elements in colonial architecture and artisanry is a constant source of fascination. Something that claimed such an inconceivable sacrifice in peoples' ultimately unsuccessful attempt to live together nevertheless left ineradicable traces in art. Mexican baroque churches of the seventeenth century contain countless inconspicuous, syncretistic depictions which were made by indigenous artists working under commission of the clergy. The longer that one gazes at the delicately carved gold ornaments in a cathedral's interior, the more they begin to transform into a tangle of lianas in a tropical rain-forest penetrated by rays of light. The figure of an angel on the outer wall of a church proclaims the good news. The angel's coiling banner takes on an almost secret three-dimensional form where its folds end. Upon closer inspection, in the shadow of the overhanging roof, this assumes the form of the snake-like body of Quetzalcoatl, the feathered dragon-god of the Aztecs.

There is a fantastical, magical and spiritual side to life on the entire continent, not only among artists but also among farmers and craftsmen. It influences modern-day political and economic decisions. Sometimes it stands in the way of real progress, but sometimes it also prevents bad decisions from being made in the name of progress.[11]

Such a fantastical component in the sand images of Colombian children, in the form of multifaceted and frequently contradictory narrative levels, often surprised and sometimes confused us therapists: buried treasures need to be kept secret although they have long since been plundered, generally peaceful pets suddenly attack humans, people's living quarters are ruled by rats and spiders, and one keeps encountering abandoned babies and little children. There are guerrilleros everywhere, in homes and far away; they are frightening, but can also arouse a longing for adventure and discipline.

The underlying connections between children's symbolic depictions and the actual social and political situations in their countries cannot be overlooked.

Latin America's vast mineral resources are dumped on the world market at dirt-cheap prices instead of being processed in new industries. Spectacular ecological diversity is forced to make way to monocultures and social utopias have become stuck in a dead end. The *campesinos*, the small farmers who never wanted anything else than to work their own land, have always been and still always are the victims. Of course they are no longer sent down into the silver mines as slaves, but they crowd the cities in a futile search for work after having lost their debt-ridden patch of earth to huge companies. They are the parents and grandparents of today's neglected children.

When I asked for DVDs about Colombia in a store, the obliging young salesperson asked me an apparently routine question: 'Violence or tourism?' How deeply cynicism, indifference and cruelty can be rooted even in a society's hierarchies of power, is illustrated by an example from Colombia: the events surrounding the *falsos positivos* in the summer of 2008, which received very little attention in European media. The scandal led to the resignation of twenty-seven Colombian military officials, three of them generals.

A group of young men looking for work in Soacha, a poor area in the south of Bogotá, were offered seasonal work in another part of Colombia. Not one of these young men, who were driven away in a truck that same day, ever returned home again. Their families searched for them in vain over the next weeks and months. At more or less the same time in Ocaña, a little village in the north of Colombia, the military was able to boast a great success in their war against guerrillas. They had succeeded in killing a particularly large number of guerrilla fighters during one combat mission. Although autopsies showed that each of the under-age guerrilla fighters had died from a shot in the neck, the officers nevertheless stated that they had been heavily armed and killed in combat. The quota of killed rebels had been met and there were bonus payments for all involved.

In this case, the Commission for Human Rights was finally able to determine the true identity of the alleged guerrilleros – the population had already been reporting similar mysterious disappearances for years. They were the jobless young men from Soacha.

Living out violence compared to expressing it in sandwork

The following account comes from a psychologist who worked in a private, but publicly financed care centre for street children in a Colombian city. There are many such institutions today, which all follow very different pedagogical ideals and criteria. Some are run by the church, others by private organizations. The ideal behind the day-care centre and boarding home described here was that neglected children and young people need to feel above all else that they are loved and accepted. The centre's founders were convinced that it was sufficient to offer children physical closeness, hugs and trust in order to overcome behavioural disorders. No form of psychological treatment was deemed necessary. There had already been a number of conflicts between the centre's administrators and the psychologist working there, who did not share this view. The psychologist recounts an example:

A 17-year-old boy had sought acceptance into the care centre. He wanted to live there at least for this one last year, because when he turned 18 this would no longer be possible. The psychologist asked him about his motivations and he explained that he didn't really have any personal problems; the only thing was that he had killed a boy from an enemy gang the day before and that the boy's friends were now looking for him. The psychologist insisted that the boy be denied acceptance – and she won through. She was not prepared to have the other children's lives put in danger by the boy's presence. One of her colleagues, who had advocated accepting the boy, took him home and hid him in his house for a year. On his eighteenth birthday, when he finally dared go 'outside' again for the first time, the boy was killed.

This principle of unconditional acceptance for which the institute's management strived was an advantage for some children. But it was of no use to the aggressive children and adolescents. On the contrary, they became an increasing danger to the younger children.

Juan was one such violent boy. Although he was only 8 years old, even the adults were afraid of him. He spoke with no one and came to the day-care centre only for meals. Even the most harmless objects turned into weapons in Juan's hands. He had already injured two younger children so badly that they needed to be taken to the emergency ward of the hospital.

The psychologist insisted on doing therapy work with Juan. She had heard of sandplay therapy and had read quite a bit about it. One day she brought a wooden box with sand and some play figures to the day-care centre. Within moments Juan had claimed the sandbox and figures entirely for himself. No other child dared approach when he was there.

Juan began using the sandtray in the way that children would normally play. But he had no idea of the play content that would usually be considered normal. His play probably corresponded precisely to what he had learnt so far in his life. He threw a handful of animals into the sand and began stabbing them with his knife, one at a time. The psychologist watched from a distance, sitting at her desk. The game was over for Juan once all the animals lay scattered across the sand. He left the room – but not without first telling the psychologist that he would play with the sand again the next day. It was the first time he had ever directed words at anyone in the day-care centre.

From that day on, he left the other children alone. Juan's killing of animals in the sandtray, which had struck the psychologist as a kind of ritual, continued in more or less the same way. After a week his play began to change slightly. Juan no longer killed the animals himself; they now fought against each other. This was an enormous step in the direction of assimilating his aggressions. He was no longer the executor but had delegated his aggressions to symbolic representatives. He was no longer involved directly but had put some distance between himself and his destructive behaviour; he was an observing third party, as it were. A new level on which to carry out the conflict had appeared inside him. We recall that expression within a free and protected space already *is* change.

Simple tolerance of his destructive behaviour on the part of the adults could not lead to improvement, because this had left the boy alone with his aggressive impulses. Graphic depiction of the same behaviour, on the other hand, within a free and protected play space and in the presence of an interested adult, had an important effect. As long as his destructiveness was *acted* (he disturbed and attacked the other children), it persisted without change. However, as soon as his destructive behaviour could be *represented*, it required only a few repetitions for a new level of expression to develop by itself.

Juan continued playing. He began to build traps with which he could capture the animals. Later he built cages to house the animals. They were no longer killed; on the contrary, they were given food and water so that they could survive. The cages were furnished with everything that an animal in captivity might need. Juan's provoking behaviour had vanished. The other educators were astonished and the institute's management became interested in sandplay.

Juan's aggressions returned only when someone else dared approach the sandtray in his presence. The psychologist tried to integrate his play into a protecting and structuring framework by determining fixed times for the sessions. Juan responded to this initiative and had even started to become more communicative. One day he was working in the sand and asked for water because he wanted to make a lake. Unfortunately the psychologist was not able to grant his wish; her working conditions in the day-care centre were precarious in every respect and she didn't even have access to a water tap. So Juan made a suggestion: 'We could paint the inside of the sandtray blue, then it would be easy to make a lake.' If Margaret Lowenfeld hadn't already thought of that herself, 8-year-old Juan in Colombia would have done so without difficulty.

Once the other educators' initial astonishment at Juan's progress had subsided, their ideological attitudes prevailed once more and eventually destroyed everything that the therapeutic work had created between the therapist and Juan.

The institute's directors thought that Juan ought to share his sandplay with the other children. They did not regard it as progress if a child communicated with only one single adult. This view may be quite justified in education generally, but it came at the wrong time in Juan's situation. In his current phase of development he was not yet able to share his sandwork. The psychologist believed that it would require only a little more time before Juan would also start making progress in his social skills.

Unfortunately she was unable to assert herself in many points, and this was one of them. Her differences with the directors came to a head: an entire system of beliefs appeared to be at stake. She was told that even a boy like Juan needed to experience that love and generosity alone could solve psychological problems.

The psychologist saw no option but to quit her job. She informed Juan of her decision. The boy said: 'You can go if you want, as long as the sandtray stays here'. The sandtray did stay there but, as one might imagine, it lost its function. Juan couldn't have known that this would happen. By the time the psychologist paid the day-care centre a visit one month later, the sandtray and the figures had disappeared into a store room. Juan no longer came even for meals.

The psychologist, who now coordinates sandwork projects, has since asked around in Juan's barrio – his quarter – to try to find him again, but in vain.

Healing sleep

I will now describe a series of sandwork sessions which took place in a children's day-care centre, where neglected children from the city's barrios are cared for.

Daniel is the youngest in a group of six children. He is 5 years old. He lives with his grandmother and his elder brother in a narrow back yard, which is shared by three families. The brother has cancer and is being treated with chemotherapy. Daniel doesn't speak. If absolutely necessary he communicates with gestures. His brother confirmed that he is, however, able to speak.

We ask ourselves if Daniel will be able to engage in this new group situation. He does in fact know the other children, but they are all older. He also knows Maria, a volunteer helper who looks after the children in the day-care centre every Saturday. We believe it could be advantageous for Daniel if Maria were to stay in the room for at least the first sandwork session.

The children have already taken their seats in front of the sandtrays; some have started playing with the sand, others are standing around the table where the figures have been placed. Meanwhile Daniel is standing motionless near the door with a defiant look on his face. His hands are buried in his pockets while he observes the other children, but his gaze keeps returning to his untouched sandtray. Ten minutes go by. He appears to have something in his pocket, a small object maybe, which he is constantly moving about. This is the only visible expression of his inner tension. After a while Daniel rubs his eyes. He looks deeply unhappy. Those adults who are sitting further away from him are convinced that he is crying. Later they say that they hardly had the heart to leave the child standing there looking so sad and alone. A therapist sitting close to him, on the other hand, thinks that something might be causing his eyes to sting, and so she offers him eye drops. He accepts them gladly. Maria asks Daniel for the third time – contrary to all instructions we had previously agreed on – if he wouldn't like to play in the sand after all. The stance that we strive at in sandwork is quite the opposite of such an intervention: first we try to accept whatever happens by itself, even if it isn't exactly what we expect and even if we find it hard to do so. In this case we had to accept the fact that Daniel couldn't play. Encouraging him even more only seemed to have the opposite effect anyhow.

Having the freedom to say 'No' at first is often the condition for being able to say 'Yes' to something later. In a sandwork session we let the child's psyche take the lead. We assume that something in the child knows what the child needs. This attitude prevents premature intervention, but in some cases doesn't exactly make the whole thing easier to bear.

After a while – almost as if Daniel has realized that his 'No' had been accepted – the little object suddenly falls out of his pocket to the ground. It is a coin, and it now rolls directly towards his therapist, who is sitting alone on a stool next to the sandtray. She picks up the coin and hands it back to Daniel. A few minutes later the coin falls to the floor again and this time it appears to find its way to the therapist on purpose. Once more she picks up the coin and hands it back to Daniel. While the other children continue playing, the sound of the coin falling to the floor in regular intervals almost starts to have a rhythmic quality to it. Daniel has started to partake in his own way. After about 20 minutes of this, he starts to look very tired and somewhat troubled. I ask him if he would like to sit down. Daniel answers by nodding his head, and he takes a seat. After a while he looks like he is barely able to keep himself from sliding off the chair. Every fibre in his body seems to be calling out to be held, so I ask him if he would like to sit on the therapist's lap. One must consider that Daniel had never met either the therapist or me before that day. But he nods, and the therapist lifts him on to her lap. As he is sitting there with her on the chair, his back leaned against her, he looks just like a few-months-old baby. He is apparently in the process of returning to his early childhood. After a while the therapist puts her arms around him, just like one would hold a very small child. She tries to synchronize her breathing with his, and after a few minutes he falls asleep. His facial expression is reminiscent of infants in deep sleep, content and satisfied. The other children have already begun to explain their sand images to the therapists, the finished images have been photographed and every-thing has already been cleared away – yet Daniel is still fast asleep. Only then do we wake him. It takes a while for Daniel to comprehend where he is and what is happening. After a meal, which he and the other children eat together, Daniel – to everyone's astonishment – says that he had a dream. He had been in a house and the therapist had been there as well.

For Daniel, the free and protected space of the sandwork group had become a place for necessary regression. In just two hours he had been able to return to his infancy and had made up for a missed experience. A feeling of 'being accepted' by his strange environment must have set in when his coin rolled to the therapist. The experience that actions can have an effect is one of the basic identity-forming experiences in early childhood. Small children find it irresistibly captivating to discover that an effect results from their own actions, for example that a light will go on when a light switch is pushed. It tells them something like: 'I exist! I am, because I have an effect on something.' Another important experience for young children is that their physical needs can be understood by adults. Children thereby learn to perceive and understand these needs themselves, and can then begin to react adequately to them. Young children often do not *know* that they are tired or cold or hungry. They might only sense a general state of unease, which can often be connected with feelings of emptiness and fear. In Daniel's case, for example, it took an adult to know that his eyes were stinging, that his legs were tired from standing, that the sandtray felt strange and that Daniel envied the other children. Emotionally neglected children are not used to being aware of their own inner states and feelings, which is why it is often difficult for them to desire change. An emotionally deprived child will rarely try to change his or her situation.[12] Daniel was swaying between desire and apathy during that session. The fact that an adult had realized this conflict had finally allowed him to 'relax' into a dimension hitherto unknown to him. This is illustrated by Daniel's dream: the house and the therapist are his newly found protection.

We thought it safe to assume that Daniel would already be better prepared for the next session. Nevertheless we also expected that his regressions might continue, so we brought along a blanket for him to cuddle up in. We also placed Daniel's sandtray on the floor so that he could sit and play there if he preferred. We placed a little basket next to the tray with which he could get his miniature figures from the table. That way he would have to go and stand only once at the table with all the other children choosing their miniatures. At the beginning of the session Daniel initially stayed standing at the door again. The therapist showed him the basket and asked him if he would like to go with her to the table to choose play material. He accepted and stayed very close to her as he quickly placed a few random cars in the basket. Then he sat down in front of his sandtray on the floor, his basket with the cars beside him. He took one of the cars in his hand and looked at it for a long time. Daniel kept looking for eye contact with the therapist, as if he were asking for her permission, but eventually he placed the car in the sand. The therapist was relieved. Daniel had caught up to the other children: he began to play.

Before we come to the descriptions of further sandwork sessions I would like to make some general comments on the play behaviour of Colombian children and on how this behaviour can be understood.

From everything that has been said so far, it should be self-evident that the assisting adult cannot expect a coherent story to be told in the course of play. The content of play will be far more like something that we know from our own dreams: fragments, contradictory and illogical themes, shifts in time, and confusion of different places and people.

If we expect a continuous narrative in sandwork, introverted children will feel overwhelmed by our questions, while extroverted children will try to invent a story in order to please us. But we will soon realize that such a story has little or nothing to do with what would have been depicted in the sand otherwise.

Thus, the assisting adult needs to record all fragments and unconnected images and scenes, but without wanting to force them into a logical and rational form by doing so. It is inevitable that the therapist's notes will therefore also be unstructured and fragmentary. The method that therapists choose to record the process differs greatly from one to another. Some find it important to allow their own flow of thoughts to run free, and to write down everything as it comes to them. Others prefer to write down only what they believe they have already understood. Others draw many little diagrams recording the course of play, because they find it easier to remember things visually.

What are we actually trying to record? Basically it is the child's interaction with everything that he or she encounters during the sandwork session: the sand, the sandtray, the play figures, the group, the therapist. Naturally we also pay attention to the constantly changing dynamics of relationship in the sandwork image itself: which figures are communicating with each other, which ones are fighting, threatening or attacking each other, which ones are friendly, curious or playful, who is looking after whom and who is separated, abandoned, cast out, killed, eaten, excluded or loved and fed by whom.

Not least of all, we observe in the long term how individual themes develop over the course of successive sand images. These themes include forms of instinctive and cultural behaviour unique to humans, like acquiring food and eating, celebration and happiness, rivalry and collaboration, creation and destruction, fighting (for and against something), love, sexuality and family life, religion and ceremonies, death and resurrection.

To order, structure and find protection

During the first sandwork session, we quickly realized that there were nowhere near enough tongue depressors (from the pharmacy) available with which to build all the walls and fences that appeared to be necessary. The children used them in great quantities and we needed to get fresh supplies before the second session. The working atmosphere is greatly disturbed if the children need to worry that there is not enough play material available for all of them. It is better to provide just a few, simple objects but each of them in a sufficient quantity.

Apparently it was important to these children to create clearly separated spaces: for example to separate different animal species from each other, 'so that they don't fight'. They also separated living quarters from roads or partitioned houses into different rooms 'where people could eat' or 'where they sleep'. We knew that most families actually only lived in a single room and that incestuous situations often arose because children and adults slept in the same bed or on the floor. Demarcating, separating and structuring things obviously had a stress-reducing effect for the children (Picture 52). They were trying to counterbalance their environment's material and emotional chaos with order. The strength of these barriers, the amount of time it took a child to build them and the emotions that the adults felt while observing the process allowed us to infer how great a danger for the child emanated from such a place that apparently needed to be walled in. Even if therapists consider all these things and are able to follow them through play, they

Picture 52

will still often be able only to guess at the true meaning of individual newly
created scenes. A bull surrounded by three walls, for example, could pertain to a
concrete outer or to an inner psychological occurrence, or to both (Picture 53). It
could represent a threat posed to the child by a certain adult. But it could also be
the child's own energy and anger that need to be suppressed in order to prevent
the child from becoming exposed to even worse emotional outbursts on the part
of certain adults. Which of the two hypotheses is right will become apparent once
numerous consecutive sessions have taken place and once more has been learnt
about the child's surroundings.

Recognizing psychological connections in a play process can often also happen
all by itself, especially in very dramatic situations. If something wants to be
expressed, it will sooner or later take on a form that can be understood. Children
will not package their problems in riddles or conceal their suffering if there is
even the slightest prospect that someone will listen to them. Children mostly
cannot express their problems in words, they cannot say what they are lacking, but
they can very well express this in play. Everything in a child's body and psyche is
directed at growth and development. No child becomes stuck at a certain age level
or falls back in development unless he or she has run into the most serious and
difficult obstacles that make psychological progress impossible. If such an
obstacle can be removed through a change of structures in the child's environment, the psyche will immediately mobilize all its self-regulating powers and will

Picture 53

quickly catch up on everything that it needs in order to progress. As the examples from South Africa have already shown us, in areas where violence is commonplace, many children's depictions pertain foremost to their real situations. But these terrible experiences are often only hinted at.

Alicia, a 14-year-old girl, used glass mosaic stones to make a lake in the middle of her image. She commented that people drowned there, but said this with a smile, as if she wanted to make it sound harmless. Alicia lives in her grandfather's house together with her three younger cousins. After their parents – both of them heroin addicts – had tried to drown the children in a bath tub, a family court had appointed the grandfather as their custodian. Of course Alicia knew why her cousins were now living with her and her grandfather, and she tried to process the shock in her sandwork. Even if the assisting adult knows this background, it would not be fitting to try to motivate Alicia to talk about it. She has indicated something for the first time and will find a way to continue processing it further – provided her message has been received. It is enough if the therapist does not return Alicia's smile when she is talking about drowning people. The therapist is free to convey his feeling of concern about the fact that people drown in this lake. But he cannot expect that this will directly influence Alicia's attitude. Once more we rely on the fact that the child's psyche 'knows' which themes can be approached when and in what form.

Before we come to the description of the next sandwork sessions, let us first further discuss the therapist's attitude. In the sandwork images of Colombian children, one scene was so quickly followed by the next that it was difficult to keep up. As therapists we are in fact accustomed to really *understanding* only a small part of the sandwork's events as they appear. This can be a frustrating feeling, but it can be counteracted if one practises tuning one's antennae to non-rational and non-analytical perceptions. This is a bit like trying to follow the gist of a conversation in a foreign language intuitively without knowing the actual words. The more one strives at definite 'interpretations', the less satisfying the whole thing will become. If, for example, soldiers appear in play, it may feel tautological to think: 'So this shows the child's aggressions'. It feels better to replace such a labelling attitude with a phenomenological one: soldiers are people who mostly fight an opponent together with other soldiers, sometimes of their own free will but more often because they have to follow orders. Or, what effect does a landscape have, now that there are plants growing in it? Is it refreshing and more alive, or confusing and a little unsettling like a jungle? One should always try to keep an eye open for at least two different, contrary, possible meanings.

If therapists are patient enough, they will surely find access to at least one sequence per session, either on an emotional or a rational level of understanding. This is sufficient. It is not necessary – or indeed even possible – to understand the symbolism behind every element of play, especially when different scenes come in such rapid succession. Themes from previous sessions will often be revisited in the following ones, thus giving the therapist a chance to compare. What can be perceived and understood in any case are children's emotional states, which can be expressed in their facial expressions, gestures, body language, the noises they make and even in their smell.

The horsey has come

I will describe 6-year-old Marcelo's sandwork sessions in a slightly different way than I have described other sessions until now. After a detailed description of Marcelo's first sandwork, I will isolate and describe single, important themes from his further nine sessions. Most of these themes were already hinted at in the first session and developed over the following five months. The themes are *being abandoned as a child* and *parental care; aggression, killing* and *being killed*; and *solidarity* and *friendship*.

Marcelo is one of three children whose mother lived on the streets just a year ago but is now able to earn a living for her children. Her partner lives with her with his two further children, but he does not work. All five children are neglected. Marcelo shows signs of physical maltreatment and his performance at school lags far behind that of other children his age. He often makes an absent impression. During sandwork as well, there are moments in which he seems to forget where he is: he stands in the middle of the room with a play figure in his hand, and appears to be dreaming. As an observer, one has the impression that these are defence mechanisms without which he would not be able to endure the aggressions directed at him from the outside. Displaying these aggressions in play was a great relief for Marcelo, and it enabled him slowly to reopen himself to his environment and thereby also to accept the positive opportunities it offered.

Marcelo begins playing with cars and motorcycles which can be seen at the lower edge of the image. He drives them back and forth. This slow but continuous movement creates a feeling of space and also produces certain roads and pathways that are driven again and again. Next, Marcelo adds excavators, trucks and workmen to the scene. Marcelo has provided each of the workmen with a shovel, all of them the same colour. He does not dig the sand himself but has it dug by the hands of the workmen. This scene is about working and digging downwards. This can be understood in a figurative sense. Psychological work has begun and Marcelo has readied himself with all the necessary tools. Such a beginning is quite astonishing for a child who appears so passive, and it must be considered promising. Marcelo begins to arrange the top half of the sand tray. He places different animals there, especially predators and some black spiders (see plate section: p. 14, Plate 27).

From the therapist's notes:

> I am happy to see him play. He is highly concentrated. I notice how carefully and patiently he places the different figures. He also takes the time to choose his figures carefully. I think of how he was described to me by his teacher, and how she complained that he never did anything. But here I see a child with well-developed mental and motor skills. He is very observant and likes to probe the sand with his fingers. He seems to have a need for things to belong together. If an action is begun, he wants it to be completed. If something falls over or is moved accidentally, he places it back – no matter how often this has to be repeated.

Unexpectedly for the therapist, Marcelo takes two little children's beds with two babies inside them and places them in the lower left corner, as far away from the spiders as possible. He then builds a square wall of bricks around the beds. Then he takes a handful of wooden sticks and pushes them into the sand around the square. A high wall with something like a roof has been created around the tiny children. He seems to be content with this scene and returns his attention to a tower that he had begun earlier.

This tower had already taken him a great deal of effort beforehand. But he seems to have gained new strength from the scene with the children. No matter how often the tower collapses just as it has reached the proper height, Marcelo does not give up. He rebuilds it again and again until it finally stays upright. Now a soldier with a machine gun is to be placed at the top. He too keeps falling down, so Marcelo places just the machine gun on the tower. This means that Marcelo does not cling stubbornly to an impossible undertaking. He can also say to himself, this will do as well. Once more, he seems content.

The session is now almost over and Marcelo has turned back to the two small children in the lower left corner. He has taken away the protective wall and now overturns the two beds with the children inside and pushes them head down into the sand. The therapist feels like she is about to suffocate. Then Marcelo lifts the children back out of the sand – they are unharmed – and places them gently back in their square of bricks and begins to rebuild the wooden stick fence. The therapist notices how Marcelo is anxious to complete everything in time. All the other children have already stood up and left their completed sandwork images. She reassures him that he could still continue working (see plate section: p. 14, Plate 28 (detail)).

In sandwork, the lower left corner has often proven to be the place where something new shows itself for the first time. This is often unconscious content which is crossing the threshold to consciousness for the first time, as it were, in an as yet primitive and raw form.

In Marcelo's case it was something very simple of which he had had a lack in his life until now – a lack which therefore had to be made up for. It is the simple fact that small children require protection.

His sudden act of 'pushing the children into the sand' is probably a story from his own life – the physical and mental maltreatment on the part of adults around him. It is also possible that this was a reaction to the approaching end of the session. His anger that play would now soon be over had let him maltreat the children for just a moment. However, the fact that he was then able to care for the children again himself was the great achievement of this session.

The theme 'early childhood' also appears in another scene in this sandwork. On the right side of the image one sees a pram holding a baby dinosaur and a green dinosaur beside it, looking at the little one (see plate section: p. 15, Plate 29 (detail)).

The little dinosaur in the pram could be figurative of how Marcelo used to feel – and still feels – regarding his infantile needs: not like a human child. This corresponds to his real surroundings. He was only ever given the bare, primitive essentials for survival, as if he were a young animal. At least a dinosaur mother is present, which is surely better than no mother at all. That he was *not* a young animal, however, but a human child, was something that Marcelo must have had to discover all by himself. This achievement is shown by the two babies whom he protected by erecting a fence around them. One could even say that Marcelo – despite being just 6 years old – behaved like a father towards these tiny children (representing his own infantile needs), a father who knows what his children need.

The only sentence that Marcelo uttered, when he was asked if he would like to explain anything in the image, was: 'The horsey came to have a look at the babies, and then it left again.' One can see the horse not far from the pram (see plate section: p. 15, Plate 29 (detail)).

Thereby, he has expressed what appears to be of primary importance to him: that the babies' existence be witnessed. Not only by the therapist and himself – who both belong to the outside world – but also by a symbolic representative in the sandwork itself, a figure from his inner, psychological reality. A lasting change can take place only on this mental level. Play will develop its healing effect only once his conscious person has stepped back and allowed the individual play figures to move about as if autonomously. 'The horsey has come!' One could also imagine that Marcelo's action – gently laying down the babies and erecting a protective wall – attracted the horse (a mental or spiritual energy), as it were. It came to bear witness that the protected babies now really do exist in this reality of the psyche.

This means that a perception of his own infantile neediness appeared for the first time in Marcelo's consciousness. The horse is like a pre-stage to the missing figures of parents. It is the vital force of nature. But it is also more than nature. The horse in Marcelo's play does not behave like a horse in the animal world. It behaves like a horse from a fairy tale, a mythological figure with human qualities. The horse's symbolic significance could be described as 'the spirit inherent in instinctual nature'.

When we speak of a symbol and of something being symbolic, we must remember that we do not mean a sign that can be described in other words, but rather, following C.G. Jung's definition, the best possible expression of an unknown psychological circumstance. A symbol is not 'interpreted' but 'amplified': it is enriched with similar elements from different levels and tentatively placed in different contexts.

We will come back to the further development of this *care* theme in Marcelo's sandwork. But first we will turn to some of the other occurring themes. *Movement and autonomy* seems to be expressed by the many different transport vehicles that appeared to be important to the boy, especially in the first few sessions. They gradually disappear, making way for people and plants. Cars and motorbikes as well as excavators and trucks appeared primarily in the first four sessions, but they appeared to have a different function in the first image than in the third, for example. In the first session, the cars were driven back and forth along the lower edge of the sandtray: to create space through movement was the underlying desire here. In addition to this there was the digging and working in the sand, which expressed how things can be moved and changed with one's own actions. This was a new and important experience for Marcelo in his passive attitude.

In the two following images, the geometric shape that is eventually created by the cars seems to be the more important factor. The cars have altered their level of expression, as it were (see plate section: p. 15, Plate 30). Marcelo uses their movement to create a circle that separates the inside from the outside. In the third image, the apparently aggressive animals – the spiders and the biting cow – are trapped inside the circle. This means quite simply that they can no longer move freely and that they have therefore become less dangerous for all the other figures. For Marcelo himself, this means that he is trying to create an almost magical border around aggressiveness in order to contain it and to protect himself from it. What is more, he is now able to distinguish inwardly his own aggressive impulses from other impulses. Things no longer merge and become mixed up in his emotional life.

The *tower* that Marcelo wanted to build very high in the first sand image, but that kept falling down, represents yet another theme. The tower is already more stable in the second image and in the third there is only a single stick pointing upwards. The fourth image shows another broad and stable tower, and in the following images many smaller towers fit into the overall picture without being conspicuous for their height. For Marcelo, these vertical elements could signify a means of escape from everyday life down below. They could also express his *desire to attain a better overview and a different perspective on things*, or also to see his manliness demonstrated. Marcelo's self-esteem fluctuates between fantasies of grandeur (a huge tower) and a sense of failure (the tower collapses). The machine gun that he was eventually able to place at the top of the tower possibly indicates one of his most powerful and dangerous fantasies: to be able to defend himself from a great height, unreachable by all, and possibly to take revenge for all the wrongs he has experienced.

Another figure that might be related to the tower is the big elephant. *Power* and a *will to assert oneself* seem to emanate from this animal. In one image, the elephant is being ridden by a 'superhero'. This figure can be seen not only as Marcelo's fantasies of his own power and strength, but also as an actual, real psychological potential.

Two quarrelling elephants appear in the seventh image. They mark the beginning of a new important theme: *duality*. For his last four images, Marcelo always spends a long time trying to find animals of which there are two individual figures. This theme eventually develops into the themes of *friendship* and *solidarity*.

These themes express that he now feels strengthened from the inside and – on that basis – is therefore also now able to cooperate and show solidarity with other children.

It is also interesting to observe the *relationships* between the different creatures in Marcelo's play. The depicted relationships between people, animals and plants take place on many different, distinct levels. The first images show biting and eating, fighting, shooting and killing. The over-whelming superiority of the aggressors attacking a single defenceless victim is especially impressive. Then a new form of interpersonal behaviour arises: the figures start to save and protect one another; even a tree's leaves must be protected from an animal wanting to eat them. One creature helps another to find food. Even an animal family already occurs in one of the last images.

One cheerful scene, which appears unchanged and independently from all the others from the second image onwards, has to do with *physical and mental wellbeing*: a colourful fish in a small pond of glass marbles (see plate section: p. 16, Plate 31 (detail) see also Picture 59 detail 1 on p. 162). The tenderness that Marcelo displays when he is playing with this fish, and the happiness that seems to emanate from it, touch the therapist every time. This element can be seen as a psychological representation of an inner wholeness, a spiritual core that Jung termed the 'Self'. The colourful fish in its glistening pond amidst all the chaos, violence and squalor is a symbol in the truest sense of the word, because everything that can be good and beau-tiful in the life of a child 'falls together' in it.[13] Marcelo has hardly experi-enced any of these things in his outside reality, but in his inner life there is still an unharmed, soothing place that – quite like the water surrounding our prenatal state – provides an almost magical protection.

This brings us back to the theme of care. We recall the two scenes that have already been described from the first sand image: the two human babies in their little beds and the little dinosaur in its pram. Precisely where the young dinosaur had been in the first image, there is now a pram containing a human baby in the second image. When looking for a person in the baby's environment with whom he can relate, one finds nothing but a tiger (Picture 59, see also Picture 59 detail 2 on p. 162). A possible explanation for this could be that Marcelo no longer needs to hide his feelings beneath the skin of a dinosaur and can start to feel like a human child, but this brings with it certain new dangers at first. To Marcelo, the aggressiveness of his surroundings may make him feel like being exposed to the eyes of a tiger. At the same time, the second image also introduces the new element we have just encountered – the colourful fish in its pond – which evokes a feeling of comfort and cheerfulness.

In the third sand image one sees another baby in a pram, this time however placed in the upper left corner, in an enclosed space where there are no threats. There are two adults next to the child. Marcelo comments that the woman is telling the man to go to find something for the baby to eat. The

Picture 59

adults obviously stand in some sort of relation to the child, even if there is no direct eye contact. It is the first time that a human figure perceives the baby's existence. Another step of progress is made in the fourth image where, in the centre of the image, there is a woman holding a baby in her arms. (Unfortunately she is hard to see in the photo because she is covered by the elephant.) Marcelo says that she is afraid of the tiger.

This is significant for the baby in the woman's arms because it means that an adult is now caring for him. This adult knows life's dangers and is therefore able to feel the baby's fears in his stead. She can act as a mediator between the child's fears and reality. Finally a psychological situation has been reached, such as a child would have the right to expect in life: it is the precondition for psychological development.

The care theme receives further differentiation in the fifth image. One can see three prams with children inside them. This time there are no adults near by. However – and this is a new element – a bottle of milk has been laid in front of each child. This means that adults had certainly been there at some point and that the children are somehow being nourished. The woman from the last image with the child in her arms can be seen again. This time she tells a large, female figure nearby (a sort of 'super-heroine' with superhuman abilities) to 'look after her baby because she no longer wants it'.

When the real mother no longer can or 'wants to' take care of her child, then a superhuman force should do so: this super-heroine must represent a kind of rescuing angel in Marcelo's imagination. Marcelo says that one of the other babies, sitting in its pram and supplied with a bottle of milk, has been left by his mother and that this stone is now looking after the child.

Apparently, if things are particularly bad, even inorganic matter can assume a kind of maternal role. A mother 'who has left' is still better than no mother at all. We have already seen this in the example of orphaned African children. This is actually the first time that Marcelo ever used the word 'mother' in sandwork. Marcelo is not an orphan, but on the whole he grew up quite like one. Almost no one was ever there to perceive his needs. Compared to the first image, where there was no one but the horse to witness the babies, there is now talk of a mother – even if this mother is particularly defined by her not wanting and having abandoned the child.

Fatherhood is also indicated for the first time in the same image: 'This black and white bull is the son of this other bull, and he would like to meet his father.' As always, since the second image, the colourful little fish is swimming around its pond of glass marbles, weightless and light-hearted, protected and free.

In the second last image one sees another child in a pram, but this time with eye contact to a female figure. Marcelo comments: 'This is this woman's child and she takes care of it.'

The theme of solidarity and the word 'friend' also appear for the first time in the same image. 'This tiger is looking for his friend. This horse is looking for his friend because he has something to eat. This man must find this other man because he is afraid of the enemies.'

And on a prehistoric evolutionary level, there is also something like the earliest form of a normal family in this image: 'This dinosaur is looking for food for its children.'

The fact that Marcelo's life will continue to be characterized by conflict, threat and neglect continued to fill the therapists with feelings of helplessness, sadness and anxiety.

But the following can be achieved and was achieved in this case with sandplay: *apart from* the anger and the feeling of being at the mercy of others, *other* inner dispositions (potentials) of perception were also activated. Marcelo now has the inner freedom to approach another child in friendship. His awareness is no longer restricted to the polarity of being suppressed and being the suppressor. He managed to experience by himself that 'one friend goes looking for another friend', for example. This means that a notion of solidarity has formed in his mental view of the world. This is a central point: it is hard to imagine a form of pedagogic intervention that could have achieved this much in such a short time in a child who is so strongly inhibited. One could, for example, tell a frightened and withdrawn child stories in which children or animals quarrel and fight, but then become friends. Or one could encourage an inhibited child to join other children in playing games in which cooperation is the key to making the best progress, and not rivalry. Would Marcelo have been able to make the best use of such offers? Until now he had used almost his entire mental energy to block as effectively as possible anything approaching him from the outside: he had managed to hide in his apathy. His behaviour at school was the same. What could have convinced him to give up this defensive attitude? Words? Role models?

The immense advantage of sandwork is that a child is never asked to accept anything from the outside. From the first moment onwards Marcelo was allowed to be entirely with himself, to dig for his own resources (like in the first sand image) undisturbed and proceeding at his own speed. What is most impressive about the whole thing – and it is this book's purpose to point this out – is that, without *any* form of direct influence, precisely those forms of behaviour were activated in Marcelo that any parent or educator would have wanted to activate.

Paradoxically, the precondition for this had precisely been an abstinence from any pedagogic stance during the sandwork session; not because this is in itself something that ought to be avoided, but simply because it would not have come at the right time for a child in Marcelo's situation. Every outside input must meet with an inner readiness, otherwise it cannot be integrated.

In the future, if a sports teacher, for example, were to say to Marcelo that it is better to strive for cooperation than for rivalry, Marcelo will intuitively *know* what this adult is talking about, because he has already experienced it inwardly. The same teacher's words might have no effect on other young people who have only ever experienced that the stronger one wins; they will not understand them even if they are punished. But such words can meet with resonance within Marcel, because the idea of friendship *has* already existed there: even more importantly, friendship between two people has in fact already materialized on the level of psychological reality.

If Marcelo's environment should improve even slightly in the future, he will be able to feel like the little fish in the water. If he should become a father, he will be a more caring father than the man with whom he grew up. If, however, his environment should not improve, the fears that Marcelo expressed in his last sand image may become reality.

But first we come to the eighth and penultimate image: there are no more disputes or confrontations among humans or animals. The colourful fish is still in its pond and there is a shell close by. I will recount Marcelo's words directly at this point. On the one hand this should show how clearly new achievements can express themselves and, on the other hand, how difficult it can be to feel one's way into a child's world and how much concentration it takes to understand a child's statements figuratively on a meta-level.

These are the guards of this house.

These animals (an iguana and a bull) are being held captive here because they killed the people.

This big horse is looking for food and these smaller horses have already found food.

This goat is taking care that they don't take away his little ones.

This is the guard of the trees, who is taking care that nobody eats even a single leaf.

The spiders are going past here, but they can't get into the house because it is closed.

This child is the child of this woman.

This woman is the mother of these babies and, so that he can't steal them, she hides the children with her horn.

This fish drinks water and spouts it out again.

This man repairs cars and washes them.

This dog is going on holidays with the bag. Where to? To the animals.

This child says that when that person over there has stopped killing, then he will go and take away his bullets.

In the last session, Marcelo seems to sum up everything that he has achieved so far. Unfortunately, after five months the children's stepfather could no longer be persuaded to bring Marcelo and his sisters to the sandwork sessions. Marcelo knew that this would be his final session.

He begins with four palm trees, each one standing in a different corner of the sandtray. Then he places churches, bushes and some people along the edges. He then uses wooden blocks and sticks to make a barrier which encloses a large square space with a kind of corridor leading around its outside. The inside space has a further separation – and also a bridge – between people and animals. Again, Marcelo tried to find as many of the animals as possible in pairs. All of the shells are made up of two parts and he placed a little stone in each of them (see plate section: p. 16, Plate 32).

There are no more babies or little children.

There are soldiers, who 'want to kill the animals, but the people prevent this.'

Only the caiman has become more dangerous: 'he pretends to be a toy, but when the horse comes by, looking for food, the caiman eats it.'

The therapist is struck by this statement in particular. What makes this scene so frightening is that the threat is directed especially at children. One cannot even trust toys, which means there is no safety in life whatsoever, not even in childhood. The horse that is searching for food – probably an expression of Marcelo's newly achieved vitality – must beware of an animal on a lower evolutionary level: at any moment, primitive impulses could destroy a differentiated attitude to life that is orientated along emotions and towards relationship.

But the caiman's cunning, his wilful disguise and deceit, can also be seen from another aspect: Marcelo may have become less naive and more cunning in his behaviour. Will both the horse and the caiman – vitality and destructive force – be able to coexist inside him?

'The lower animal will eat the one on the higher evolutionary level of development, if it isn't careful.' If one relates this statement of Marcelo's to the entire cultural history of humanity, then Marcelo is not entirely alone with his fear.

The educators were able to confirm without doubt that Marcelo had become more open and active during the five months of his sandwork.

Picture 59 detail 1

Picture 59 detail 2

Chapter 10

Practical instructions for an Expressive Sandwork project

A self-contained project consisting of a *series of four sandwork sessions* in a group of four to eight children is helpful in emergency situations (for example as a means of crisis intervention after an earthquake). Such a project can take place in just ten days – including team discussions and supervisions of every single sandwork. A therapist coming from outside is thus able to carry out such a project,[1] but the therapist must ensure that the assistants (facilitators) receive enough training and preparatory work that they can continue working independently – provided an *online supervision* is guaranteed throughout.

In situations of chronic destitution, a self-contained series of four sessions is both a *short-term therapy* and *diagnostic assessment* at the same time. After four sandplay sessions, one is generally able to tell which children will be able to make further steps of development by themselves, and which children would require further psychological help or some different form of care.

Indication

All people of at least 3 years of age, who are in any way 'difficult', can participate. There is no real contraindication for Expressive Sandwork, of neither a psychiatric nor a psychological nature. The only condition is that a participating person must be able to let the rest of the group be undisturbed in their work.

Material

Sandtrays made of wood or plastic containing slightly moist, fine-grained, clean sand are required. Light blue, rectangular tubs can often be found in shops selling household goods or photography accessories. The *miniatures* or other play objects should be chosen by the fact that they, for the most part, *occur in the children's everyday lives*.

What is needed in any case: large amounts of stones, simple building material, bits of metal (wheels, screws, nails), wooden blocks, string, vegetation (leaves, pine cones, roots, seeds, branches – these can all be freshly collected on the day), shells and bottle corks. One also requires objects that represent humans and animals and, if available, human and animal babies, fighting people (soldiers), as well as protective and frightening figures.

Of course the objects will vary depending on geographical or practical circumstances, but it is important that *no new material be added or taken away* during the four sessions. An exception is made when one replenishes material or increases the amount of a certain material of which there had been too little in the previous session.

The objects are placed either along a wall or on a table in the middle of the room, so that they can be reached easily by all children at any time without disturbing anyone else in the process. The different *categories* should be separated as well as possible so that things are clear and that no child need search too long for what he or she wants.

Room

Sandwork in a group can take place in any kind of room, or even outdoors if there is no other possibility. The distances between the trays depend on the size of the room. The important factor is that every child has a private space, and that the children are not able to observe each other's play too easily, but that each child nevertheless should be aware of the group and able to feel protected by it. It is optimal if the children can work on all four sides of their trays if they wish.

The children can sit in front of their sandtrays if there are enough stools, or they can stand. Some of the sandtrays should be variable in their height, so that smaller children can still work comfortably. Should this not be possible, the sandtray can be placed on the floor.

Each individual facilitator remains seated or standing close to his or her appointed child. The facilitators should not change their position during the course of the sessions. If, for some reason, they should nevertheless have to change their position, this fact should be recorded in the notes. It has proven beneficial for the *facilitator* to be *positioned at the upper right corner of the sandtray* (from the child's point of view). Each child is always free to talk quietly to his or her facilitator. The children will usually tell their facilitator when they have finished their sand image and, if they wish, they can then explain their image, while the facilitator listens intently, takes notes and perhaps asks open questions. *Each child must have the same facilitator throughout all of the sessions.*

Technical equipment

A digital camera is important; computer and printer are useful because the pictures can then be immediately printed and discussed. If possible, it is better to photograph the sand images without using a flash. The images are photographed from the position where the child had been working. If a child was working on all four sides, this should be mentioned in the notes.

Writing pads with a solid back are useful, because notes often have to be taken while standing. Colour pens, pencils and paper, or play dough could be provided for the children who are finished before the others.

Introductory words

Before the children take their positions at the sandtrays, the group receives a brief introduction to the procedure. What is said in detail depends on many different variables. Because sandwork – no matter whether it takes place in a group or individually – is always about the relationship between the player and the therapist, this introduction should not be merely about giving a standard explanation of a set of rules. Rather, the words should be chosen carefully in each individual situation to help create an atmosphere in which the 'free and protected space' can best be established. Some therapists prefer to hold a longer introduction, while others say just the bare minimum. The introduction must be suited to the social and cultural ways of the given geographic location. Whenever the head therapist is an outsider, a foreigner working with local facilitators, it has proven beneficial for someone else who is familiar with the children's social surroundings to speak the opening words: this person will also be more familiar with the children's own vocabulary.

It suffices to tell younger children that this will be a *game in which everyone can create their own world*. One might add that some children may take longer to know what and how they want to play, while others may know immediately what they need. But neither the one nor the other is better or worse and nothing is beautiful or ugly. One is allowed to do anything one can think of, except throw sand out of the sandtray, destroy things wilfully, or disturb others. There should be no speaking among the children, but the children are always free to talk quietly to their facilitator if they require something.

One can tell older children that they will have the *opportunity to learn something about themselves*, to express things that are rarely spoken about, like worries or wishes. They will be able to create their own worlds – the word 'play' might not be entirely suitable for adolescents – or can simply do whatever they think of, without having to worry about knowing why: just have fun. When they have finished, they are free to explain to their facilitator what they have created and how they felt while doing so. In the end – after all four sessions – each child will again have a chance to talk to his or her facilitator individually about the four sessions, or about other things.

Time and memory

An hour, or one and a half hours at most, should be reserved for sandwork itself – including individual explanations of the sand images. After this, there is time for photographing and clearing up. This should not be done by the children themselves, and should only be begun once the last child has left the room.

When taking the photos, it is a good idea to write down immediately which photo goes with which child. Even if therapists initially believe they will surely be able to remember the content of a child's sandplay, and especially by which child it was made, this impression can be misleading. Even experienced therapists often forget important scenes, especially if there are a lot of processes and images within just a few days. It may have to do with the very special form of observation and listening that takes place in a semi-conscious state and is therefore not as readily accessible to conscious memory. It is important not to overestimate one's powers of recollection and to take *precise notes*.

Notes

As ever, a maximum of individuality in one's approach also goes for the way one takes notes. It can be helpful to separate each *page of notes* into at least *two columns*. One column is for objective observation, for example which figures are placed in the sand in what order, or how the child works. The other column is reserved for the facilitator's own subjective impressions, thoughts and feelings that are aroused by what is happening in the sand. What should also be noted here, for example, is how concentrated the facilitators felt themselves to be or what distracted them. Diagrams of the sand image can also be drawn. After the image is completed, the facilitator tries to write down the child's explanations as exactly as possible in the child's own words, as well as recording the manner in which the child explains or does not explain.

When taking notes, as with so many other factors, one tries to find the right balance midway between an obsessive recording of every smallest detail and the conveyance of a vague, general impression. A printed photo is attached to the notes of every session.

Discussing the sand images

At the end of the four sessions, the photos and notes of the individual sand images are *discussed in the team*. One will often be able to perceive a development from initial chaos to some first rudimentary – or even quite differentiated – structures. Apart from the development that can be read in the sand images, the *focus* of these discussions also lies on the facilitator's subjective *thoughts, feelings and emotional sensations*. It can occur that a facilitator may feel called upon to take concrete actions outside of sandplay to help the child assigned to him or her. Impulses such as these must also be questioned.

Limits

A special situation arises when children show progress during the first two or three sessions, but undo these achievements in the later sessions. In these cases, we can assume that the children are trapped in an outside situation which they cannot overcome by themselves, and in which they cannot allow themselves such a fantasy of development. To maintain their equilibrium, defence mechanisms are activated (e.g. identification with the aggressor, or displacement). The psyche has learned that it is better to have no hope at all than to have one's hopes disappointed. Thus, children who indicate development in the first images, only to destroy it all in the last one, are especially in need of urgent help. Paying a home visit is particularly called for in these cases to clarify whether there is a persistent source of acute traumatization involved, for example continuous abuse or a constant threat to the child's life.

In some cases it is difficult to understand what it is that a child needs. This can be the case when a child does not seem to feel like playing, or tends towards disturbing the other children. Such children might require a different kind of approach. They may first need to be strengthened on their ego-level, for example by learning a skill; making or repairing things, sports, sewing, painting or making music may be more appropriate in such cases.

Training

Volunteers can be trained within any such project. They are not assigned a child at first, but observe the group as a whole and carry out assisting work, for example setting up, taking down and sorting play material and sandtrays, and caring for the children who either do not want to play in the sand or have already finished their images. The volunteers also take part in the team discussions.

Expressive Sandwork involves a *great expenditure of practical work*. One must repeatedly set up and take down the sandtrays, transport bags of sand, and arrange the miniatures on tables and then clear them away again. On top of this, there is documentation: every session must be recorded in notes or drawings, every sand image must be photographed at the end of each session, transferred to a computer, printed out, and sorted together with the hand-written notes.

Nevertheless, the experience for psychology students is hard to surpass. There are not many situations in which they can learn as much theory and practical work in such a short time. The training of facilitators includes an entrance interview with two therapists, a minimum of four sandplay sessions in the role of the 'patient', about forty hours of theory, participation in one sandplay project as an observer and in a further project as facilitator for a child, and joining in the team discussions of both sessions under the supervision of the therapist. Finally, the facilitator must write a case report about the sandworks of the assisted child.

Information on Expressive Sandwork projects and training of facilitators can be found in the website of the International Association for Expressive Sandwork (www.sandwork.org).

Notes

I The social aspect of psychoanalysis: Freud's polyclinic

1 Freud, S., 'Wege der psychoanalytischen Therapie', Internationaler Kongress für Psychoanalyse, Budapest, 28 September 1918, *Internationale Zeitschrift für Psychoanalyse*, 1919, 5 (2): 61–68, in *Gesammelte Werke*, 1947, Vol. 12: 183–194. Freud, S., 'Lines of advance in psychoanalytic psychotherapy', 1918, in *The Standard Edition of the Complete Psychological Works of Sigmund Freud*, Vol. 17, p. 164.
2 'They now think that they can use us for practical purposes but they appear to have no sense of the value of a scientific study of war neuroses.' Lou Andreas-Salomé (4 October 1918) from Sigmund Freud Chronology (1918), Sigmund Freud Museum Vienna, Vienna IX, Berggasse 19.
3 Sanitätsbericht über das deutsche Heer im Weltkriege 1914–1918, Vol. 3: Heeressanitätsinspektion des Reichswehrministeriums (ed.) *Die Krankenbewegung bei dem deutschen Feld- und Besatzungsheer*, Berlin, 1934, 145 (German army medical report from First World War).
4 Binswanger, O., 'Die Kriegshysterie', in O. v. Schjerning (ed.) *Handbuch der ärztlichen Erfahrungen im Weltkriege 1914–18*, Vol. 4: K. Bonhoeffer (ed.) *Geistes- und Nervenkrankheiten*, Leipzig, 1922.
5 Eitingon, M., 'Bericht über die Berliner Psychoanalytische Poliklinik (März 1920 – Juni 1922)', *Internationale Zeitschrift für Psychoanalyse*, 1922, 8: 506–520.
6 Ferenczi's talk at the Fifth International Congress in Budapest also dealt with a new form of analysis, which he called 'active therapy'. It was later incorporated by the Berlin Polyclinic under the name 'fractionary analysis'.
7 Freud, 'Lines of advance in psychoanalytic psychotherapy', p. 167.
8 *Zehn Jahre Berliner Psychoanalytisches Institut (Poliklinik und Lehranstalt) 1920 bis 1930*, Internationaler Psychoanalytischer Verlag, Vienna, 1930.
9 Eitingon, M., 'Report of the Berlin Psycho-Analytical Polyclinic, March 1920 – June 1922', *International Journal of Psycho-Analysis*, 1923, 4: 254–269.
10 Aerztliche Reform-Zeitung ('Doctors' Reform Newspaper'), *A Psychoanalytic Ambulatorium in Vienna*, Vols 9–10, Archiv des Psychoanalytischen Ambulatoriums, Vienna, 1922, p. 49.
11 Danto, E.A., *Freud's Free Clinics: Psychoanalysis and Social Justice, 1918–1938*, Columbia University Press, New York, 2005, p. 126.
12 Steward, R., Unpublished interview, in E.A. Danto, 'The Ambulatorium: Freud's free clinic in Vienna', *International Journal of Psycho-Analysis*, 1998, 79 (2): 287–300.
13 In 1925, he published *Wayward Youth*, where he describes the successes of the psychoanalytical technique in treating criminal adolescents in youth centres (Ober-Hollabrunn from 1918 to 1920 and St Andrä from 1920 to 1922). Aichhorn, A., *Wayward Youth*, Viking, New York, 1925.

14 Frank, C., *Melanie Klein in Berlin: Her First Psychoanalysis with Children*, New Library of Psychoanalysis, General Editor D. Birksted-Breen, Routledge, London, 2009.

15 Frank, C., *Melanie Kleins erste Kinderanalysen: Die Entdeckung des Kindes als Objekt sui generis von Heilen und Forschen*, Frommann-Holzboog, Stuttgart, 1999.

16 Frank, *Melanie Kleins erste Kinderanalysen*, p. 321.

17 Frank, *Melanie Kleins erste Kinderanalysen*, p. 322, translated by Benjamin Seaman.

18 Today, one of the basic preconditions for the psychotherapeutic treatment of children is that their parents or responsible adults be available for regular talks.

19 Freud, S., 'Einige Charaktertypen aus der psychoanalytischen Arbeit', in *Gesammelte Werke*, Vol. 10, Chapter 3, Fischer, Frankfurt, 1946, pp. 364–391.

20 Frank, *Melanie Kleins erste Kinderanalysen*, p. 323, translated by Benjamin Seaman.

21 Brecht, K., Friedrich, V., Hermanns, L.M., Kaminer, J.I. and Dierk, H.J. (eds) *Hier geht das Leben auf eine sehr merkwürdige Weise weiter ... Zur Geschichte der Psychoanalyse in Deutschland*, Michael Kellner, Hamburg, 1985.

22 Danto, *Freud's Free Clinics*, p. 301.

23 Diercks, C., 'The Vienna Psychoanalytic Polyclinic ("*Ambulatorium*"): Wilhelm Reich and the technical seminar', *Psychoanalysis and History*, 2002, 4: 67–84.

2 The cross-cultural aspect of analytical psychology: Carl Gustav Jung

1 Jung, C.G. and Jaffé, A., *Memories, Dreams, Reflections*, Random House, New York, 1965.

2 Jung and Jaffé, *Memories, Dreams, Reflections*, p. 27.

3 Jung and Jaffé, *Memories, Dreams, Reflections*, p. 27.

4 Jung and Jaffé, *Memories, Dreams, Reflections*, p. 27.

5 Jung and Jaffé, *Memories, Dreams, Reflections*, p. 28.

6 Jung and Jaffé, *Memories, Dreams, Reflections*, p. 33.

7 Jung and Jaffé, *Memories, Dreams, Reflections*, p. 42.

8 Jung and Jaffé, *Memories, Dreams, Reflections*, p. 42.

9 Jung and Jaffé, *Memories, Dreams, Reflections*, p. 38.

10 Jung and Jaffé, *Memories, Dreams, Reflections*, p. 29.

11 Jung and Jaffé, *Memories, Dreams, Reflections*, p. 29.

12 Jung and Jaffé, *Memories, Dreams, Reflections*, p. 30.

13 If one studies the exchange of letters between Jung and the Dominican monk Father White under this aspect, one can tell a connection between the shy boy Carl and the reserved, 80-year-old 'C.G.' (as he had his friends call him), who was not capable of rescuing their friendship despite their theoretical differences. Conrad Lammers, A. and Cunningham, A. (eds) *The Jung-White Letters*, Routledge, London, 2007.

14 Wickes, F., *The Inner World of Childhood*, Appleton, New York, 1927; Sigo Press, Boston, MA, 1978.

15 Jung, C.G., Foreword, in Wickes, *The Inner World of Childhood*, p. xx.

16 Jung, Foreword, in Wickes, *The Inner World of Childhood*, p. xix.

17 Jung, Foreword, in Wickes, *The Inner World of Childhood*, p. xix.

18 Wickes, *The Inner World of Childhood*, p. 170.

19 The term 'play therapy' is now understood as the 'non-directive play therapy', which was founded by Virginia Axline in the early 1970s and was orientated along Carl Rogers' 'Client Centered Therapy'. Today it is known as 'Child Oriented Play Therapy'.

20 Since most of the psychoanalysts emigrated to the USA during the war, their innovations eventually returned to Europe from there.

21 McNiff, S., 'Foreword', in C.A. Malchiodi (ed.) *Expressive Therapies*, Guilford Press, New York, 2006.
22 Malchiodi, C.A. (ed.) *Expressive Therapies*, Guilford Press, New York, 2006.
23 Wolf, R.I., Review: '*Expressive Therapy: A Creative Arts Approach to Depth-Oriented Treatment*. Arthur Robbins with Contributors. New York: Human Sciences Press, 1980', *Psychoanalytic Review*, 1983, 70: 277–278.
24 'Art expression in and of itself is considered by some practitioners to be a form of active imagination, because in art expression images arise spontaneously.' Malchiodi, *Expressive Therapies*, p. 24.
25 The fifth edition of the American Psychiatric Association's *Diagnostic and Statistical Manual of Mental Disorders* (DSM-V) is currently being prepared. It should be published in May 2013 and will supersede the DSM-IV, which was revised in 2000.
26 Papadopoulos, R.K., 'Destructiveness, atrocities and healing: Epistemological and clinical reflections', *Journal of Analytical Psychology*, 1998, 43: 455–477, p. 457.
27 Papadopoulos, 'Destructiveness, atrocities and healing', p. 458.
28 Papadopoulos, 'Destructiveness, atrocities and healing', p. 458.
29 Papadopoulos, 'Destructiveness, atrocities and healing', p. 458.

3 Margaret Lowenfeld's *World Technique* and Dora Kalff's *Sandplay*

1 Leaflet from the Clinic for Nervous and Difficult Children, 12 Telford Road, Ladbroke Grove, London, W10. Reproduced in Lowenfeld, M., *Understanding Children's Sandplay: Lowenfeld's World Technique*, Sussex Academic Press, Portland, OR, 2007, p. xii.
2 Evans, R.I., *Freedom to Choose: The Life and Work of Dr. Helena Wright, A Pioneer of Contraception*, Bodley Head, London, 1984.
3 Lowenfeld, *Understanding Children's Sandplay*, p. 1.
4 Mitchell, R.R. and Friedman, H.S., *Sandplay: Past, Present and Future*, Routledge, London, 1993.
5 Wells, H.G., *Floor Games*, Palmer, London, 1911; Arno Press, New York, 1976.
6 Lowenfeld, M., *The World Technique*, Institute of Child Psychology, Allen & Unwin, Boston, MA, 1979, p. 3.
7 Lowenfeld, *Understanding Children's Sandplay*, p. 280, emphasis in the original.
8 Urwin, C. and Hood-Williams, J. (eds) *Child Psychotherapy, War, and the Normal Child: Selected Papers by Margaret Lowenfeld*, Free Association Books, London, 1988, p. 292.
9 Urwin and Hood-Williams, *Child Psychotherapy, War, and the Normal Child*, p. 3.
10 Urwin and Hood-Williams, *Child Psychotherapy, War, and the Normal Child*, p. 293.
11 Urwin and Hood-Williams, *Child Psychotherapy, War, and the Normal Child*, p. 296.
12 Winnicott, D., *Therapeutic Consultations in Child Psychiatry*, Basic Books, New York, 1971, p. 3.
13 Urwin and Hood-Williams, *Child Psychotherapy, War, and the Normal Child*, p. 291.
14 Urwin and Hood-Williams, *Child Psychotherapy, War, and the Normal Child*, p. 297.
15 Urwin and Hood-Williams, *Child Psychotherapy, War, and the Normal Child*, p. 300.
16 See, for example, Stern, D.N., *Diary of a Baby*, Basic Books, New York, 1990.
17 See, for example, Stern, A., *Der Malort*, Daimon, Einsiedeln, 1998.
18 Lowenfeld, M., *Play in Childhood*, Sussex Academic Press, Portland, OR, 2008, p. 232.
19 Lowenfeld, *Understanding Children's Sandplay*, p. vii.
20 Lowenfeld, M., *Play in Childhood*, Sussex Academic Press, Portland, OR, 2008, p. 232.
21 Winnicott, D., *Playing and Reality*, Tavistock, London, 1971.

22 The sandtray's measurements were exactly defined, as was the light blue colour on the inside. The miniatures were all listed and the therapist's non-interpretative attitude was exactly described.

23 Mitchell and Friedman, *Sandplay*.

24 Lowenfeld, *The World Technique*.

25 Dora Kalff's life is described in detail in Mitchell and Friedman, *Sandplay*.

26 Kalff, D., 'The archetype as a healing factor', *Psychologia*, 9, 177–84, in A. Guggenbühl-Craig (ed.) *The Archetype: Proceedings of the Second International Congress of Analytical Psychology*, Karger, Basel, 1966.

27 Navone, A., 'Matter and the psyche: A feasible therapy', in E. Pattis Zoja (ed.) *Sandplay Therapy: Treatment of Psychopathologies*, Daimon, Einsiedeln, 2002.

28 Pattis Zoja, E. (ed.) *Sandplay Therapy: Treatment of Psychopathologies*, Daimon, Einsiedeln, 2002.

29 Kohut, H., *The Analysis of the Self*, International Universities Press, New York, 1971.

4 Psychotherapy in precarious situations

1 Tricario, G., *Daídalon: L'archetipo della possibilità*, Moretti & Vitali, Bergamo, 2009.

2 *Rhythm Is It!*, a film by Thomas Grube and Enrique Sánchez Lansch, with Sir Simon Rattle and Berlin Philharmonic Orchestra, 2004.

3 *El Sistema*, a film by Paul Smaczny and Maria Stodtmeier, with José Antonio Abreu, Gustavo Dudamel and Simon Bolivar Youth Orchestra, 2008

4 For example, the theatre production of *Hamlet Noir* in Burkina Faso, 2004.

5 Wikipedia, 'Lay Community Counsellor Model'.

6 Ahmed, S.H. and Siddiqi, M.N., 'Essay: Healing through art therapy in disaster settings', *Lancet*, 2006, 368: S28–S29.

7 Jung, C.G., 'The relations between the Ego and the Unconscious', in C.G. Jung, *Two Essays on Analytical Psychology*, in *Collected Works of C.G. Jung*, Vol. 7, Routledge, London, 1953.

8 Kalsched, D., *The Inner World of Trauma: Archetypal Defenses of the Personal Spirit*, Routledge, London, 1996.

9 Jung, 'The relations between the Ego and the Unconscious'.

10 Pattis Zoja, E., 'What can a Jungian analyst learn from sandplay?', *Journal of Sandplay Therapy*, 2002, 11: 29–41, p. 29.

11 Hillmann, J., *Healing Fiction*, Spring, Dallas, TX, 1983.

12 'Free and protected space': see Kalff, D., *Sandplay: A Psychotherapeutic Approach to the Psyche*, Temenos Press, Cloverdale, CA, 2003.

5 Trauma and 'newly contained time'

1 Char, R., 'L'Eternité à Lourmarin' (April 1960). The poem is available in M.A. Caws and T. Jolas (eds) *Selected Poems of René Char*, New Directions, New York, 1992.

2 The two poets had been like brothers: see Todd, O., *Albert Camus: Une vie*, Gallimard, Paris, 1996, Chapter 35, 'Tres amis', p. 484. Albert Camus (1913–60) is buried in the cemetery at Lourmarin, France.

3 Char, 'L'Eternité à Lourmarin'; all the quotations from Char's poem are translated by Benjamin Seaman.

4 Allan Schore brings together psychoanalytic research, attachment theories, and brain research in showing how impairment of the right brain's stress coping systems due to relational trauma in infancy have damaging consequences for the adult. See Schore, A.N., 'The effects of early relational trauma on right brain development, affect regulation, and infant mental health', *Infant Mental Health Journal*, 2001, 22 (1–2): 201–269; Schore, A.N., 'Early trauma and the development of the right brain', address to

Understanding and Treating Trauma: Developmental and Neurobiological Approaches Conference, Department of Psychiatry and Biobehavioral Sciences, UCLA School of Medicine, Los Angeles, CA, 1998.

5 Ansermet, F. and Magistretti, P., *Neuroscience et psychanalyse: Une rencontre autour de la singularité*, Odile Jacob, Paris, 2004.

6 Mundo, E., *Neuroscienze per la psicologia clinica: Le basi del dialogo mente-cervello*, Raffallo Cortina Editore, Milan, 2009.

7 Joseph, S.A., Williams, R.M. and Yule, W., 'Normal and abnormal reactions to trauma', in S.A. Joseph, R.M. Williams and W. Yule (eds) *Understanding Post-Traumatic Stress: A Psychosocial Perspective on PTSD and Treatment*, Chichester, Wiley, 1997.

8 Papadopoulos, R.K. (ed.) *Therapeutic Care for Refugees: No Place Like Home*, Karnac, London, 2002, pp. 30 and 33.

9 Baudot, G., *Les Lettres precolombiennes*, Toulouse, 1976, in T. Todorov and G. Baudot, *Racconti aztechi della Conquista*, Enaudi, Turin, 1988, p. 97, translated from the Italian by Benjamin Seaman.

10 Baudot, *Les Lettres precolombiennes*, in Todorov and Baudot, *Racconti aztechi della Conquista*, p. 97, translated by Benjamin Seaman.

11 Baudot, *Les Lettres precolombiennes*, in Todorov and Baudot, *Racconti aztechi della Conquista*, p. 98, translated by Benjamin Seaman.

12 Zoja, L., 'Trauma and abuse: The development of a cultural complex in the history of Latin America', in T. Singer and S.L. Kimbles (eds) *The Cultural Complex: Contemporary Jungian Perspectives on Psyche and Society*, Routledge, London, 2004.

13 Zoja, 'Trauma and abuse', p. 39.

14 Guggenbühl-Craig, A., *Power in the Helping Professions*, Spring, Dallas, TX, 1986.

15 Bauer, J., *Das Gedächtnis des Körpers: Wie Beziehungen und Lebensstile unsere Gene steueren*, Piper, Stuttgart, 2004; Panksepp, J., *Affective Neuroscience: The Foundations of Human and Animal Emotions*, Oxford University Press, Oxford, 1998.

16 Kalsched, D., *The Inner World of Trauma: Archetypal Defenses of the Personal Spirit*, Routledge, London, 1996.

17 Only when the girl started school and moved to her parents in a nearby industrial town, where her dog was forcibly taken away from her, did she begin to develop disorders which more than once in the following years brought her close to a complete psychological collapse. Although she had no chance in her childhood to rebel against her parents' severe pathology, something inside her remained protected and whole: she kept alive her sensibility, her emotional warmth and her exceptional capacity for introspection all the way into adulthood. Far away from her home country, she gradually succeeded in making her own way through life.

18 Jung, C.G., 'Flying saucers: A modern myth of things seen in skies', in *Collected Works of C.G. Jung*, Vol. 10, Routledge, London, 1958.

19 Lorenzo Lotto, *Il Vizio e la Virtù* ('Allegory of Virtue and Vice'), 1505.

6 Expressive Sandwork

1 Kalff, D., *Sandplay: A Psychotherapeutic Approach to the Psyche*, Temenos Press, Cloverdale, CA, 2003, p. 9.

2 Lowenfeld, M., *Understanding Children's Sandplay: Lowenfeld's World Technique*, Sussex Academic Press, Portland, OR, 2007, p. 4.

3 This training consists of approximately forty hours of theoretical teaching by a therapist, and a minimum of four Expressive Sandwork sessions of self-experience.

4 Lowenfeld, M., *Play in Childhood*, Sussex Academic Press, Portland, OR, 2008, p. 3.

5 Winnicott, D., *Playing and Reality*, Tavistock, London, 1971.

6 Kalff, *Sandplay*, p. 9.

7   Lowenfeld, *Understanding Children's Sandplay*, p. 2.
8   Lowenfeld, *Understanding Children's Sandplay*, p. 4.
9   Kalff, *Sandplay*, p. 8.
10 Kalff, *Sandplay*, p. 10.
11 Lowenfeld, *Understanding Children's Sandplay*, p. 6.
12 Kalff, *Sandplay*, p. 9.
13 Kalff, *Sandplay*, p. 7.
14 This is referring to 'interest' in the entymological sense: *inter-esse* in Latin means 'being in the middle of something'.
15 Winnicott, *Playing and Reality*.
16 Stern, A., *Der Malort*, Daimon, Einsiedeln, 1998.
17 von Gontard, A., *Theorie und Praxis der Sandspieltherapie: Ein Handbuch aus kinderpsychiatrischer Sicht*, Kohlhammer, Stuttgart, 2007.
18 Pattis Zoja, E., 'The good and the beautiful in sandplay therapy', *Journal of Sandplay Therapy*, 2010, 19: 33–46.

7 Expressive Sandwork in South Africa

1   Lorenz, K., *Das sogenannte Böse: Zur Naturgeschichte der Aggression*, Taschenbuch, Frankfurt, 1998.
2   A psychological-anthropological attempt at describing what developed in this situation can be made by the term *pseudo-speciation* (Erik Erikson): a person, or group of people, behaves as if the other people do not merely belong to a different ethnic group, but to a different *species*. In conflicts between ethnic groups, each group's subjective perception that the others are not even 'real humans' reduces not only any feelings of guilt the attackers might have, but also the natural, instinctive inhibition preventing all species from eating their fellow species-members.
3   Sandplay therapy was interrupted for months after this incident because the Expressive Sandwork project leader, Imme Thom, had been threatened. Each side accused her of helping the other group.
4   The following stories of Baito, Chlony, Tumi, Refilve and Jeremy are based on the notes of Imme Thom, an art therapist who began using sandplay therapy to help neglected children in Krugersdorp in the year 2000.
5   This sandplay process was first published in German: Thom, I. and Kendler, M., 'Sandspieltherapie in einer fremden Welt', *Zeitschrift für Sandspieltherapie: Zeitschrift für Wissenschaft und Praxis einer Methode*, 21, Verlag Linde von Keyserlingk, Stuttgart, 2006.
6   Thom and Kendler, 'Sandspieltherapie in einer fremden Welt', p. 55.
7   Thom and Kendler, 'Sandspieltherapie in einer fremden Welt', p. 56.
8   Eliade, M., *Le Sacré et le profane*, Gallimard, Paris, 1965.
9   This broom head was used by other children over and over again in the following weeks.

8 Expressive Sandwork in China

1   Museum of the Cultural Revolution.
2   Kalsched, D., *The Inner World of Trauma: Archetypal Defenses of the Personal Spirit*, Routledge, London, 1996.
3   The records of this case study were kindly provided to me by Professor Gao Lan.
4   Winnicott, D., *Playing and Reality*, Tavistock, London, 1971.
5   Kalff, D., *Sandplay: A Psychotherapeutic Approach to the Psyche*, Temenos Press, Cloverdale, CA, 2003.
6   Winnicott, *Playing and Reality*.

7 If Liu were a European child, we could add that the word 'sea' is etymologically related to the word 'mother'. There are, however, no such linguistic derivations in Chinese as we know in western languages. But a range of associations can be derived from the Chinese characters for the words.

9 Expressive Sandwork in Colombia, Latin America

1   ¿Solo así he de irme?
    ¿Como las flores que perecieron?
    ¿Nada quedará en mi nombre?
    ¿Nada de mi fama aquí en la tierra?
    ¡Al menos flores, al menos cantos!

Translated by Benjamin Seaman.
2 Encyclopedia Britannica, 'Dobyns, Henry', *Encyclopedia Britannica Online*, 2010: www.britannica.com/EBchecked/topic/1397520/Dobyns-Henry
3 Gambini, R., *Anima e cultura*, Moretti & Vitali, Bergamo, 2005, p. 19, translated by Benjamin Seaman.
4 'Expulsion of the Indios' is the title of his book: Gambini, R., *O espelho índio: Os jesuitas e a destruição da alma indígena*, Espaço e Tempo, Rio de Janeiro, 1988.
5 Gambini, *Anima e cultura*, p. 20, translated by Benjamin Seaman.
6 Galeano, E., *Las venas abiertas de America latina*, Ciudad de Mexico-Madrid, Siglo XXI Editores, 1994.
7 Bolivar, G., *Sin tetas no hay paraíso*, Editora Oveja Negra, Bogotá, 2008.
8 Comunidad de Sant'Egido is a non-church-affiliated relief organization founded in Rome in the 1970s by Andrea Riccardi. It is internationally known in particular for its peace negotiations.
9 Zoja, L., *The Father: Historical, Cultural, Psychological Perspectives*, Routledge, London, 2001.
10 In *Tocar y luchar* ('To Play and to Fight', 2006), a film by Alberto Arvelo Mendoza, the conductor Simon Rattle says: 'If there is one place in the world where something really new is happening in classical music today, it is Venezuela.'
11 Barloewen, C., *Kulturgeschichte und Modernität Lateinamerikas*, Matthes & Seitz, Munich, 1992.
12 Peterson, C., Maier, F. and Seligman, M.E.P., *Learned Helplessness: A Theory for the Age of Personal Control*, Oxford University Press, Oxford, 1993.
13 The word 'symbol' comes from the Ancient Greek, *syn-ballein*, to throw together.

10 Practical instructions for an Expressive Sandwork project

1 'Therapists' in this case means members of an internationally recognized society for psychoanalysis or psychotherapy, for example the International Association for Analytical Psychology (IAAP) or the International Society for Sandplay Therapy (ISST), who also have experience in sandplay.

Bibliography

Aerztliche Reform-Zeitung ('Doctors' Reform Newspaper'), *A Psychoanalytic Ambulatorium in Vienna*, Vols 9–10, Archiv des Psychoanalytischen Ambulatoriums, Vienna, 1922.

Ahmed, S.H. and Siddiqi, M.N., 'Essay: Healing through art therapy in disaster settings', *Lancet*, 2006, 368: S28–S29.

Aichhorn, A., *Wayward Youth*, Viking, New York, 1925.

American Psychiatric Association (APA), *Diagnostic and Statistical Manual of Mental Disorders*, Text Revision (DSM-IV-TR), APA, Washington, DC, 2000.

Ansermet, F. and Magistretti, P., *Neuroscience et psychanalyse: Une rencontre autour de la singularité*, Odile Jacob, Paris, 2004.

Barloewen, C., *Kulturgeschichte und Modernität Lateinamerikas*, Matthes & Seitz, Munich, 1992.

Baudot, G., *Les Lettres precolombiennes*, Toulouse, 1976, in T. Todorov and G. Baudot, *Racconti aztechi della Conquista*, Enaudi, Turin, 1988.

Bauer, J., *Das Gedächtnis des Körpers: Wie Beziehungen und Lebensstile unsere Gene steueren*, Piper, Stuttgart, 2004.

Binswanger, O., 'Die Kriegshysterie', in O. v. Schjerning (ed.) *Handbuch der ärztlichen Erfahrungen im Weltkriege 1914–18*, Vol. 4: K. Bonhoeffer (ed.) *Geistes- und Nervenkrankheiten*, Leipzig, 1922.

Bolivar, G., *Sin tetas no hay paraíso*, Editora Oveja Negra, Bogotá, 2008.

Brecht, K., Friedrich, V., Hermanns, L.M., Kaminer, J.I. and Dierk, H.J. (eds) *Hier geht das Leben auf eine sehr merkwürdige Weise wetter ... Zur Geschichte der Psychoanalyse in Deutschland*, Psychosozial Verlag, Giessen, 2009.

Conrad Lammers, A. and Cunningham, A. (eds) *The Jung-White Letters*, Routledge, London, 2007.

Danto, E.A., *Freud's Free Clinics: Psychoanalysis and Social Justice, 1918–1938*, Columbia University Press, New York, 2005.

Diercks, C., 'The Vienna Psychoanalytic Polyclinic ("*Ambulatorium*"): Wilhelm Reich and the technical seminar', *Psychoanalysis and History*, 2002, 4: 67–84.

Eitingon, M., 'Bericht über die Berliner Psychoanalytische Poliklinik, März 1920 – Juni 1922', *Internationale Zeitschrift für Psychoanalyse*, 1922, 8: 506–520.

Eitingon, M., 'Report of the Berlin Psycho-Analytical Polyclinic, March 1920 – June 1922', *International Journal of Psycho-Analysis*, 1923, 4: 254–269.

Eliade, M., *Le Sacré et le profane*, Gallimard, Paris, 1965.

Encyclopedia Britannica, 'Dobyns, Henry', *Encyclopedia Britannica Online*, 2010: www. britannica.com/EBchecked/topic/1397520/Dobyns-Henry

Evans, R.I., *Freedom to Choose: The Life and Work of Dr. Helena Wright, A Pioneer of Contraception*, Bodley Head, London, 1984.

Frank, C., *Melanie Kleins erste Kinderanalysen: Die Entdeckung des Kindes als Objekt sui generis von Heilen und Forschen*, Frommann-Holzboog, Stuttgart, 1999.

Frank, C., *Melanie Klein in Berlin: Her First Psychoanalysis with Children*, New Library of Psychoanalysis, General Editor D. Birksted-Breen, Routledge, London, 2009.

Freud, S., 'Wege der psychoanalytischen Therapie', Internationaler Kongress für Psychoanalyse, Budapest, 28 September 1918, *Internationale Zeitschrift für Psychoanalyse*, 1919, 5 (2): 61–68, in *Gesammelte Werke*, 1947, Vol. 12: 183–194.

Freud, S., 'Lines of advance in psychoanalytic psychotherapy', 1918, in *The Standard Edition of the Complete Psychological Works of Sigmund Freud*, Vol. 17, p. 164.

Freud, S., 'Einige Charaktertypen aus der psychoanalytischen Arbeit', in *Gesammelte Werke*, Vol. 10, Chapter 3, Fischer, Frankfurt, 1946, pp. 364–391.

Galeano, E., *Las venas abiertas de America latina*, Ciudad de Mexico-Madrid, Siglo XXI Editores, 1994.

Gambini, R., *O espelho índio: Os jesuitas e a destruição da alma indígena*, Espaço e Tempo, Rio de Janeiro, 1988.

Gambini, R., *Anima e cultura*, Moretti & Vitali, Bergamo, 2005.

Guggenbühl-Craig, A., *Power in the Helping Professions*, Spring, Dallas, TX, 1986.

Hillmann, J., *Healing Fiction*, Spring, Dallas, TX, 1983.

Joseph, S.A., Williams, R.M. and Yule, W., 'Normal and abnormal reactions to trauma', in S.A. Joseph, R.M. Williams and W. Yule (eds) *Understanding Post-Traumatic Stress: A Psychosocial Perspective on PTSD and Treatment*, Chichester, Wiley, 1997.

Jung, C.G., 'The relations between the Ego and the Unconscious', in C.G. Jung, *Two Essays on Analytical Psychology*, in *Collected Works of C.G. Jung*, Vol. 7, Routledge, London, 1953.

Jung, C.G., 'Flying saucers: A modern myth of things seen in skies', in *Collected Works of C.G. Jung*, Vol. 10, Routledge, London, 1958.

Jung, C.G. and Jaffé, A., *Memories, Dreams, Reflections*, Random House, New York, 1965.

Kalff, D., 'The archetype as a healing factor', *Psychologia*, 9, 177–184, in A. Guggenbühl-Craig (ed.) *The Archetype: Proceedings of the Second International Congress of Analytical Psychology*, Karger, Basel, 1966.

Kalff, D., *Sandplay: A Psychotherapeutic Approach to the Psyche*, Temenos Press, Cloverdale, CA, 2003.

Kalsched, D., *The Inner World of Trauma: Archetypal Defenses of the Personal Spirit*, Routledge, London, 1996.

Kohut, H., *The Analysis of the Self*, International Universities Press, New York, 1971.

Lorenz, K., *Das sogenannte Böse: Zur Naturgeschichte der Aggression*, Taschenbuch, Frankfurt, 1998.

Lowenfeld, M., *The World Technique*, Institute of Child Psychology, Allen & Unwin, Boston, MA, 1979.

Lowenfeld, M., *Understanding Children's Sandplay: Lowenfeld's World Technique*, Sussex Academic Press, Portland, OR, 2007.

Lowenfeld, M., *Play in Childhood*, Sussex Academic Press, Portland, OR, 2008.

McNiff, S., 'Foreword', in C.A. Malchiodi (ed.) *Expressive Therapies*, Guilford Press, New York, 2006.

Malchiodi, C.A. (ed.) *Expressive Therapies*, Guilford Press, New York, 2006.

Mitchell, R.R. and Friedman, H.S., *Sandplay: Past, Present and Future*, Routledge, London, 1993.

Mundo, E., *Neuroscienze per la psicologia clinica: Le basi del dialogo mente-cervello*, Raffallo Cortina Editore, Milan, 2009.

Navone, A., 'Matter and the psyche: A feasible therapy', in E. Pattis Zoja (ed.) *Sandplay Therapy: Treatment of Psychopathologies*, Daimon, Einsiedeln, 2002.

Panksepp, J., *Affective Neuroscience: The Foundations of Human and Animal Emotions*, Oxford University Press, Oxford, 1998.

Papadopoulos, R.K., 'Destructiveness, atrocities and healing: Epistemological and clinical reflections', *Journal of Analytical Psychology*, 1998, 43: 455–477.

Papadopoulos, R.K. (ed.) *Therapeutic Care for Refugees: No Place Like Home*, Karnac, London, 2002.

Pattis Zoja, E. (ed.) *Sandplay Therapy: Treatment of Psychopathologies*, Daimon, Einsiedeln, 2002.

Pattis Zoja, E., 'What can a Jungian analyst learn from sandplay?', *Journal of Sandplay Therapy*, 2002, 11: 29–41.

Pattis Zoja, E., 'The good and the beautiful in sandplay therapy', *Journal of Sandplay Therapy*, 2010, 19: 33–46.

Peterson, C., Maier, F. and Seligman, M.E.P., *Learned Helplessness: A Theory for the Age of Personal Control*, Oxford University Press, Oxford, 1993.

Sanitätsbericht über das deutsche Heer im Weltkriege 1914–1918, Vol. 3: Heeressanitätsinspektion des Reichswehrministeriums (ed.) *Die Krankenbewegung bei dem deutschen Feld- und Besatzungsheer*, Berlin, 1934.

Schore, A.N., 'Early trauma and the development of the right brain', address to Understanding and Treating Trauma: Developmental and Neurobiological Approaches Conference, Department of Psychiatry and Biobehavioral Sciences, UCLA School of Medicine, Los Angeles, CA, 1998.

Schore, A.N., 'The effects of early relational trauma on right brain development, affect regulation, and infant mental health', *Infant Mental Health Journal*, 2001, 22 (1–2): 201–269.

Stern, A., *Der Malort*, Daimon, Einsiedeln, 1998.

Stern, D.N., *Diary of a Baby*, Basic Books, New York, 1990.

Steward, R., Unpublished interview, in E.A. Danto, 'The Ambulatorium: Freud's free clinic in Vienna', *International Journal of Psycho-Analysis*, 1998, 79 (2): 287–300.

Thom, I. and Kendler, M., 'Sandspieltherapie in einer fremden Welt', *Zeitschrift für Sandspieltherapie: Zeitschrift für Wissenschaft und Praxis einer Methode*, 21, Verlag Linde von Keyserlingk, Stuttgart, 2006.

Todd, O., *Albert Camus: Une vie*, Gallimard, Paris, 1996.

Tricario, G., *Daídalon: L'archetipo della possibilità*, Moretti & Vitali, Bergamo, 2009.

Urwin, C. and Hood-Williams, J. (eds) *Child Psychotherapy, War, and the Normal Child: Selected Papers by Margaret Lowenfeld*, Free Association Books, London, 1988.

von Gontard, A., *Theorie und Praxis der Sandspieltherapie: Ein Handbuch aus kinderpsy-chiatrischer Sicht*, Kohlhammer, Stuttgart, 2007.

Wells, H.G., *Floor Games*, Palmer, London, 1911; Arno Press, New York, 1976.

Wickes, F., *The Inner World of Childhood*, Sigo Press, Boston, MA, 1978.

Winnicott, D., *Playing and Reality*, Tavistock, London, 1971.

Winnicott, D., *Therapeutic Consultations in Child Psychiatry*, Basic Books, New York, 1971.

Wolf, R.I., Review: '*Expressive Therapy: A Creative Arts Approach to Depth-Oriented Treatment*. Arthur Robbins with Contributors. New York: Human Sciences Press, 1980', *Psychoanalytic Review*, 1983, 70: 277–278.

Zehn Jahre Berliner Psychoanalytisches Institut (Poliklinik und Lehranstalt) 1920 bis 1930, Internationaler Psychoanalytischer Verlag, Vienna, 1930.

Zoja, L., *The Father: Historical, Cultural, Psychological Perspectives*, Routledge, London, 2001.

Zoja, L., 'Trauma and abuse: The development of a cultural complex in the history of Latin America', in T. Singer and S.L. Kimbles (eds) *The Cultural Complex: Contemporary Jungian Perspectives on Psyche and Society*, Routledge, London, 2004.

Index

For Product Safety Concerns and Information please contact our EU
representative GPSR@taylorandfrancis.com
Taylor & Francis Verlag GmbH, Kaufingerstraße 24, 80331 München, Germany